CONSTRUCTION ENGINEERING & MANAGEMENT

AUTHOR

Dr. Sparsh Johari
Assistant Professor
Department of Civil Engineering,
Indian Institute of Technology Guwahati, Guwahati

REVIEWER

Dr. Senthilkumar V
Associate Professor
Department of Civil Engineering,
Indian Institute of Technology Palakkad, Palakkad

All India Council for Technical Education
Nelson Mandela Marg, Vasant Kunj,
New Delhi, India

Dear Readers,

To prevent the piracy, this book is secured with HIGH SECURITY HOLOGRAM on the front title cover. In case you don't find the hologram on the front cover title, please write us to at contact@khannabooks.com or whatsapp us at +91-99109 09320 and avail special gift voucher for yourself.

Specimen of Hologram on front Cover title:

Moreover, there is a SPECIAL DISCOUNT COUPON for you with EVERY HOLOGRAM.

How to avail this SPECIAL DISCOUNT:

Step 1: Scratch the hologram

Step 2: Under the scratch area, your "coupon code" is available

Step 3: Logon to www.khannabooks.com

Step 4: Use your "coupon code" in the shopping cart and get your copy at a special discount

Step 5: Enjoy your reading!

ISBN: 978-93-5538-530-7

Book Code: UG487EN

Construction Engineering & Management

by Dr. Sparsh Johari

First Edition: 2026

Originally Published by:
All India Council for Technical Education, Ministry of Education, GOI

Exclusively Published & Distributed by:
Khanna Book Publishing Co. (P) Ltd.
4C/4344, Ansari Road, Daryaganj,
New Delhi (INDIA)

Visit us at: **www.khannabooks.com**
Write us at: **contact@khannabooks.com**

To view complete list of books,
Please scan the QR Code:

Printed in Bharat.

प्रो. टी. जी. सीताराम
अध्यक्ष
Prof. T. G. Sitharam
Chairman

आज़ादी का अमृत महोत्सव

अखिल भारतीय तकनीकी शिक्षा परिषद्
(भारत सरकार का एक सांविधिक निकाय)
(शिक्षा मंत्रालय, भारत सरकार)
नेल्सन मंडेला मार्ग, वसंत कुंज, नई दिल्ली–110070
दूरभाष : 011–26131498
ई–मेल : chairman@aicte-india.org

ALL INDIA COUNCIL FOR TECHNICAL EDUCATION
(A STATUTORY BODY OF THE GOVT. OF INDIA)
(Ministry of Education, Govt. of India)
Nelson Mandela Marg, Vasant Kunj, New Delhi-110070
Phone : 011-26131498
E-mail : chairman@aicte-india.org

FOREWORD

Engineers are the backbone of any modern society. They are the ones responsible for the marvels as well as the improved quality of life across the world. Engineers have driven humanity towards greater heights in a more evolved and unprecedented manner.

The All India Council for Technical Education (AICTE), have spared no efforts towards the strengthening of the technical education in the country. AICTE is always committed towards promoting quality Technical Education to make India a modern developed nation emphasizing on the overall welfare of mankind.

An array of initiatives has been taken by AICTE in last decade which have been accelerated now by the National Education Policy (NEP) 2020. The implementation of NEP under the visionary leadership of Hon'ble Prime Minister of India envisages the provision for education in regional languages to all, thereby ensuring that every graduate becomes competent enough and is in a position to contribute towards the national growth and development through innovation & entrepreneurship.

One of the spheres where AICTE had been relentlessly working since past couple of years is providing high quality original technical contents at Under Graduate & Diploma level prepared and translated by eminent educators in various Indian languages to its aspirants. For students pursuing 2nd year of their Engineering education, AICTE has identified 87 books, which shall be translated into 12 Indian languages - Hindi, Tamil, Gujarati, Odia, Bengali, Kannada, Urdu, Punjabi, Telugu, Marathi, Assamese & Malayalam. In addition to the English medium, books in different Indian Languages are going to support the students to understand the concepts in their respective mother tongue.

On behalf of AICTE, I express sincere gratitude to all distinguished authors, reviewers and translators from the renowned institutions of high repute for their admirable contribution in a record span of time.

AICTE is confident that these outcomes based original contents shall help aspirants to master the subject with comprehension and greater ease.

T.G. Sitharam

(Prof. T. G. Sitharam)

ACKNOWLEDGEMENT

I am deeply grateful to the authorities of AICTE, particularly Prof T G Sitharam, Chairman; Dr Abhay Jere, Vice-Chairman; Prof. Rajivc Kumar, Member-Secretary, Dr. Ramesh Unnikrishnan, Advisor-II; and Dr. Sunil Luthra; Director, Training and Learning Bureau, for allowing me to write this book. Their meticulous planning and unwavering support in publishing the book on 'Construction Engineering & Management' has been instrumental. I also extend my sincere appreciation to the book reviewer, Dr Senthilkumar. V., Associate Professor, Department of Civil Engineering, Indian Institute of Technology Palakkad, for his invaluable inputs across all book units.

This book is a testament to the collective wisdom and shared vision of the Government of India, AICTE members, experts, and authors who have generously shared their insights to advance engineering education in our country. I extend my heartfelt acknowledgements to the numerous contributors in this field whose published books, review articles, papers, photographs, footnotes, references, advice, and other valuable information have enriched my work.

I wish to acknowledge the support and great love of my family: my wife, Mrs Shikha Mittal; my mother, Mrs Nidhi Johari; my father, Mr Ashok Kumar Johari; my sister-in-law, Mrs Shubham Srivastava; and my brother, Mr Utkarsh Johri. I am also thankful to my kid, Mr Ridhaan Johari, nephew, Mr Ivaan Johri, and maternal uncle, Late (Col) N B Saxena. They kept me going, and this work would not have been possible without their love and support.

Dr. Sparsh Johari

CONTRIBUTORS

I want to thank the following faculties, independent researchers, and students for their contribution in shaping this book:

Faculties

Dr Chirag Kothari, Assistant Professor, IIT Kanpur

Dr Srinivas Mantrala, Professor of Practice, IIT Kanpur

Independent researchers

Dr Abhilasha Panwar (PhD, IIT Delhi)

Dr Nivea Thomas (PhD, IIT Delhi)

Students

Mr Ashwini Kumar (Research scholar, IIT Guwahati)

Mr Siddhartha Kashyap (Research scholar, IIT Guwahati)

Mr Sudarshan Saikia (Research scholar, IIT Guwahati)

Mrs Shikha Mittal (Research scholar, IIT Delhi)

Mr Aman Jaiswal (Master's student, IIT Guwahati)

Mr Shivam Gupta (Master's student, IIT Guwahati)

Mr Vaibhav Singh (Master's student, IIT Guwahati)

Dr. Sparsh Johari

PREFACE

Welcome to the world of construction engineering and management, a dynamic field at the intersection of engineering, business, and project management. This book serves as a comprehensive guide to understanding the intricate processes, principles, and practices that underpin the successful execution of construction projects.

Construction engineering & management have always been integral to human civilisation, shaping the built environment and facilitating societal progress. However, in today's fast-paced world, with ever-evolving technologies, heightened sustainability concerns, and increasingly complex projects, the need for proficient construction engineers and managers has never been greater.

This book aims to provide a holistic overview of construction engineering and management, covering various topics ranging from project planning and scheduling to cost estimation, risk management, and sustainability considerations. Whether you're a student embarking on a career in construction, a seasoned professional seeking to enhance your skills, or an enthusiast eager to delve into the intricacies of building projects, this book offers valuable insights and practical knowledge.

My approach to presenting the material is both comprehensive and accessible. I blend theoretical concepts with real-world examples, case studies, and practical applications to ensure students understand the subject matter deeply. Moreover, I have incorporated the latest industry trends, best practices, and technological advancements to provide students with up-to-date information that reflects the field's current state.

Readers will encounter various topics throughout the book, including project delivery methods, construction contracts, quality management, safety regulations, and emerging trends such as Building Information Modeling (BIM) and sustainable construction practices. Each chapter is meticulously crafted to offer a balance of theoretical foundations and practical insights, equipping students with the knowledge and skills needed to navigate the complexities of construction projects effectively.

I want to express my sincere gratitude to the AICTE and many professionals, educators, and researchers whose contributions have enriched the content of this book. I also thank the students for their interest in this fascinating field and commitment to advancing their knowledge and expertise in construction engineering and management.

I hope this book serves as a valuable resource and inspires students to embark on a fulfilling construction engineering and management journey. Whether you're involved in building towering skyscrapers, intricate infrastructure projects, or sustainable residential developments, I trust that the insights gleaned from this book will empower you to tackle challenges, drive innovation, and contribute to the continued advancement of the construction industry.

Happy reading, and best wishes for your construction engineering & management endeavours!

Dr. Sparsh Johari

OUTCOME BASED EDUCATION

For the implementation of an outcome based education the first requirement is to develop an outcome based curriculum and incorporate an outcome based assessment in the education system. By going through outcome based assessments evaluators will be able to evaluate whether the students have achieved the outlined standard, specific and measurable outcomes. With the proper incorporation of outcome based education, there will be a definite commitment to achieve a minimum standard for all learners without giving up at any level. At the end of the programme running with the aid of outcome based education, a student will be able to arrive at the following outcomes:

PO1. Engineering knowledge: Apply the knowledge of mathematics, science, engineering fundamentals, and an engineering specialization to the solution of complex engineering problems.

PO2. Problem analysis: Identify, formulate, review research literature, and analyse complex engineering problems reaching substantiated conclusions using first principles of mathematics, natural sciences, and engineering sciences.

PO3. Design / development of solutions: Design solutions for complex engineering problems and design system components or processes that meet the specified needs with appropriate consideration for the public health and safety, and the cultural, societal, and environmental considerations.

PO4. Conduct investigations of complex problems: Use research-based knowledge and research methods including design of experiments, analysis and interpretation of data, and synthesis of the information to provide valid conclusions.

PO5. Modern tool usage: Create, select, and apply appropriate techniques, resources, and modern engineering and IT tools including prediction and modeling to complex engineering activities with an understanding of the limitations.

PO6. The engineer and society: Apply reasoning informed by the contextual knowledge to assess societal, health, safety, legal and cultural issues and the consequent responsibilities relevant to the professional engineering practice.

PO7. Environment and sustainability: Understand the impact of the professional engineering solutions in societal and environmental contexts, and demonstrate the knowledge of, and need for sustainable development.

PO8. Ethics: Apply ethical principles and commit to professional ethics and responsibilities and norms of the engineering practice.

PO9. Individual and team work: Function effectively as an individual, and as a member or leader in diverse teams, and in multidisciplinary settings.

PO10. Communication: Communicate effectively on complex engineering activities with the engineering community and with society at large, such as, being able to comprehend and write effective reports and design documentation, make effective presentations, and give and receive clear instructions.

PO11. Project management and finance: Demonstrate knowledge and understanding of the engineering and management principles and apply these to one's own work, as a member and leader in a team, to manage projects and in multidisciplinary environments.

PO12. Life-long learning: Recognize the need for, and have the preparation and ability to engage in independent and life-long learning in the broadest context of technological change.

COURSE OUTCOMES

After completion of the course the students will be able to:

CO-1: Understand the importance of construction management

CO-2: Able to plan, schedule and monitor a construction project with minimum cost and time

CO-3: Select the right equipment and method for different construction scenarios

CO-4: Understand basic construction methodology for safe and quality construction

CO-5: Adopt the latest construction methodology and equipment

CO-6: Understand a requirement of the construction contract

Course Outcomes	Expected Mapping with Programme Outcomes (1- Weak Correlation; 2- Medium correlation; 3- Strong Correlation)											
	PO-1	PO-2	PO-3	PO-4	PO-5	PO-6	PO-7	PO-8	PO-9	PO-10	PO-11	PO-12
CO-1	3	1	2	1	1	3	1	-	2	1	-	1
CO-2	3	3	3	3	-	-	-	-	2	1	-	-
CO-3	3	3	3	2	2	-	1	-	-	-	3	1
CO-4	3	2	3	1	1	1	2	2	2	-	2	3
CO-5	3	2	2	1	3	-	-	-	-	-	2	1
CO-6	3	1	2	1	-	-	1	1	2	2	2	3

GUIDELINES FOR TEACHERS

To implement Outcome Based Education (OBE) knowledge level and skill set of the students should be enhanced. Teachers should take a major responsibility for the proper implementation of OBE. Some of the responsibilities (not limited to) for the teachers in OBE system may be as follows:

- Within reasonable constraint, they should manoeuvre time to the best advantage of all students.
- They should assess the students only upon certain defined criterion without considering any other potential ineligibility to discriminate them.
- They should try to grow the learning abilities of the students to a certain level before they leave the institute.
- They should try to ensure that all the students are equipped with the quality knowledge as well as competence after they finish their education.
- They should always encourage the students to develop their ultimate performance capabilities.
- They should facilitate and encourage group work and team work to consolidate newer approach.
- They should follow Blooms taxonomy in every part of the assessment.

Bloom's Taxonomy

Level	Teacher should Check	Student should be able to	Possible Mode of Assessment
Create	Students ability to create	Design or Create	Mini project
Evaluate	Students ability to justify	Argue or Defend	Assignment
Analyse	Students ability to distinguish	Differentiate or Distinguish	Project/Lab Methodology
Apply	Students ability to use information	Operate or Demonstrate	Technical Presentation/ Demonstration
Understand	Students ability to explain the ideas	Explain or Classify	Presentation/Seminar
Remember	Students ability to recall (or remember)	Define or Recall	Quiz

GUIDELINES FOR STUDENTS

Students should take equal responsibility for implementing the OBE. Some of the responsibilities (not limited to) for the students in OBE system are as follows:

- Students should be well aware of each UO before the start of a unit in each and every course.
- Students should be well aware of each CO before the start of the course.
- Students should be well aware of each PO before the start of the programme.
- Students should think critically and reasonably with proper reflection and action.
- Learning of the students should be connected and integrated with practical and real life consequences.
- Students should be well aware of their competency at every level of OBE.

LIST OF FIGURES

LIST OF TABLES

CONTENTS

1 BASICS OF CONSTRUCTION

UNIT SPECIFICS

The introduction to the basics of construction management serves as a gateway to understanding the intricate processes and responsibilities involved in overseeing construction projects. This chapter comprehensively overviews the fundamental principles and practices essential for effective construction management. From project initiation and feasibility studies to procurement, scheduling, budgeting, and quality control, construction managers play a vital role in orchestrating the various facets of construction projects.

RATIONALE

To start a construction project, one must know the types, features, phases, and agencies involved in construction project.

PRE-REQUISITE

Nil

UNIT OUTCOMES

List of outcomes of this unit is as follows:

U1-O1: Understand uniqueness in construction

U1-O2: Describe different types and phases of a construction project

U1-O3: Understand different types of stakeholders involved in construction

Unit Outcomes	Expected Mapping with Course Outcomes *(1- Weak Correlation; 2- Medium correlation; 3- Strong Correlation)*					
	CO-1	CO-2	CO-3	CO-4	CO-5	CO-6
U1-O1	3	1	3	1	1	2
U1-O2	3	3	2	2	2	3
U2-O3	3	3	1	2	1	3

1.1 CONSTRUCTION

In its simplest terms, construction refers to the process or method of building or assembling structures. This practice is as ancient as humanity, with evidence tracing back to the Stone Age. The earliest known instance of construction is believed to be a stone circle found at Olduvai Gorge, which represents the remains of a windbreak.

In the context of the Indian subcontinent, the Indus Valley Civilisation, dating back to 2800 BC, showcases remarkable advancements in construction. The civilisation boasted houses made of burnt bricks, cities planned on a grid layout pattern, and a sophisticated drainage system, demonstrating a level of urban planning and construction prowess that was truly ahead of its time.

Fast forward to the present day, the methodology involved in constructing the structures has evolved exponentially. Modern construction incorporates various materials and technologies, from concrete and steel to advanced polymers and composites. We have moved from building simple dwellings to constructing towering skyscrapers, expansive bridges, and intricate transportation networks.

Moreover, the advent of digital technology has revolutionised construction processes. Building Information Modelling (BIM), 3D printing, and prefabrication are just a few examples of how technology shapes the future of construction. Sustainability has also become a key focus, with green building practices and renewable energy sources becoming increasingly prevalent. India's first 3-D-printed post office is shown in Fig. 1. 1.

Fig. 1.1: India's first 3-D printed post office

The construction journey from the Stone Age to the present is a testament to human ingenuity and innovation. As we continue to push the boundaries of what is possible, one can only imagine what the future holds for this ever-evolving field.

Try to find out!

Which is the World's first 3-D printed building?

1.2 CONSTRUCTION PROJECT

A construction project involves a coordinated effort to build or assemble infrastructure. It includes several stages, from initial planning and design to financing and execution, and continues until the project is completed and ready for use. The size of construction projects can vary greatly, ranging from small projects such as home renovations to large projects such as skyscrapers or bridges. Each project requires a diverse team of experts, including architects, engineers, and construction managers, to work together to achieve the project's objectives while adhering to the specified budget and timeline. Amid this diverse team and complex tasks, construction management becomes crucial. Construction management is the field of study that involves overseeing the day-to-day operations, coordinating with various teams, and ensuring that the project stays on schedule and within budget with the required standards of quality and safety.

1.3 FEATURES OF A CONSTRUCTION PROJECT

1.3.1 Uniqueness

Every construction project is unique, meaning it has a specific purpose, location, design, construction methodology, and set of conditions. No two projects are identical, even if they are of the same type. For example, the construction of two identical residential buildings differs in various ways, such as the teams involved, the different sets of contracts, the different locations of the project, and the different ways adopted to construct the facility.

1.3.2 Complexity

Construction projects involve various tasks that must be coordinated and managed simultaneously. This includes everything from the design and planning of the facility to the procurement of materials and equipment to the construction of the facility, all requiring different skills and expertise. In addition, managing and working with different teams to build one entity under harsh weather conditions brings more complexity to construction.

1.3.3 Multidisciplinary Team

A diverse team of professionals, each with expertise, are involved in a construction project. This can include architects, engineers, project managers, and construction workers. Each team member plays a crucial role in ensuring the project's success.

1.3.4 Resource Constraints

Every construction project operates within certain constraints, such as a fixed budget or a set timeline. These constraints often include labour, material, and equipment resources, significantly affecting the project's success. Managing these constraints effectively ensures the project is completed on time and within budget.

1.3.5 Significant Investment

Construction projects often involve substantial financial investment. This includes the cost of materials, labour, equipment, and other resources. A small house construction can cost a few lakhs, while a big construction project can cost thousands of crores. Therefore, financial risk in construction projects is high, making effective cost management crucial.

1.3.6 Risk and Uncertainty

Construction projects face uncertainties due to various factors such as weather conditions, availability of materials, changes in design, scope change, and unforeseen site conditions. These uncertainties can introduce risks that can impact the project's timeline and cost, making risk management a crucial aspect of construction project management.

1.3.7 Stakeholders

A construction project involves multiple stakeholders, including the client, contractors, sub-contractors, consultants, suppliers, and regulatory authorities. Each stakeholder has different interests and expectations from the project. Though stakeholders work together to build a construction entity, their motives for work differ. For example, the client focuses more on quality, and the contractor's motive is to earn more profit in terms of money. Effective stakeholder management is essential to ensure clear communication, manage expectations, and facilitate smooth project execution.

1.3.8 Untrained Labour

Construction projects involve labourers with varying levels of skill and training. It is a fact that most contractors do not have their labourers. Whenever the contractors start any construction project, they hire locally available labour. Typically, the primary occupation of the locally available labourers is not construction. The presence of untrained labour can introduce productivity, quality of work, and safety challenges. Therefore, proper training and skill development are crucial for the project's success.

1.4 CONSTRUCTION PROJECT TYPES AND FEATURES

1.4.1 Residential Construction Projects

Residential construction projects include structures built for living purposes, such as individual homes and apartment buildings. The scale can vary from single-unit dwellings to large residential complexes.

1.4.2 Commercial Construction Projects

Commercial construction projects involve creating structures for business use, such as office buildings, shopping malls, and hotels. These projects often have additional complexities due to requirements for safety, environmental considerations, energy efficiency, and accessibility.

1.4.3 Institutional Construction Projects

The public sector typically commissions institutional construction projects, which involve the construction of structures such as educational institutions, healthcare facilities, government buildings, and other public service utilities. These projects are subject to specific requirements for accessibility, safety, and functionality. It's worth noting that institutional projects can also be privately owned, developed, and operated, which may lead to overlap with commercial projects.

1.4.4 Mixed-Use Construction Projects

Mixed-use construction projects blend residential, commercial, and sometimes industrial spaces into one development. They aim to create a balanced work, living, and leisure environment. However, incorporating multiple end uses can make the project more complex, thus creating problems in the project's phases.

There are mainly three types of mixed-use construction projects:

Vertical Mixed-Use

Vertical mixed-use projects layer different uses in a single building, such as retail on the ground floor, offices in the middle, and residences on top. They're prevalent in urban areas where space is limited.

Horizontal Mixed-Use

Unlike vertical projects that build up, horizontal mixed-use spread out, making them common in suburbs where space is abundant. Each building typically has a specific use.

Transit-Oriented Developments (TODs)

Transit-oriented development projects, often a mix of vertical and horizontal developments, are built near public transit hubs to reduce car dependency. They may be developed in conjunction with a new transit station or to rejuvenate an underused one.

1.4.5 Industrial Construction Projects

Industrial construction projects include factories, power plants, and warehouses. These projects require specialised expertise due to their large scale and the specific nature of industrial operations. Industrial projects frequently face stringent government regulations, particularly concerning environmental implications. Such projects generally necessitate specialised engineering expertise because such projects involve manufacturing various hazardous materials, which are not commonly found in other projects, like manufacturing structural steel, metal sheets, bitumen, and fly ash.

1.4.6 Heavy Civil Construction Projects

Heavy civil construction projects refer to large-scale public infrastructure projects that are critical for the functioning of a society and its economy. Heavy civil construction projects present significant engineering challenges due to their scale and complexity. Moreover, they can substantially impact the surrounding environment, necessitating careful planning and execution to minimise adverse effects. It's important to note that these projects are typically subject to rigorous regulatory oversight, particularly concerning environmental impact assessments. These projects can be further divided into two subcategories:

1.4.7 Transportation Projects

Transportation projects are designed to facilitate the movement of people and goods. They play a crucial role in connecting different regions and promoting economic growth. Examples of transportation projects include highway, bridge, railway, and port projects.

1.4.8 Utility Projects

Utility projects provide essential services required for society's day-to-day functioning. They involve the construction and maintenance of facilities for the delivery of public utilities. Examples of utility projects include water pipelines, sewage, and other public utility projects.

1.4.9 Monumental Construction Projects

Monumental construction projects include structures built to commemorate a person, event, or idea, such as monuments, statues, and memorials. These projects often have artistic, historical, or cultural significance and require careful design and craftsmanship.

Each type of construction project has its unique characteristics and requirements, making the construction industry a diverse and dynamic field. Every construction project, whether it's residential, commercial, institutional, industrial, heavy civil, or monumental, is unique. A few examples are shown in Fig. 1.2. Each has specific needs and challenges. For example, residential projects often focus on comfort and functionality, while commercial projects may prioritise efficiency and design. On the other hand, heavy civil projects require robust engineering solutions for large-scale public works. This variety makes the construction industry diverse, always adapting to new requirements and technologies.

(a) Residential Project

(b) Institutional Project

(c) Industrial Project

(d) Road Project

Fig. 1.2: Types of construction projects

1.5 PHASES OF A PROJECT

Phases of the construction are broadly divided into three phases, further divided into a few subcategories. All the phases are shown in Fig. 1.3.

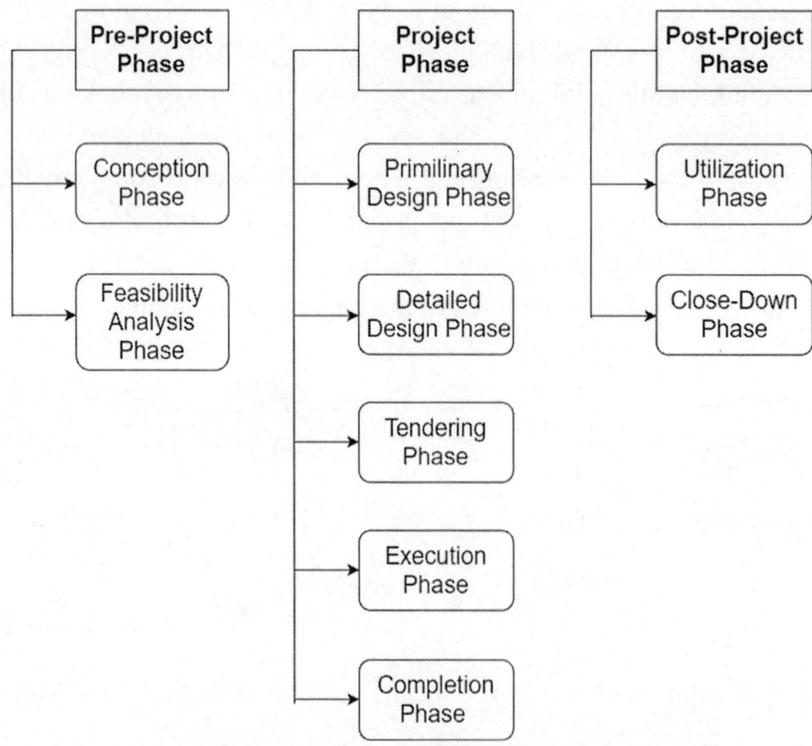

Fig. 1.3: Phases of construction

1.5.1 Pre-Project Phase

Conception phase

The conception phase identifies potential projects by examining needs and possible solutions. For instance, a city authority may explore various solutions to a parking issue near a popular landmark. These solutions should align with the authority's mission, vision, and budget. Some of the ideas generated are selected based on their benefits to the organisation. This phase is crucial for new construction projects as it influences the final cost and future uncertainty.

Feasibility Analysis Phase

The feasibility analysis phase evaluates the selected project ideas in the organisation's context. It considers the organisation's needs, strategic goals, and capabilities. Based on feasibility analysis, decision-makers can decide whether to proceed with the proposed project.

1.5.2 Project Phase

Preliminary Design Phase

The preliminary design phase involves the preparation of tendering and contracting documents. Basic design calculations, tender drawings, and design and material specifications are performed. Any changes from the initial scope of work are documented.

Detailed Design Phase

Detailed designs can be done internally or by giving a contract. The detailed design provides the final specifications and drawings for constructing any structure or equipment installation. For "item rate" contracts, this happens before tendering. For "design-build" or "lump sum" contracts, tendering starts after basic design and specifications. The definition and types of contracts are elaborated in Unit 7.

Tendering Phase

The tendering phase involves issuing tenders if a contractor executes the project. In a construction project, many stakeholders are involved. Therefore, to do different jobs in a construction project, various contracts are signed between other parties to work. Offering a contract to any party comes under the tendering phase. The tender documents should be clear and precise to avoid any disputes about the scope of work.

Execution Phase

The execution phase begins after the contract is awarded. If the detailed design and drawings were not part of the tender document, the contractor prepared them and followed them with the construction. In this phase, the structure comes from the drawings and is built on the ground.

Completion Phase

The completion phase involves testing, commissioning the major equipment, and handing the constructed facility to the client. The client checks the work and issues a completion certificate and approval.

1.5.3 Post-Project Phase

Utilisation Phase

The utilisation phase involves the client or end-user utilising the completed project. The facility's performance is regularly monitored and maintained throughout the project's life.

Close-down Phase

The close-down phase occurs when the project has served its purpose. It is then dismantled and disposed of, and the cycle of phases is repeated.

Note

It's important to understand that a project cycle has no universally agreed-upon number of phases. The division into phases can vary greatly depending on the nature of the project, the industry, the organisation, and the project management methodology used. Some project management methodologies propose a simple three-phase model (pre-project, project, and post-project). In contrast, others may break the project cycle into five, six, or even more phases. These can include the initiation phase, planning and budgeting phase, design phase, bid phase, execution, monitoring and control phase, and closure, among others.

Try to find out!

Under which category can the world's tallest statue be classified?

1.6 AGENCIES INVOLVED AND THEIR METHODS OF EXECUTION

There are many agencies involved in a construction project. Their roles, responsibilities, and methods of execution are different from each other. Evolving agencies may vary based on the nature of projects and corporate policies. The agencies involved in a typical construction project are shown in Fig. 1.4.

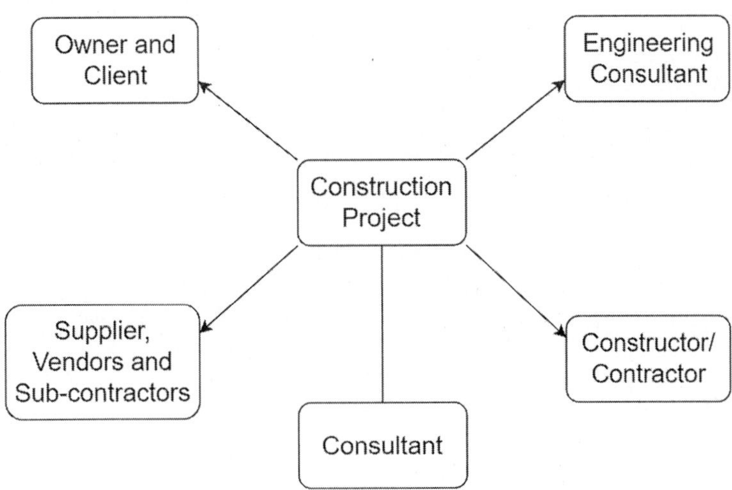

Fig. 1.4: Agencies involved in a construction project

1.6.1 Owner and Client

The entity or individual accountable for initiating and funding the planning and construction of the building is commonly known as the Client. In building contracts, the Client is typically identified as the Owner. The client plays a crucial role in construction projects by assuming responsibility for three key areas: funding, specification, and scope determination. Some clients in the construction industry are private organisations, public corporations, cooperative societies, legal entities, banks, local governments, individuals, etc. The primary obligations of clients are defining project goals, securing funding, creating budgets, managing financial risks, acquiring land, and navigating permits and regulations.

1.6.2 Consulting Agencies

Consulting agencies involving engineers and architects who provide technical services on behalf of the client as well as a constructor. Consultants are primarily responsible for feasibility study, planning, technical surveys, designing, drawing, tendering, evaluations, quality control, supervision, etc. Consultants help translate the owner's vision into technical blueprints and specifications, ensuring structural integrity and functionality. The expertise provided by a consultant may vary from project to project. For example, the expertise of a consultant required for a residential housing development may include designing functional and aesthetically pleasing homes, creating plans that maximise space efficiency, and ensuring compliance with local building codes and regulations. For a bridge construction project, the expertise of a consultant could be involved in designing a bridge that meets safety standards and environmental considerations.

1.6.3 Constructor/Contractor Agencies

The constructor/contractor overseeing the construction of the works utilises a blend of its internal resources and those of subcontractors. In other words, the contractor is responsible for constructing or building the structure on the ground. The contractor may engage consultants to contribute to the design development. The constructor must finish the project on time, ensure quality, and follow local laws to protect the environment. It's important not to harm the interests of owners, local communities, or employees during the project. The contractor to which the client gives the contract is also known as a general contractor or main contractor.

1.6.4 Legal Agencies

The legal agency plays a crucial role in enforcing contractual agreements. Legal agencies are responsible for dispute and claim settlement. When it comes to managing and controlling building projects, legal organisations are essential. These organisations are in charge of making sure that construction-related operations follow all applicable laws, rules, and specifications. These might be governmental organisations, regulatory agencies, or legal establishments that uphold zoning laws, building codes, safety rules, and environmental laws. In construction projects, legal firms play a crucial role in safeguarding the public's interests, guaranteeing the security of buildings, and promoting fair and ethical practices within the construction industry.

In addition, conflicts and disputes are unavoidable due to the involvement of various stakeholders with different objectives for a project (the client's object is to get quality construction while the contractor aims to earn more profit). The legal agencies get involved in construction projects to settle disputes.

1.6.5 Suppliers, Vendors, and Sub-contractors

Collaborating with vendors, subcontractors, and suppliers is critical to successfully executing projects. Suppliers provide the necessary materials and resources, and vendors offer a wide range of products and services for the project's progress.

In the context of significant construction endeavours, it is not anticipated that any single contractor would possess the expertise encompassing all specialised trades and techniques necessary for project completion. In such instances, the services of specialised contractors are enlisted through distinct agreements, referred to as subcontracts. In these scenarios, an overarching contract, denoted as the prime contract, is established between the project owner and the general contractor. Consequently, the contractor assumes responsibility to the owner for all work within the contractual scope. This accountability extends to the tasks executed by the contractor's workforce and subcontractors. The main contractor manages their work and schedules and coordinates the subcontractor's activities. Coordination assumes particular significance, notably in large-scale construction projects requiring diverse specialised trades at specific phases. These trades include mechanics, fabrication and erection, electrical work, air conditioning, foundation treatment, and piling. Conversely, the prime contractor executes tasks such as concreting, carpentry, painting, and masonry.

SUMMARY

The construction industry, with roots dating back to the Stone Age, has evolved significantly, showcasing human ingenuity and innovation. From the Indus Valley Civilisation to modern times, construction has advanced in materials, technologies, and sustainability practices. Digital technology, including Building Information Modelling (BIM) and 3D printing, has revolutionised processes. Construction projects, characterised by uniqueness, complexity, and multidisciplinary teams, involve various types such as residential, commercial, institutional, industrial, and heavy civil. The basics of construction management revolve around efficient organisation, coordination, and supervision of construction projects from inception to completion. It encompasses key principles such as project planning, scheduling, budgeting, procurement, and quality control. Construction managers play a pivotal role in liaising between clients, architects, engineers, contractors, and subcontractors to ensure that projects are delivered on time, within budget, and to the required quality standards. Effective communication, risk management, and conflict resolution are essential skills for construction managers to address challenges and mitigate potential delays or cost overruns. Additionally, construction management involves compliance with regulatory requirements, safety standards, and environmental regulations to ensure workers' well-being and the project's sustainability. Construction management basics are essential for overseeing successful construction projects and delivering value to stakeholders.

EXERCISE

Make a few groups of students, each having five students. The students take on different roles in managing a construction project. Assigning each group, a specific construction project scenario (e.g., building a school, constructing a bridge, renovating a historic building). In their roles:

a) Identify and discuss the unique features of their assigned construction project.

b) Determine the most appropriate project type and justify their decision.

c) Outline the key phases of the project and allocate responsibilities for each phase among the group members.

d) Simulate interactions between stakeholders, including the owner/client, architect, contractor, and regulatory agencies, to negotiate project requirements, resolve conflicts, and ensure compliance with regulations.

MULTIPLE CHOICE QUESTIONS

1. Which of the following is NOT a unique feature of construction projects?

   A) Temporary nature
   B) Large-scale equipment usage
   C) High predictability in outcomes
   D) Unique project requirements

2. What construction project involves residential homes, apartments, or condominiums?

   A) Civil construction
   B) Commercial construction
   C) Industrial construction
   D) Residential construction

3. During which phase of a construction project are bids solicited from potential contractors?

A) Pre-construction phase
B) Design phase
C) Construction phase
D) Post-construction phase

4. Which of the following is NOT a phase of the construction project lifecycle?

A) Planning
B) Procurement
C) Development
D) Post-construction

5. What is the primary goal of value engineering in construction projects?

A) Maximize project duration
B) Minimize project cost without sacrificing quality
C) Increase project complexity
D) Maximize project scope

6. What type of construction project involves the construction of office buildings, retail stores, or shopping centres?

A) Civil construction
B) Commercial construction
C) Industrial construction
D) Residential construction

7. Which stakeholder in a construction project is responsible for designing the building?

A) Architect
B) Owner
C) Contractor
D) Engineer

8. What is the primary function of the planning phase in a construction project?

A) Develop detailed construction plans
B) Acquire necessary permits and approvals
C) Identify project stakeholders

D) Establish project budget and timeline

9. Which phase of a construction project involves obtaining necessary approvals and permits from regulatory authorities?

   A) Design phase
   B) Pre-construction phase
   C) Construction phase
   D) Post-construction phase

10. Who is typically responsible for managing the finances and budget of a construction project?

   A) Owner
   B) Architect
   C) Construction Manager
   D) Contractor

ANSWERS TO MULTIPLE CHOICE QUESTIONS

1	2	3	4	5	6	7	8	9	10
C	D	A	C	B	B	A	D	B	A

SHORT ANSWER TYPE QUESTIONS

1. Which phases include tasks such as "conducting a feasibility study of the proposed project", "reviewing design documents", "pre-qualifying contractors", and "concession agreement"?
2. Name three digital technologies transforming construction processes.
3. Provide one example of a multi-purpose construction project.
4. What is the difference between leadership and management?
5. How is the construction industry different from the manufacturing industry?
6. Briefly explain the role of an architect in a construction project and highlight one key task they perform during the design phase.

7. Identify two major stakeholders in a construction project other than the client or owner and describe their roles and responsibilities.
8. Describe the Design-Build (DB) method of construction execution and explain its advantages compared to other methods.

LONG ANSWER TYPE QUESTIONS

1. Mention the primary challenges associated with untrained labour.
2. Identify the primary responsibility of legal agencies in construction.
3. List ten real examples of heavy civil infrastructure projects of different sectors with their completion time (in years) and involved stakeholders.
4. Explore the historical significance of construction from the Stone Age to modern times, highlighting key milestones.
5. Discuss the advancements in construction during the Indus Valley Civilisation, emphasising architectural achievements.
6. Analyse the impact of digital technology on the construction industry, citing specific examples like BIM and 3D printing.
7. Compare and contrast the features of residential, commercial, and industrial construction projects, including their purposes and complexities.
8. Take an example of any actual ongoing or completed construction project, detailing the activities involved in each phase and the difficulties the contractor faces.

TUTORIAL

You are part of a construction project team that renovates a historic building into a museum. As part of your responsibilities, you must address various challenges and considerations specific to this project. You need to develop a phased timeline for the renovation project, including key milestones and activities for each phase, from planning to post-construction. In addition, you need to analyse the roles of regulatory agencies involved in preserving historic buildings and explain their methods of execution to ensure compliance with preservation standards during the renovation process.

KNOW MORE

For more information related to this topic scan the QR code.

OR

Type this link in your browser

https://www.routledge.com/rsc/downloads/An_Introduction_to_Construction_Management.pdf

BIBLIOGRAPHY

- Abdullahi, A. H. (2014). Review of subcontracting practice in the construction industry. *Journal of Environmental Sciences and Resources Management*, 6(1), 23-33.
- Bennett, F. L. 2003. *The management of construction*, Butterworth Heinemann.
- Dubois, A., and Gadde, L. E. (2002). The construction industry as a loosely coupled system: implications for productivity and innovation. *Construction Management & Economics*, 20(7), 621-631.
- Hughes, J. M. Will. (2001). *Roles in construction projects: analysis and terminology*, Construction Industry Publications: London.
- Jha, K. N. (2015). *Construction project management: theory and practice*, Pearson India Education Service Pvt. Ltd: New Delhi.
- Kwofie, T. E., Fugar, F., Adinyira, E., and Ahadzie, D. K. (2014). Identification and classification of the unique features of mass housing projects. *Journal of Construction Engineering*, 2014(2), 1-11.
- Yang, H. Y. L. Z. Jie. (2020). Influence factors on general contractor capability in the context of transforming China. *Advances in Civil Engineering*, 11(18), 8874579.

CONSTRUCTION PROJECT PLANNING

UNIT SPECIFICS

The process of methodically arranging and defining every action and resource needed to execute a construction project effectively is known as construction project planning. This planning step must be undertaken to guarantee that the project is managed effectively, stays within budget, fulfils the highest quality requirements, and is finished within the allotted period. This unit deals with the different methods and processes to plan an effective construction project.

RATIONALE

To execute a successful construction project, understanding tools and techniques for effecting planning and scheduling is necessary.

PRE-REQUISITE

Basics of probability

UNIT OUTCOMES

List of outcomes of this unit is as follows:

U2-O1: Understand the stages of project planning

U2-O2: Develop project plans and schedules through various techniques

U2-O3: Adjustment of schedules based on available resources

U2-O4: Estimation of project delays

Unit Outcomes	Expected Mapping with Course Outcomes *(1- Weak Correlation; 2- Medium correlation; 3- Strong Correlation)*					
	CO-1	CO-2	CO-3	CO-4	CO-5	CO-6
U2-O1	3	1	1	1	1	2
U2-O2	3	3	2	1	2	1
U2-O3	2	3	3	1	3	1
U2-O4	2	2	2	2	3	3

2.1 STAGES OF PROJECT PLANNING

2.1.1 Pre-tender Planning

The groundwork for A successful tendering process is laid during the pre-tender phase. It entails actions and choices that must be made before the official release of the tender. Pre-tender planning is an essential stage of the construction project lifecycle before the official bidding or tendering procedure. Making sure the project is prepared for prospective contractors to bid on requires careful planning and organisation. Doing a comprehensive requirements assessment is essential before starting a tender process. This entails determining the company's needs and precisely outlining the project's parameters. Establishing the goals, requirements, and outcomes probable contractors or service providers anticipate meeting is crucial in pre-tendering.

2.1.2 Pre-construction Planning

Pre-construction planning is essential to the project control procedure and, consequently, the project's success. In this pre-construction planning phase, the project is defined, possible problems are identified, planning and scheduling are done, the scope is estimated, costs are calculated, and the job demands are analysed. The finest opportunity to put the project on a successful path is through preconstruction planning, which is the initial measurement.

2.1.3 Detailed Construction Planning

The act of creating and recording a detailed plan for carrying out a building project is known as "detailed construction planning." This planning stage is essential to guarantee that the project is finished effectively, on schedule, within budget, and with the necessary quality standards. Coordination between multiple parties and a multidisciplinary approach are essential for detailed construction planning. The objective is to develop a thorough plan that directs the project from start to finish, considering every facet of construction management and guaranteeing project success.

2.2 ROLES OF CLIENT AND CONTRACTOR

The client and the contractor are the most important stakeholders of a construction project. As stated in Unit 1, understanding the roles and duties of all parties involved before starting a construction project is essential for an effortless procedure, adhering to legal standards, and, eventually, completing the project successfully. Clients are responsible for verifying the qualifications of the individuals they choose, guaranteeing appropriate project management frameworks, allocating ample time and resources for every phase, ensuring quality in the project, and furnishing designers and contractors with pre-construction data. During the planning and construction phases, as well as the upkeep and use of a building once it is constructed, clients should remove, minimise, or regulate hazards and risks. Additionally, they ought to furnish details regarding the residual hazards. Contractors should plan, manage, and oversee their duties and that of their staff; verify the qualifications of all employees and staff; train staff; adhere to all on-site health and safety regulations; and ensure sufficient welfare facilities for their staff.

2.2.1 Client

The client's role and obligations are vital in guaranteeing the project's safety and effective completion. Some of the key roles of a client are listed below:

Project Management

The client must efficiently manage the project. This means ensuring safety rules are followed, providing enough time and resources for the project, and verifying that construction is done as safely as possible. In addition, the client must guarantee that all project participants have adequate channels for collaboration and communication.

Finance, Budget and Decision making

The client must ensure sufficient finance for the completion of the project. Therefore, the client must work with project participants to create a reasonable budget aligned with the project's objectives. The client also determines the project's layout, makes significant adjustments, and approves project designs, plans, and alterations that might occur while constructing.

Selection of Project Team and Contractor

The client selects the principal members of the project team, such as contractors, planners, engineers, and project supervisors. The client also ascertained that the project team had the knowledge and experience required to fulfil the project's objectives.

Adherence to Regulations and Contractual Conditions

The client verifies that all applicable laws, ordinances, and standards are followed during construction and acquires the project's required licenses and permissions. The client also sets the terms and conditions of payment, duties, deadlines for the project, and roles for contractors and subcontractors in contracts in conjunction with legal experts.

Health and Safety and Conformity with Welfare Regulations

Throughout the project, the client is responsible for taking appropriate steps to maintain and evaluate health and safety protocols. This entails assessing the effectiveness of the measures regularly and making reasonable adjustments. In addition to other services, this entails offering enough and appropriate hygienic and laundry facilities, drinking water, and rest areas.

2.2.2 Contractor

In a construction project, a contractor must ensure the work is done efficiently and safely. Organisations or individuals that manage building projects as part of their business are known as contractors. A key player in a construction project is the contractor, who brings together different components to produce a final product that satisfies the client's time frame, budget, quality, and artistry requirements. To effectively carry out these duties, a contractor must have strong communication skills, project management skills, and the ability to pay attention to detail. The key roles of a contractor in a construction project are:

i. Bidding and proposal submission
ii. Pre-construction planning and project scheduling
iii. Ascertain the client's understanding of their responsibilities
iv. Organizing, supervising, and monitoring construction activities
v. Training of workers
vi. Complying with the safety and health regulation

2.2.3 Level of Details

The degree of accuracy and intricacy in the project's preparation, layout, paperwork, and implementation is the level of detail in a construction project. The amount of detail may change depending on the project's requirements, scale, and complexity. The qualities of the project, the needs of the client, and the demand for control and precision will determine the right level of detail. To effectively manage time, assets, and expenses and guarantee the successful completion of the construction project, it is imperative to strike a balance with the level of detail.

2.3 PROCESS OF DEVELOPMENT OF PLANS AND SCHEDULES

A systematic and controlled procedure is used to create plans and schedules in construction project management to guarantee that the work is well-planned, continues to be on requirements, and is finished within the allotted time. The sequencing of tasks in a construction project is arranged through construction scheduling, which guides the project's execution in project management. The project's general timeline, including milestones, is arranged along with the tasks and activities in a project schedule. The construction project schedule monitors the progress of a project to ensure that the project is completed on time, and if not, compute the delays in the project.

2.3.1 Work Breakdown Structure

An organised, hierarchical, and deliverable-focused project breakdown is called a work breakdown structure, or WBS. The ability to deconstruct the scope of a project and see every activity needed to finish it makes it a valuable diagram for project managers. The work breakdown structure is a crucial project planning tool because it details every step of the project's work. The WBS diagram shows the ultimate project deliverables, tasks, and work packages. The main components and concepts of a work breakdown structure are as follows:

The order of the hierarchy

The project is divided into successively smaller and more manageable components by the hierarchical structure of the WBS. Each level below the top level delves deeper into specifics, while the top level reflects the project as a whole.

Sub-project level and deliverables

The primary project phases or stages are usually represented at the top level of the WBS. Each phase is divided into deliverables at later stages, each phase's definitive outcomes.

Work Package

The most basic elements of the WBS are work packages, which stand for discrete, achievable objectives. Every job package needs to be precisely defined, with obvious limitations and a quantifiable result.

Decomposition and Manage Plans

Disassembling higher-level components into smaller, more manageable parts is called decomposition. This process is repeated until the job packages are small enough for efficient management and control. The scope, budgetary constraints, actual expenditures, and timeline are linked and compared to earned value for performance evaluation at control accounts, which are management control points. These checkpoints are frequently in line with significant outcomes or benchmarks.

Level of activity

A work package can be subdivided into numerous steps or smaller activities requiring time and resources. Every one of these tasks is referred to as an activity.

Operational level

Generally speaking, the operational level stands for the lower tiers of the hierarchy where particular task packages are established. An activity consists of one or more stages in each operation. For instance, the following activities are included in "earthmoving" for a road construction project:

i. digging,
ii. filling,
iii. grading, and
iv. compacting

Fig. 2.1 shows a typical WBS of construction of a small house.

2.3.2 Bar Chart

When rectangular bars with heights or lengths proportionate to the values they represent are used to display categorical data, the resulting chart or graph is called a bar chart or bar graph. One may layout the bars horizontally or vertically. Comparisons between distinct categories are presented in a bar graph. The categories under comparison are displayed on one axis of the chart. At the same time, a measured value is represented on the other—several bar graphs display bars grouped into multiple groups, displaying the values of various measured variables. To be completed, a project often comprises several clearly defined, manageable components or tasks that must be carried out or finished in a specific order. In 1910, Mr. Henry L. Gantt designed a bar chart to facilitate an improvised model of planning and controlling the production at the ordinance factory of the U.S. Navy. This straightforward chart, often known as a Gantt chart, shows the activity schedule. A horizontal bar chart called a Gantt chart is used in project management to show the project's schedule over time visually. Fig. 2.2 shows a typical Gantt chart with a project of 22 days' duration. Each activity is indicated by a blue colour bar.

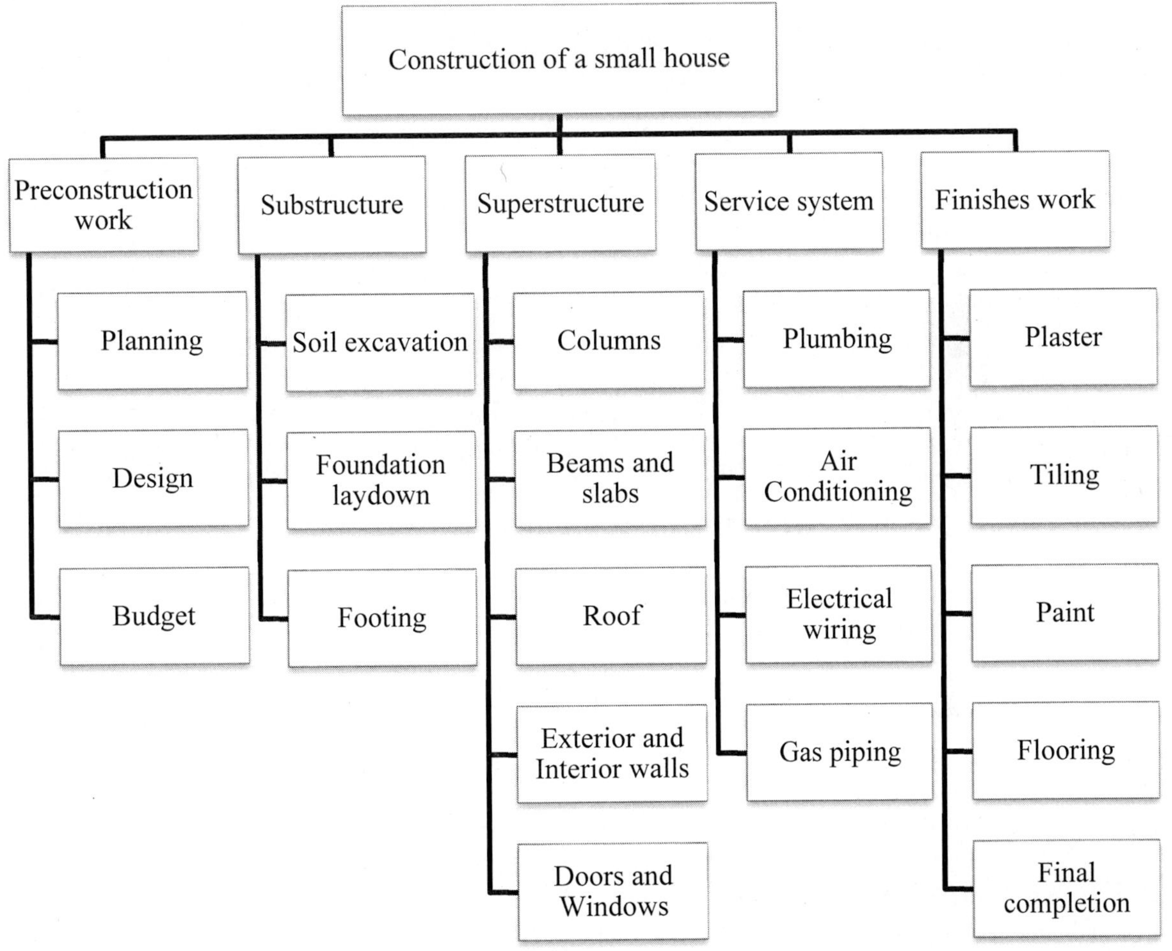

Fig. 2.1: Work breakdown structure

Try to find out!

Which of the two software are commonly used for project planning, scheduling, and monitoring?

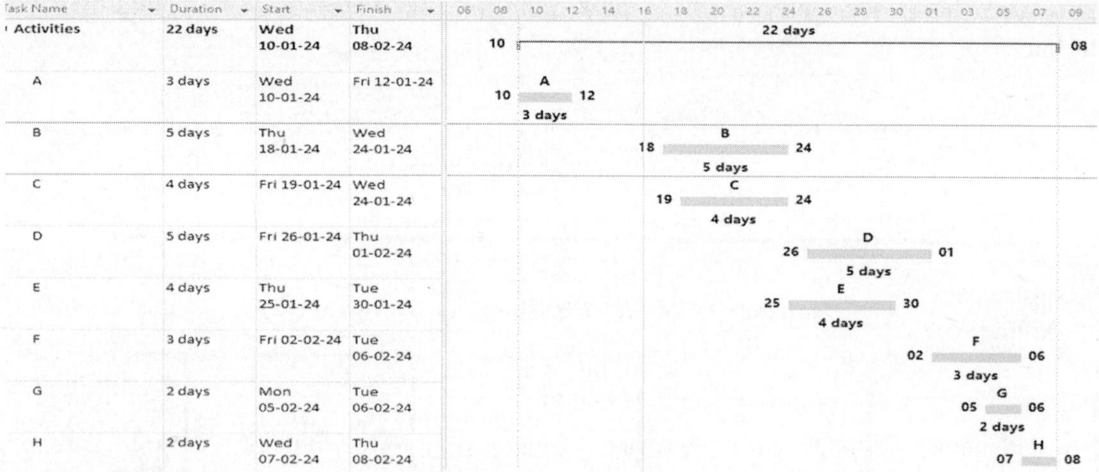

Task Name	Duration	Start	Finish
Activities	22 days	Wed 10-01-24	Thu 08-02-24
A	3 days	Wed 10-01-24	Fri 12-01-24
B	5 days	Thu 18-01-24	Wed 24-01-24
C	4 days	Fri 19-01-24	Wed 24-01-24
D	5 days	Fri 26-01-24	Thu 01-02-24
E	4 days	Thu 25-01-24	Tue 30-01-24
F	3 days	Fri 02-02-24	Tue 06-02-24
G	2 days	Mon 05-02-24	Tue 06-02-24
H	2 days	Wed 07-02-24	Thu 08-02-24

Fig. 2.2: Gantt chart

2.4 CONCEPT OF PRODUCTIVITY

In the construction sector, productivity is referred to by various words, including production rate, labour-hour (l-h) rate, performance factor, etc. Productivity is the ratio of output/input, or actual output (in terms of creating economic value), to the input of an associated resource (often, but not always, represented in l-hr).

Several factors impact project productivity. A project manager must understand each factor and try to control them to enhance productivity. These are as follows:

2.4.1 Inadequate Planning

A successful project in the future depends on preconstruction planning. Starting a construction project without proper planning is one of the biggest mistakes that may happen. This could result in several difficulties and delays at the location. A lack of critical equipment on hand when needed or skilled workers, for instance, could result from inadequate project planning. This can result in a significant loss in output.

2.4.2 Overtime and Stress

Construction is a physically demanding job that primarily uses manual labour. Overworked and tired construction workers can hurt their output. Overly high expectations from construction managers ultimately have a detrimental impact on labour productivity.

Construction businesses should put worker well-being first, use good project management techniques, think about fair working hours, and create a positive, encouraging work atmosphere to lessen the harmful impacts of overtime and stress. Construction teams can function better and produce more when workloads are balanced, proper rest times are given, and stress-related issues are addressed.

2.4.3 Sluggish Decision Making

There are inevitable obstacles in the path of construction projects. Contractors must act quickly and decisively in each situation when this occurs. Contractors' quick decision-making skills are one of the significant factors that could affect construction productivity. This can be attributed to their lack of access to appropriate information, which would prevent them from making a snap judgment.

2.4.4 Inventory and Machinery Management

Adequate inventory and machinery management guarantees timely resource availability, lowers downtime, controls costs, fosters better teamwork, and improves project efficiency and quality. All of these factors boost construction productivity. Using best practices and contemporary technology in these domains can significantly enhance the execution of construction projects.

2.4.5 Lack of Communication

On a construction site, poor communication can significantly and detrimentally impact output, effectiveness, and project success. As several stakeholders work on a project, effective communication becomes imperative. Construction project managers should prioritise open, honest, and transparent communication at every project step. This entails utilising digital communication tools, holding frequent project meetings, offering efficient communication training, and encouraging information sharing and teamwork among all parties involved.

2.4.6 Slow Digital Transformation

The decreased use of digital tools can negatively impact construction productivity. In a field where technology is increasingly used to improve productivity and teamwork, underusing digital technologies might result in problems and lost opportunities. To increase productivity and project outcomes, construction stakeholders should prioritise adopting and routinely using digital technologies, fund training initiatives to improve team members' digital literacy and foster a culture that welcomes new technology.

2.5 NETWORK DIAGRAM

A network is a graphical representation of project activities and their logical connections (dependencies) in project management. A project network, or project network diagram, is the name given to this visual depiction. The network diagram aids in planning, scheduling, and managing the numerous jobs and activities the project manager needs to finish a project. Guidelines are followed while developing a project network. These are explained later in the current chapter. A typical network diagram consists of events and activities, as shown in Fig. 2.3. In a network, no events consume any time; only activities consume time. We will learn this later in the current chapter.

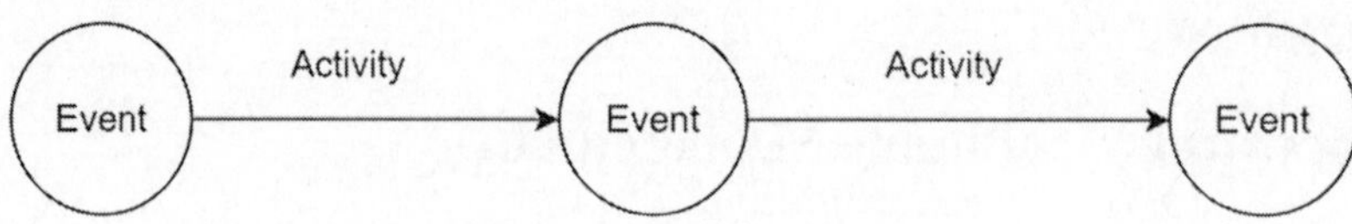

Fig. 2.3: A network diagram

2.5.1 Event

An "event" is a moment that marks the conclusion of a specific task or achievement. In a network diagram, events are shown as circles or nodes connected by arrows to demonstrate the connections and logical flow between various tasks. Events serve as the beginning or end of one or more activities and are essential in establishing the timeline for the project. Some examples of events are the foundation being completed, the slab being cast, the exterior wall being finished, etc.

Representation of Events

The events, also known as nodes, are represented by shapes like circular, rectangular, elliptical, square or any other geometrical figure, as shown in Fig. 2.4

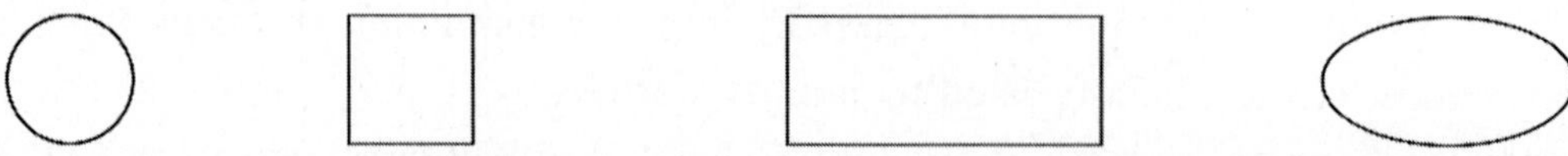

Fig. 2.4: Ways of representation of events

Type of Events

Tail event: Any event that signifies the start of an activity is called a tail event. The tail event at the beginning of a project is referred to as the initial event. Fig. 2.5 (a) shows an initial event that represents the start of a project, whereas Fig. 2.5 (b) shows a tail event that represents the beginning of any activity but not the project—understanding that an initial event represents the beginning of any activity and the whole project.

(a) Initial Event (b) Tail event

Fig. 2.5: Tail events

Head events: Every activity has an ending, which is again a particular moment in time and is signified by an event. This type of event is called a head event because it is related to the head or pointed end of the arrow in the network diagram. Fig. 2.6 (a) shows a head event, whereas Fig. 2.6 (b) shows a final event of a project. Here, the project is ending, and no other activity is emerging.

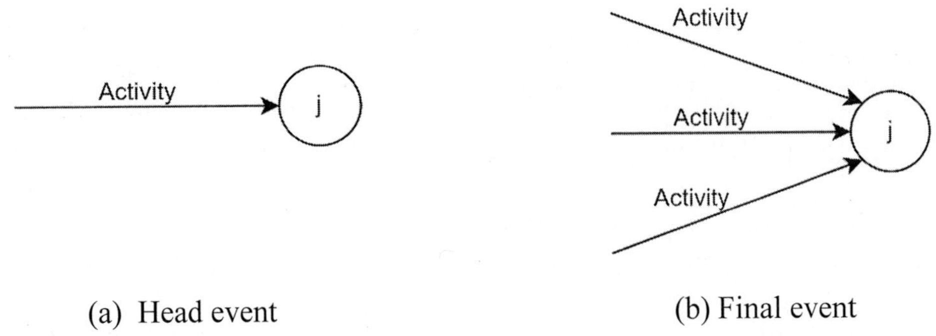

(a) Head event (b) Final event

Fig. 2.6: Head events

Predecessor events: Predecessor events are generally defined as those actions or events that must be finished before moving on to another activity or event. Immediate predecessor events occur exactly before another occurrence without any time interval.

Successor events: Successor events are defined as specific events or activities that come after another particular event or activity. The term "immediate successor events" refers to events that happen right after another event without any breaks in between.

Illustration 1

Suppose a construction project is going on. Several events will need to be done to execute the project successfully. Let's take two of them: excavation is completed, and the foundation is poured. As per the process, excavation must be finished before the foundation is poured. Therefore, among these two events, 'excavation completed' is a predecessor event, and 'foundation poured' is the successor event.

Illustration 2

Fig. 2.7 shows the network diagram drawn from the given event data.

Events	Predecessor	Immediate Predecessor events	Successor	Immediate Successor Events
1	-	-	2,3,4,5	2,3
2	1	1	4,5	4
3	1	1	4,5	4
4	1,2,3	2,3	5	5
5	1,2,3,4	4	-	-

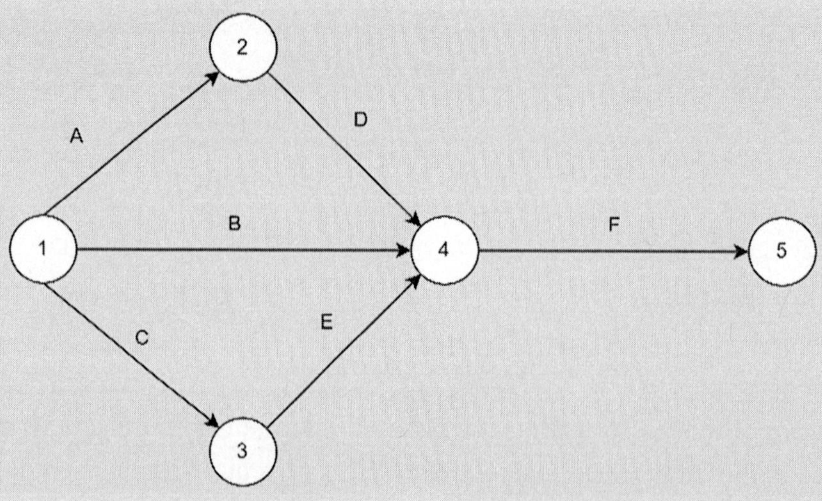

Fig. 2.7: Network diagram

2.5.2 Activity

An "activity" is a designated task or unit of work that must be finished as a larger project component. Project network diagrams show activities as nodes/arrows, the constituent parts of a project schedule. Every task has a predetermined time, depends on other tasks to be completed, and advances a certain project goal or milestone. Fig. 2.8 shows activity on the arrow – laying of foundation – of 10 days' duration.

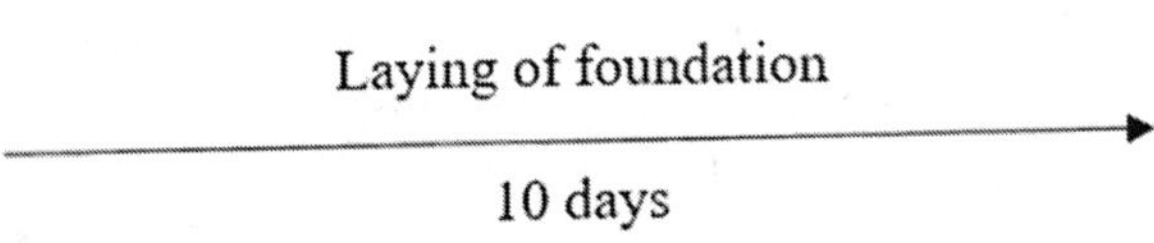

Fig. 2.8: Activity on arrow

Predecessor activities: Activities that must be completed before an activity are referred to as that activity's predecessor activities.

Successor Activities: Succeeding activities to an activity under consideration must be completed following the conclusion of the action under consideration.

Illustration 3

Fig. 2.9 shows the network diagram drawn from the given activity data.

Activities	Predecessor activity	Immediate predecessor activity	Successor activity	Immediate successor activity
A (1-2)	–	–	C (2-4) E (4-6)	C (2-4)
B (1-3)	–	–	D (3-5) F (5-6)	D (3-5)
C (2-4)	A (1-2)	A (1-2)	E (4-6)	E (4-6)
D (3-5)	B (1-3)	B (1-3)	F (5-6)	F (5-6)
E (4-6)	A (1-2) C (2-4)	A (1-2)	–	–
F (5-6)	B (1-3) D (3-5)	B (1-3)	–	–

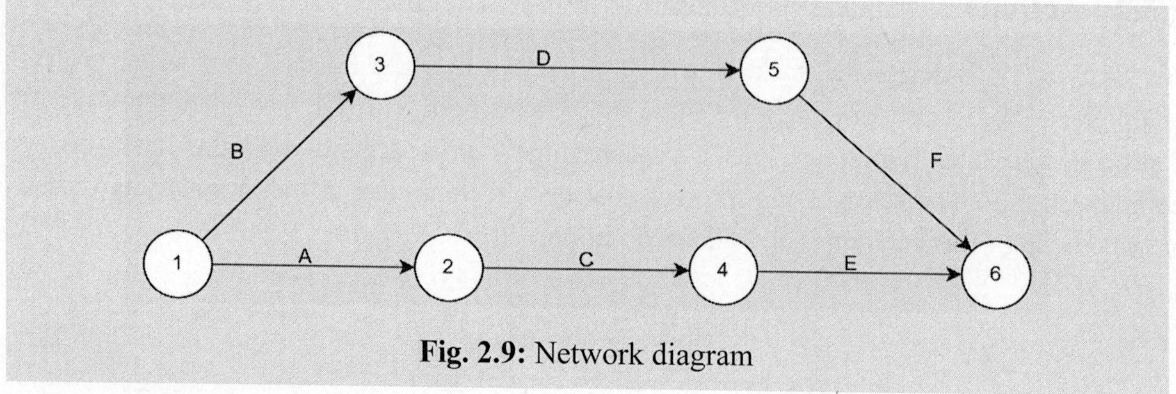

Fig. 2.9: Network diagram

2.5.3 Dummy Activity

Dummy activity defines the interdependencies between activities and is included in a network for logical and mathematical reasons. It does not require the consumption of resources and, hence, does not require any time to be completed. In a network diagram, dummies are commonly shown as dashed lines. Without a specific task, the dashed line indicates a link between the nodes representing activities. In Fig. 2.10, Activity E cannot be started until B and C are completed, whereas Activity D depends only on B. In such a case, without using the dummy activity, the logic of the network cannot be established.

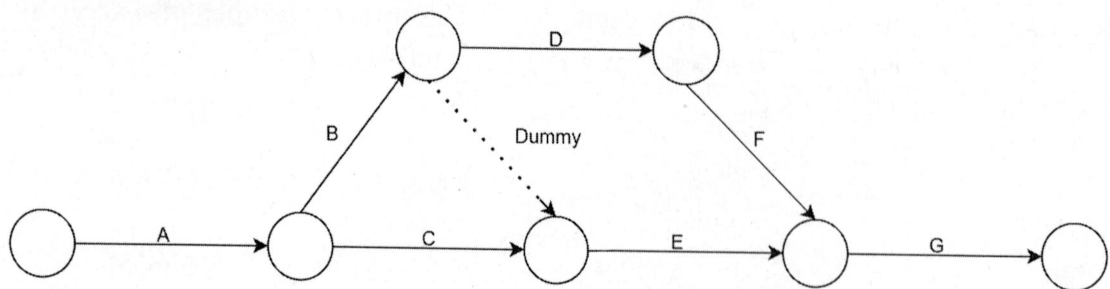

Fig. 2.10: Network with dummy activity

2.5.4 Types of Network

Two types of networks can now be used for construction planning —activity-on-arrow (AOA) and activity-on-node (AON). The nodes in AOA can be seen at either the beginning or the end of an activity because the activities are represented as arrows going from one node to another. Activities in AON are represented as nodes, and an arrow linking two nodes indicates the direct predecessor relationship between two activities.

It should be emphasised that all activities must be finished before starting a new one and that an arrow indicates a logical order; its length or direction has no bearing on how long a project will take. Time is typically shown as flowing from top to bottom and left to right when project networks are drawn.

Activity-on-Arrow (AOA)

When a roof slab is being constructed, for example, the job can be divided into easy tasks like erection of framework(A), bending of reinforcement(B), placing of reinforcement(C) and concreting(D), which must be done in that order. It takes 3, 4, 7, and 2 days to complete each task, meaning the project may be finished with 16 hours of effort. Therefore, the representation of Activity on the arrow is shown in the following Fig. 2.11.

Each activity in this model (Fig. 2.11) is specified in terms of two nodes (let's say i, j), so i and j represent the activity's beginning and end, respectively. Nevertheless, this does not imply that i or j are significant regarding the time scale. Each activity's (i, j) beginning and ending times must be determined independently. In the above example, the activities of erection of framework(A), bending of reinforcement(B), placing of reinforcement(C), and concreting(D) can be represented as (1,2), (2,3), (3,4) and (4,5) respectively.

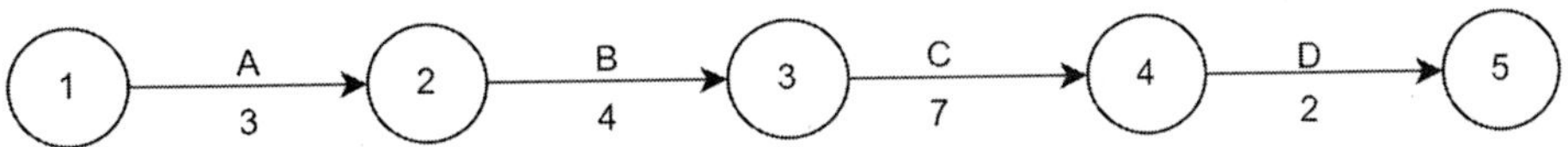

Fig. 2.11: Activity on arrow representation

Adding dummy activities to an AOA network, as shown in Fig. 2.12, are laborious operations that make the network appear long and add to the additional effort in the computational process (the computation considers both the actual and dummy activities). To circumvent these drawbacks, the AON substitute has been developed.

Activity-on-Node (AON)

The activities in the AON network are represented by circles or boxes called nodes, and an arrow connecting the two nodes indicates the direct predecessor relationship between the two activities. The diagram in Fig. 2.13 shows the AON network for the project in Fig. 212. It is evident that while AOA has used two dummy activities, d1 and d2, AON has not utilised a single dummy for the same number of activities and similar linkages.

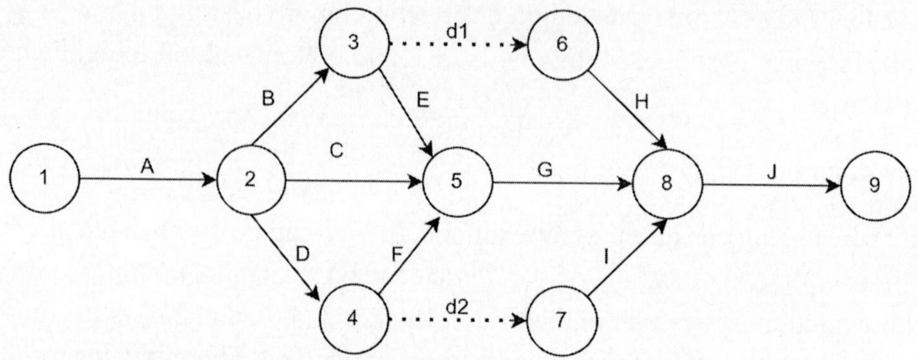

Fig. 2.12: AOA network diagram with two dummy activities

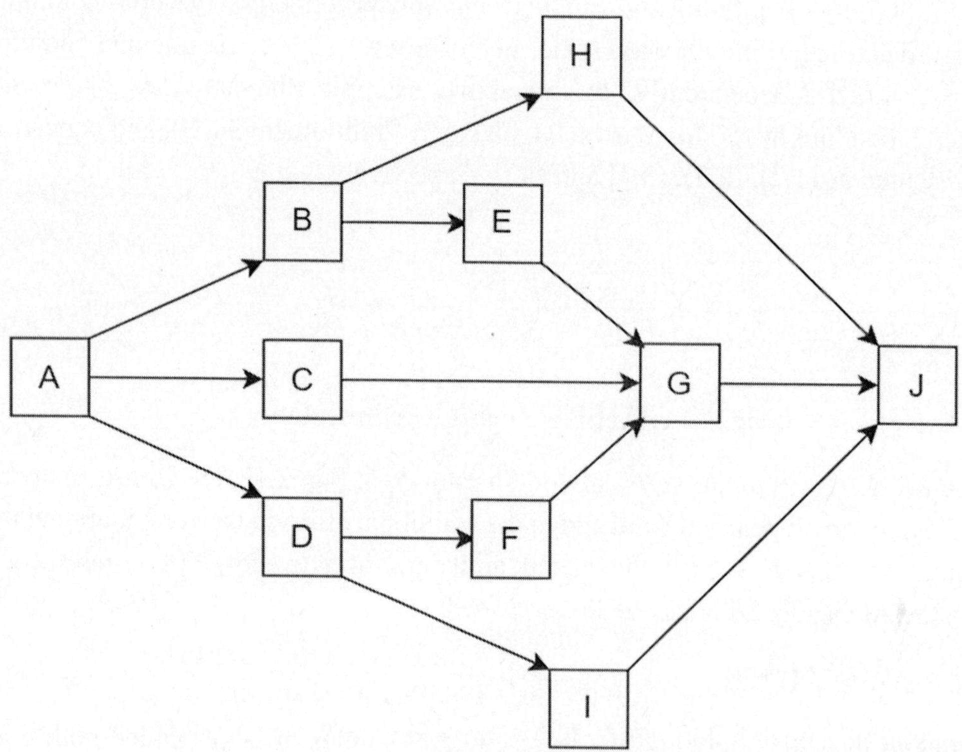

Fig. 2.13: AON network diagram example

People frequently ask which is more convenient when comparing AOA with AON. While AON is more practical in cases where the network is huge, intricate, and has several relationships, AOA appears to be the most intuitive option when building a small network manually. Additionally, it is far simpler to set up for calculation. Drawing and editing AON is easier than AOA (although computer programs can also make this an easy affair). Moreover, AON is easier to understand, and even non-technical people may grasp it easily.

2.6 NETWORK RULES

A network diagram of any project is developed based on specific rules. The following points are worth noting when drawing a network diagram:

i. Each defined activity is represented in the network by a single, unique arrow.
ii. All tasks before an activity may be started must be finished.
iii. The arrows showing different activities only show logical progression. There is no bearing on the arrows' length or direction.
iv. The arrow's direction indicates the basic temporal progression.
v. Numbers are used to identify events.
vi. The activities are distinguished by alphabet or the numbers of their beginning and ending events.
vii. A network should have just one starting and ending node else it is considered to have a dangling error. Such an error is shown in Fig. 2.14, where multiple initial and end events are available.

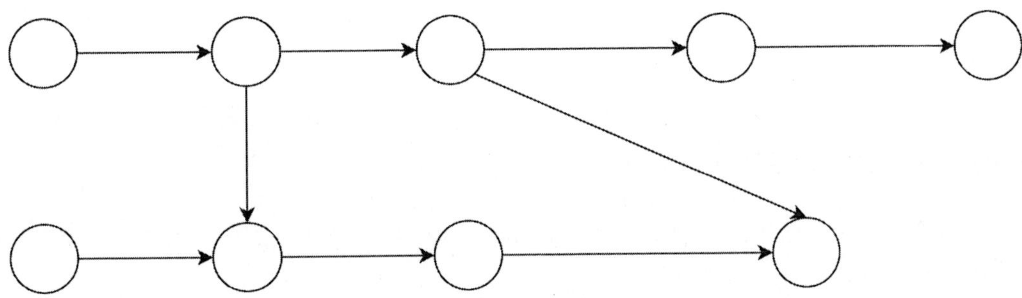

Fig. 2.14: Dangling error in a network

viii. It is not allowed to loop in a network. An event cannot happen more than once, meaning no network path can loop back to a prior event instance; otherwise, there will be a looping error in the network, as shown in Fig. 2.15.

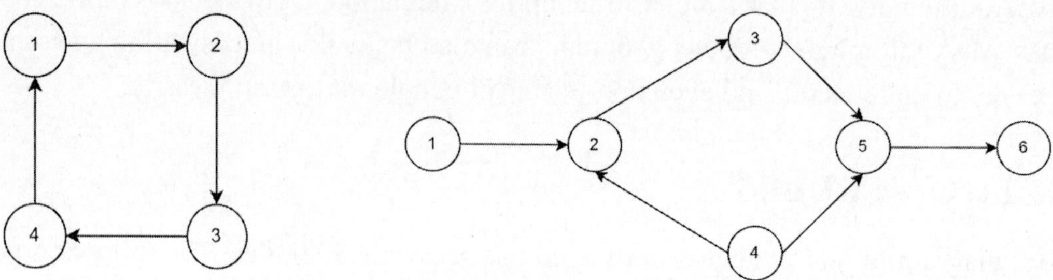

Fig. 2.15: Looping error in a network

ix. Normally, arrows shouldn't cross one another. If crossing is required, one should be built over the other by a bridge, as shown in Fig. 2.16.

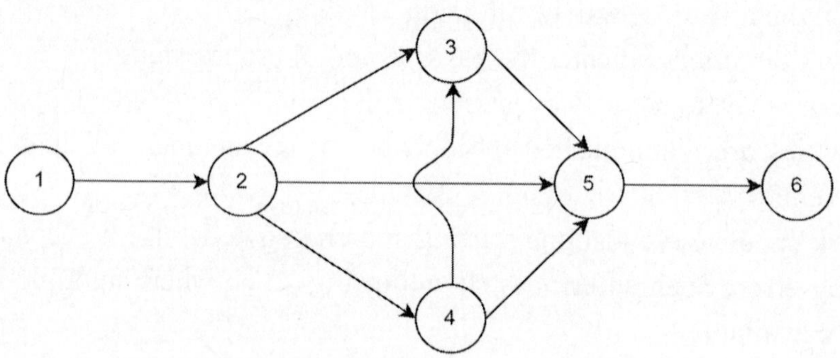

Fig. 2.16: Bridging of a network

2.7 FULKERSON'S RULE FOR SEQUENTIAL NUMBERING OF EVENTS IN A NETWORK

Fulkerson's Rule aims to give a systematic approach to numbering a network's nodes so that the numbers accurately represent the network's connection and structure. Following are the steps worth noting while numbering the events in a network:

i. The first event (initial), designated as "1," has all outgoing and no incoming arrows.
ii. Eliminate every arrow originating from node '1'. As a result, at least one more node will become an initial event. These occurrences should be numbered 2, 3,…
iii. Remove all the arrows that branch off these numbered events to add more starting events. Assign these occurrences the following numbers.
iv. Continue until you reach the last, or terminal node, which is numbered and has all of its arrows pointing inside and none outward.

Illustration 4

Giving numbers to the events for the following network diagram:

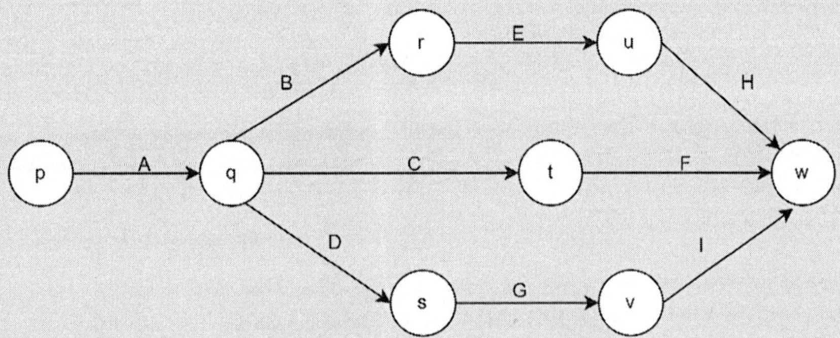

i. Event p is the initial event, so that it will be numbered 1

ii. Now, neglect the arrow (A) originating from the node p. Therefore, q will be the new initial event, so number it as 2.

iii. There are three arrows originating from event 2. Again, by neglecting this, three more new initial events are observed as nodes r, t and s, so number them as 3,4 and 5, respectively.

iv. Consider event 3 and neglect the arrow emerging from it. So, there is a new event; assign the number 6 to it. Similarly, consider event 5, an arrow emerging from it, neglect that, now we have a new event v, so assign it as 7.

v. Finally, we have an event from which no arrow emerges. Hence, this is the terminating event number 8.

The final network diagram with event numbers is shown in Fig. 2.17.

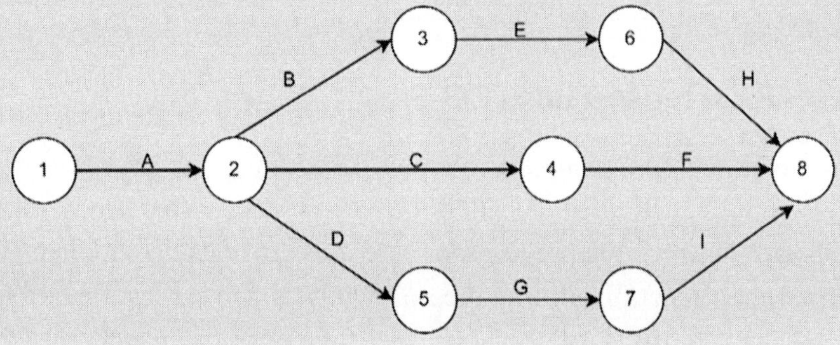

Fig. 2.17: Network diagram after numbering

Illustration 5

Fig. 2.18 shows the network diagram with event numbers of the given data.

Activities	Immediate predecessor	Activities	Immediate predecessor
A	-	F	C
B	-	G	D, E
C	A	H	D, E
D	A	I	F, G
E	B	J	H

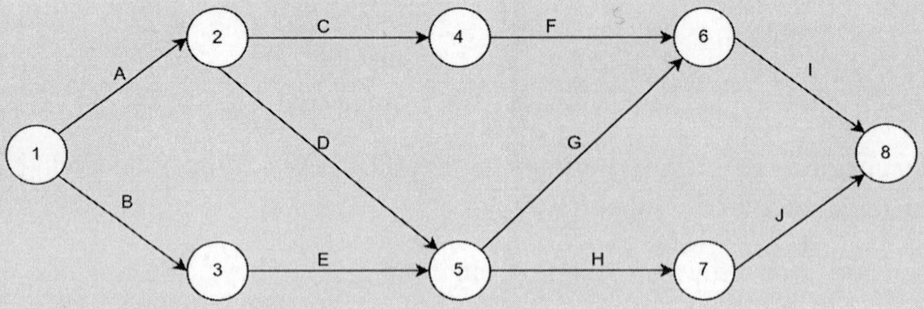

Fig. 2.18: Network diagram with relation and numbering of events

2.8 ANALYSIS OF EVENT TIMINGS

A project network diagram's time-related component is assessed as part of the time analysis of a network. This analysis is essential to efficiently manage project deadlines, identify important paths, and comprehend the project schedule. The analysis frequently involves figuring out important scheduling parameters and forward-pass and backward-pass computations. Each event is associated with it two times. These are the earliest and latest occurrence times, explained in upcoming sections.

2.8.1 Earliest Occurrence Time (EOT)

The earliest time an event can occur in a project schedule, given the project plan and the interdependencies between activities, is called the earliest occurrence time of that event. The durations and linkages between the predecessor activities are considered when calculating the earliest occurrence time. Generally, during the time analysis, the earliest time of the start event is taken as ZERO, and the EOT of the subsequent event is calculated by adding activity duration connecting the two events. When many activities end in an event, the event's EOT is the greatest value resulting from adding the duration to the EOT of each corresponding earlier event. Eq. 2.1 is used to calculate EOT. This method of calculating EOT is also called Forward Pass. Fig. 2.19 shows the nomenclature used for computing occurrence time in the forward pass.

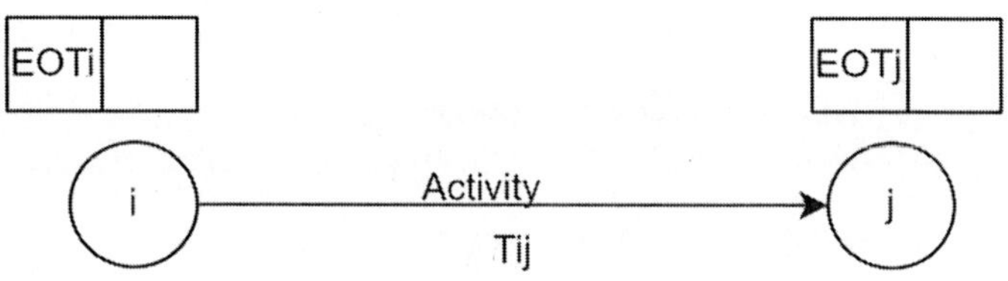

Fig. 2.19: Calculating EOT

$$EOT_j = EOT_i + T_{ij} \tag{2.1}$$

Where,
EOT_j = Earliest Occurrence Time of event j
EOT_i = Earliest Occurrence Time of event i
T_{ij} = duration of activity i-j

Illustration 6

The network with activities and their respective durations is given below. Determine the EOT of each event.

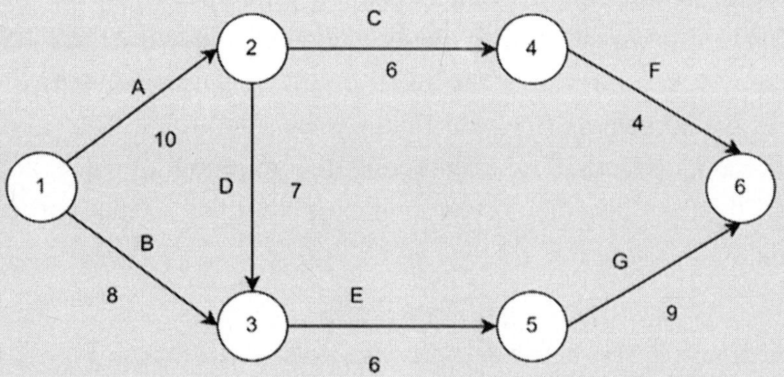

Solution:

$EOT_1 = 0$

$EOT_2 = EOT_1 + T_{12} = 0+10 = 10$

EOT_3 = maximum of $(EOT_1 + T_{13}, EOT_2 + T_{23})$ = maximum of $(0+8, 10+7) = 17$

Similarly, $EOT_4 = 16$, $EOT_5 = 23$, $EOT_6 = 32$

The EOT of all the events are shown below:

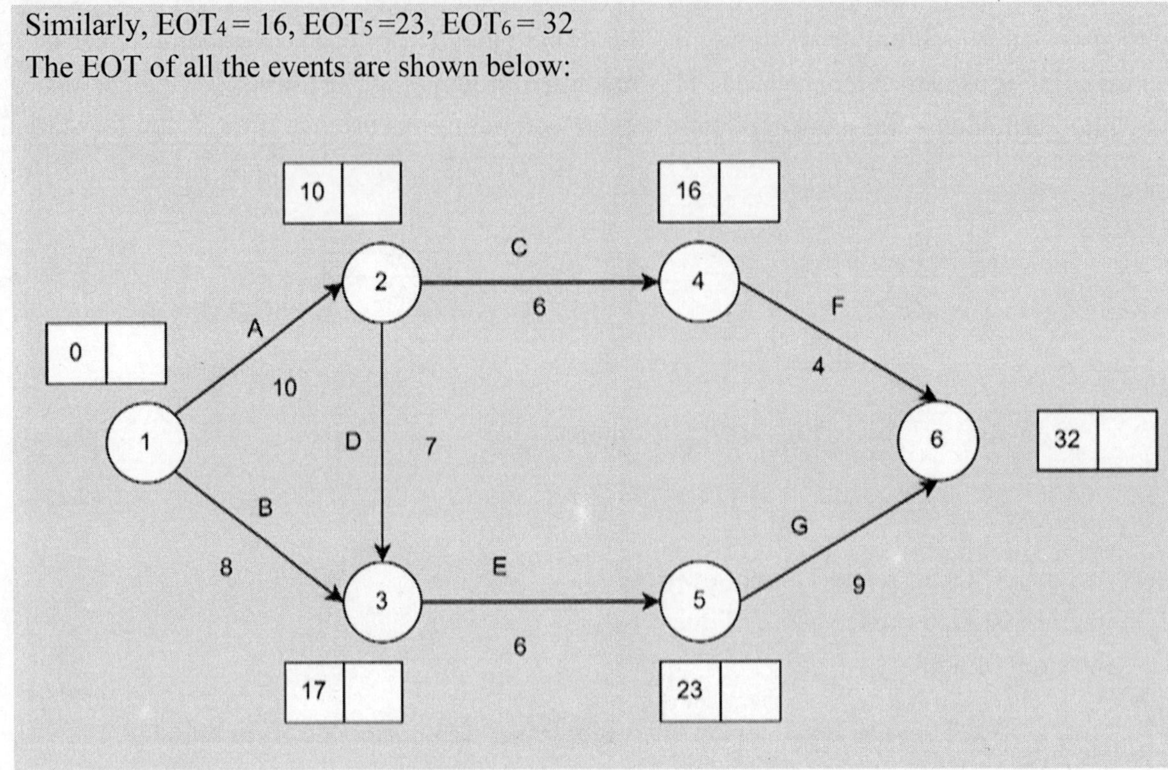

2.8.2 Latest Occurrence Time (LOT)

The latest time at which an event can occur without affecting the total project time is the latest occurrence time. The project's final event is primarily interpreted in the same way as the previous event's EOT. Moving in the opposite direction and deducting the activity length from the LOT at the activity's head yields the LOT of the remaining events. This method of calculating LOT is also known as Backward Pass. When multiple activities diverge from an event, the lowest value is found by subtracting the duration of each activity from the corresponding LOT of the subsequent event, which is the LOT of that particular event. The LOT can be calculated by using Eq. 2.2.

$$LOT_i = LOT_j - T_{ij} \tag{2.2}$$

Where,

LOT_j = Latest Occurrence Time of event j

LOT_i = Latest Occurrence Time of event i

T_{ij} = duration of activity i-j

Illustration 7

The network with activities and their respective durations is given below. Determine the LOT of each event.

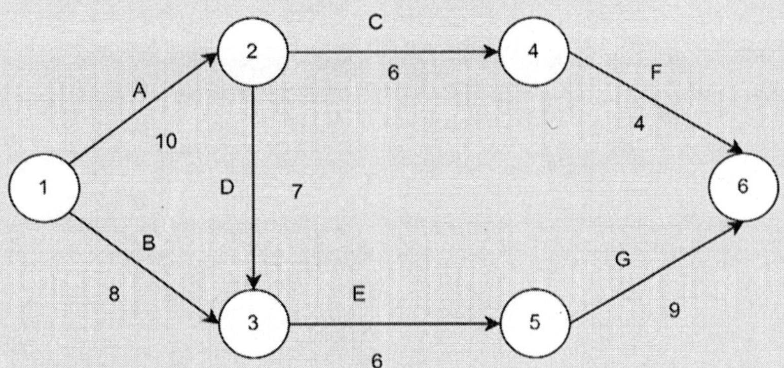

Solution:

$LOT_6 = 32$

$LOT_5 = LOT_6 - T_{56} = 32 - 9 = 23$

$LOT_5 = LOT_6 - T_{56} = 32 - 9 = 23$

$LOT_4 = LOT_6 - T_{46} = 32 - 4 = 28$

$LOT_3 = LOT_5 - T_{35} = 23 - 6 = 17$

$LOT_2 = \text{minimum of } (LOT_3 - T_{23}, LOT_4 - T_{24}) = \text{minimum of } (17\text{-}7, 28\text{-}6) = 10$

$LOT_1 = \text{minimum of } (LOT_3 - T_{13}, LOT_2 - T_{12}) = \text{minimum of } (17\text{-}8, 10\text{-}10) = 0$

The LOT of all the events are shown below:

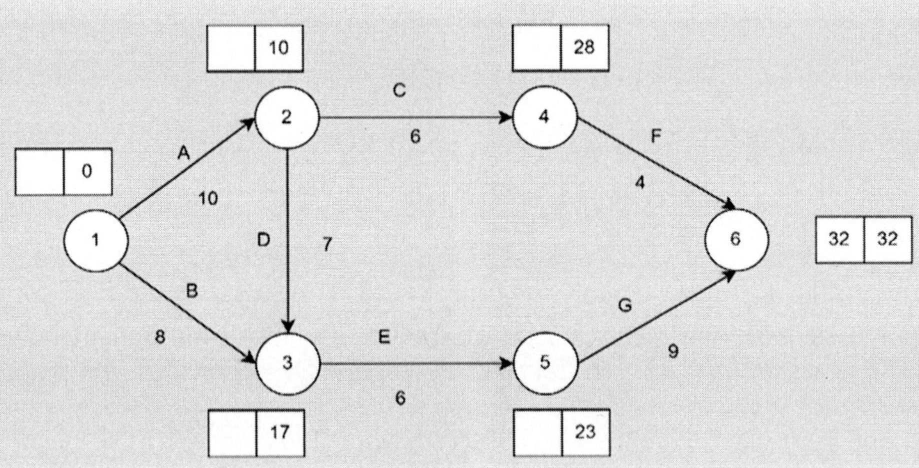

By combining the solutions of illustrations 6 and 7, the complete solution of the given network problem with all values of EOT and LOT are shown in Fig. 2.20.

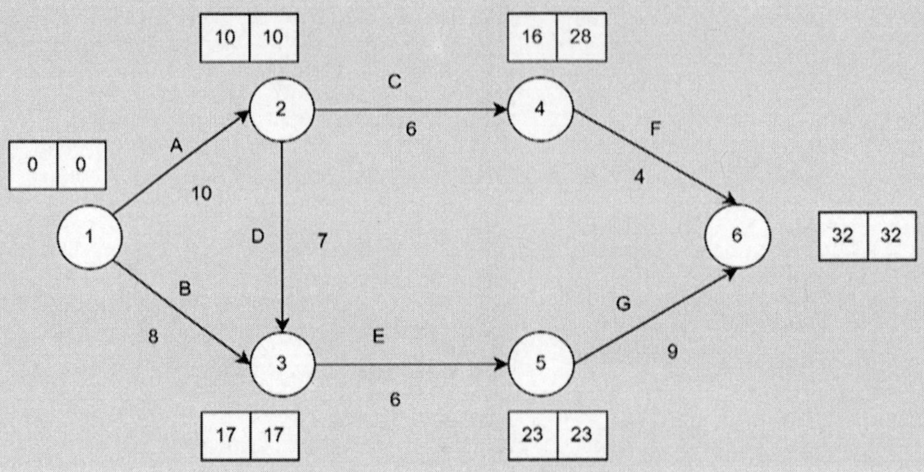

Fig. 2.20: EOT and LOT of the project

2.8.3 Slack

Slack is the term used to describe the discrepancy between an event's LOT and EOT. Slack indicates when an event must occur for the project to be finished on schedule. Project managers may evaluate the project timeline's resilience and schedule flexibility with Slack's assistance. Slack can be zero, positive or negative, depending on the relationship between LOTs and EOTs.

For example, Slack of Event 4 in Fig. 2.20 problem is given as

$$= LOT_4 - EOT_4 = (28-16) = 12$$

Positive slack: If the value of Slack is positive, i.e., if LOT is greater than EOT for an event, then it is called positive Slack. Positive slack represents that we have excess resources or a condition of being ahead of schedule.

Negative slack: If the scheduled completion time, i.e. LOT, is less than the EOT for an event, we get negative slack. It represents a lack of resources or the condition of being behind schedule.

Zero slack: The zero slack condition is observed when LOT equals EOT of an event. It represents the availability of sufficient resources or conditions on schedule.

2.9 ANALYSIS OF ACTIVITY TIMINGS

T_{i-j} represents the duration of an activity (i, j). This is the time needed to do an activity (i, j) from start to finish. Days, weeks, or months may indicate the duration, depending on the activity and level of detail in any typical construction project. It should be highlighted that while the amount of effort required for the activity and the resources used determine the actual length, a precise linear relationship is not strictly necessary in theory.

2.9.1 Start Time and Finish time

The contractor or client may wait a while before beginning an activity, but doing so will not impact the project's completion date. In conceptual terms, an activity can begin after the necessary groundwork is finished. Likewise, the activity can be completed at a different time based on when it starts and how long it lasts. The following terms are frequently used when discussing the start and finish times of an activity:

Earliest Start Time (EST)

This is the earliest time that the activity (i, j) can begin, provided all prerequisites are satisfied. In this text, EST_{i-j} denotes the earliest start time of an activity (i, j). The EST of an activity is equal to the EOT of the preceding event and can be represented as shown in Eq. 2.3.

$$EST_{i-j} = EOT_i \tag{2.3}$$

Earliest Finish Time (EFT)

This is the earliest time an activity (i, j) can be completed, provided all the activities earlier are started at their ESTs. The addition of the activity duration to EST determines the EFT of an activity. It is also equal to the EOT_j and can be represented in Eq. 2.4.

$$EFT_{i-j} = EOT_i + T_{i-j} = EOT_j \tag{2.4}$$

Latest Finish Time (LFT)

This is the latest time that an activity must be finished to ensure that there is no delay in the project and that it is completed on schedule. It is equal to the value of LOT_j and can be represented as shown in Eq. 2.5.

$$LFT_{i-j} = LOT_j \tag{2.5}$$

Latest Start Time (LST)

This is the latest time that an activity can begin to ensure the project is completed on schedule without delay. The LST of an activity is calculated by subtracting the duration of the activity from the LET of the succeeding event. It can be represented as shown in Eq. 2.6.

$$LST_{i\text{-}j} = LFT_{i\text{-}j} - T_{i\text{-}j} \tag{2.6}$$

2.9.2 Float

The term "float" describes the amount of time that can be delayed between tasks or activities without impacting the schedule or completion date of the project as a whole. It refers to the range of flexibility that allows an activity's start or finish times to change without compromising the project's completion. Float is further classified into four categories – total, free, independent, and interference floats.

Total Float (TF)

The amount of time an activity's start can be delayed without affecting the project's scheduled completion is known as its total float. The total float can be calculated using Eq. 2.7 or 2.8.

$$TF_{i\text{-}j} = LST_{i\text{-}j} - EST_{i\text{-}j} \tag{2.7}$$

$$TF_{i\text{-}j} = LFT_{i\text{-}j} - EFTi\text{-}j \tag{2.8}$$

Regarding event timings, the $TF_{i\text{-}j}$ equals the late occurrence time (LOT_j) of the successive event minus the early occurrence time (EOT_i) of the previous event minus the time the activity described between these events lasted. It is shown in Eq. 2.9.

$$TF_{i\text{-}j} = LOT_j - EOT_i - T_{i\text{-}j} \tag{2.9}$$

Free Float (FF)

The term "free float" refers to the time by which the start of one activity is delayed without affecting the start of its successor activity. Free float is defined as the earliest occurrence time of the subsequent event (EOT_j) minus the earliest occurrence time of the previous event (EOT_i) minus the duration of the defined activity between these events (Eq. 2.10). It generally represents that this float does not affect the succeeding activities.

$$FF_{i\text{-}j} = EOT_j - EOT_i - T_{i\text{-}j} \tag{2.10}$$

Independent Float (IF)

The amount of time an activity's start can be delayed without impacting its predecessor or follower is known as its independent float. At times, neither the predecessor nor the successor activity is affected by the incorporation of this float. The definition of independent float of an activity is the earliest occurrence time of the subsequent event (EOT_j) minus the latest occurrence time of the previous event (LOT_i), as well as minus the duration of the defined activity in between these events. It is shown in Eq. 2.11.

$$IF_{i\text{-}j} = EOT_j - LOT_i - T_{i\text{-}j} \qquad \textbf{(2.11)}$$

Interference Float

It is described as the difference between total float and free float. It is shown in Eq. 2.12.

$$\text{Interference Float} = TF_{i\text{-}j} - FF_{i\text{-}j} \qquad \textbf{(2.12)}$$

2.10 PROJECT PRECEDENCE NETWORK

The logical links we have learned till now suggest that one or more tasks must be finished before one activity begins. For instance, the brickwork must be completed before plastering can begin, so it makes sense that brickwork comes before plastering. However, practically, there is inevitably some overlap in time between the adjacent activities. An exercise that can start sometime after initiating another activity (which should logically come first) is one of the examples. Plastering, for instance, should be done before painting a wall, but finishing the latter before starting the former is not required. Painting can begin while plastering is being done if enough work is available.

Networks use the term delays (Lags) to describe the relationships between different start and finish activities in precedence networks. They better represent a real-time realistic plan than other project-network analysis techniques, demonstrating the interdependence and relationship between various activities. Activity representation in the Precedence Network is shown in Fig. 2.21.

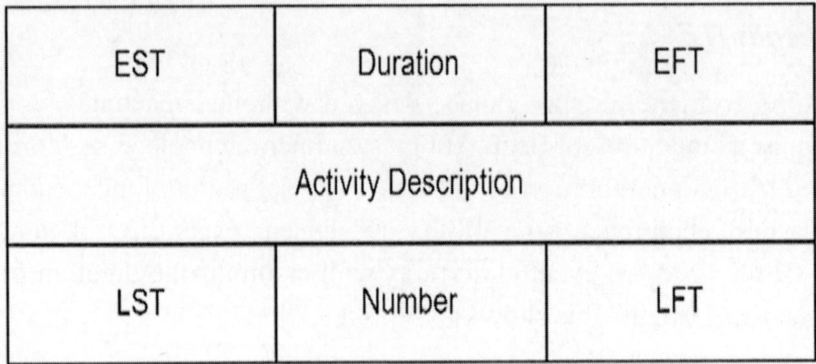

Fig. 2.21: Representation of an activity in precedence network diagram

Where,
EST = Earliest Start Time
LST = Latest Start Time
EFT = Earliest Finish Time
LFT = Latest Finish Time

In a precedence network, the logical relationship is illustrated by drawing lines from previous activity nodes to connect activity nodes. Four relationships can connect different nodes in a precedence network – finish-to-start, start-to-start, finish-to-finish, and start-to-finish.

2.10.1 Finish-to-Start

The kind of precedence relationship that is most prevalent is the finish-to-start relationship. This indicates that completing the predecessor work is a prerequisite for starting the successor task. Before beginning the curing process (successor), the concrete pouring procedure (predecessor) must be completed. Fig. 2.22 shows a finish-to-start relationship between A and B activities. In the figure, it is written as '2FS', which means there is a lag of 2 days (if the unit is taken in days) between the two activities. In other words, activity B will take 2 more days to start after activity A will finish.

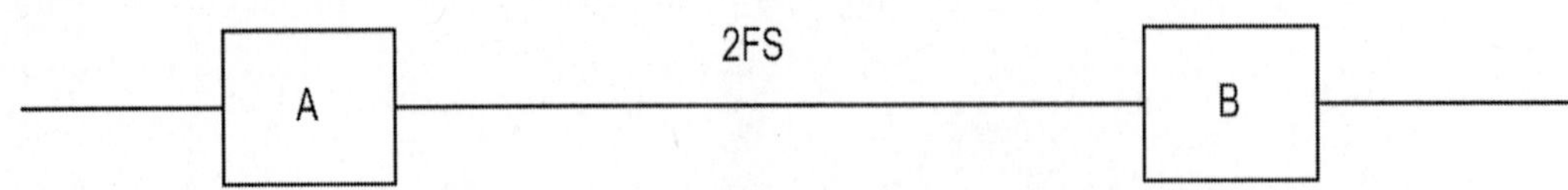

Fig. 2.22: Finish-to-start relationship

2.10.2 Start-to-Start

The two jobs may differ in duration, yet they operate concurrently. Such a relationship between the activities can be shown with the help of a start-to-start relationship. For instance, the predecessor, excavation, and the successor, foundation formwork, can begin simultaneously. Fig. 2.23 shows the start-to-start relationship. It shows that activity B will start 6 days after the start of activity A.

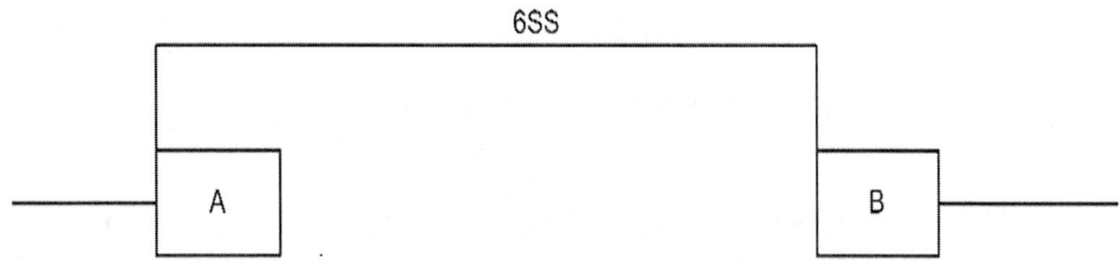

Fig. 2.23: Start-to-start relationship

2.10.3 Finish-to-Finish

The finish-to-finish relationship states that until the previous task is completed, the successor task cannot be completed. For instance, painting (predecessor) must be completed before clean-up (successor) may be achieved. Fig. 2.24 shows the finish-to-finish relationship. It shows that activity H will finish 3 days after the day activity G finishes.

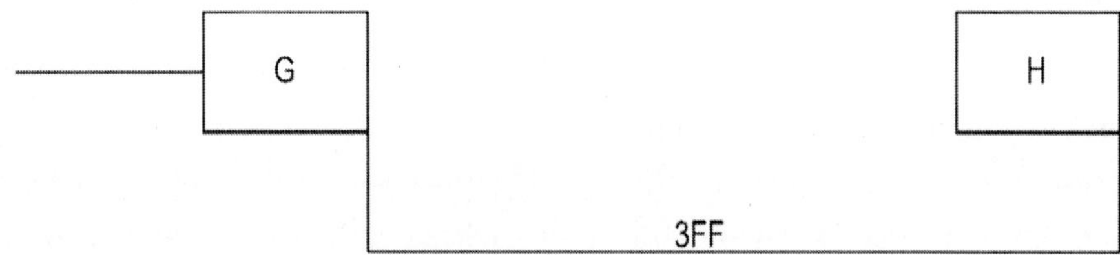

Fig. 2.24: Finish-to-finish relationship

2.10.4 Start-to-Finish

A start-to-finish relationship means the successor task cannot be finished until the predecessor task has started. Start-to-finish linkages are less common and may need to be carefully considered. For example, training (the predecessor activity) must begin before hiring (the successor activity) may conclude. It is shown in Fig. 2.25 where activity B is finishing after 2 days from the start of activity A.

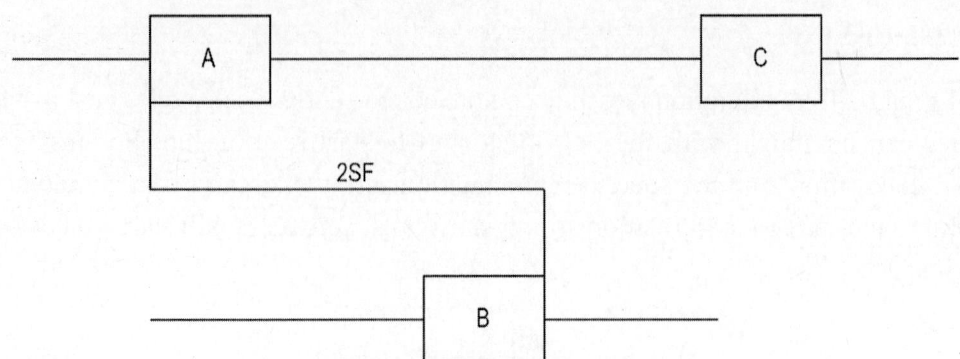

Fig. 2.25: Start-to-finish relationship

2.11 CRITICAL PATH METHOD (CPM)

The CPM was developed in the 1950s by DuPont. Creating a project model that includes a list of all activities needed to finish the project, the amount of time required for each activity, and the dependencies between the activities is a crucial step in adopting CPM. Developing a project model with the following elements is the fundamental method for utilising CPM:

i. A list of all actions necessary to finish the project (also known as Work breakdown structure),
ii. The time (length) that each activity will take to complete, and
iii. The relationships between the activities.

With these, CPM computes the beginning and ending times of every activity, ascertains which tasks are essential to finishing a project (referred to as the critical path), and identifies the tasks that have "float time" (i.e., are less critical). A critical path in project management is the order of the longest-running project network activities, which helps determine how quickly the project can be finished. The activities that lie on the critical path are known as Critical activities. There is no float on the critical path; thus, any delay in an operation there will immediately affect the anticipated project completion date. Multiple concurrent critical routes may exist in a project. The term "sub-critical" or "non-critical" path refers to an extra parallel path less in length (time to accomplish the path) than the critical path through the network.

In the beginning, only logical dependencies between terminal elements were considered by the critical path method. Since then, it has grown to provide room for adding resources relevant to every task. This feature makes it possible to investigate a related idea known as the critical chain, which establishes the duration of a project by considering both resource and time requirements. Critical Path Method estimates a project's duration and identifies any delays' most likely locations. Throughout the project, the developer will receive a visual representation of potential bottlenecks through a step-by-step process.

There may be one or more critical paths in a project, but the total time spent on each path is the same and is referred to as project time. If the following basic procedures are followed, creating a CPM can be relatively straightforward:

List the activities that must be considered in a rough sequence.
Assign a number to each event, calculate the time needed, and identify its causes.
Use connecting lines to represent the antecedent relationships, time needed, and numbered occurrences of the events arranged in a CPM network diagram.
Establish the earliest times for the events to begin and conclude.
Establish the latest times at which the events will begin.
Identify the critical route.

Illustration 8

Draw the network for the following activities and find the critical path for the project's total duration.

Activity	Duration (days)
1-2	6
2-3	5
2-4	8
3-5	6
4-5	3
4-6	7
5-7	9
6-7	4

Solution:

Drawing a network

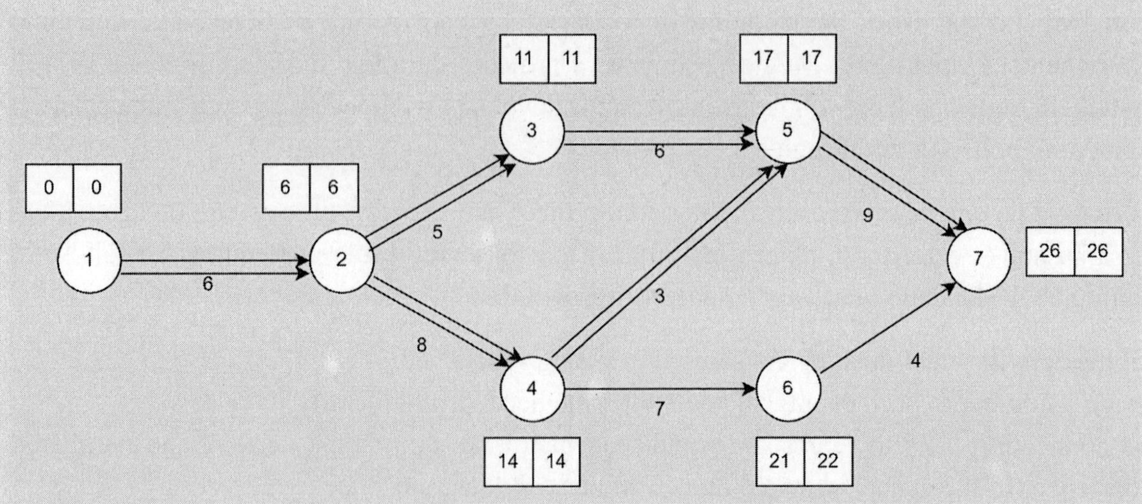

Project duration = 26 days

Critical path: There are 2 critical paths in this case, which are given below:

i) 1-2-3-5-7

ii) 1-2-4-5-7

If it is assumed that the project starts on 26/12/2023 with 5 days working days, provided that on 15th January 2024 and 26th January 2024, there is a public holiday, the completion date of the project and CPM calendar table is given as

Activity	Duration (days)	Schedule Start	Schedule Finish	Remarks
1-2	6	26/12/2023	02/01/2024	Critical
2-3	5	03/01/2024	09/01/2024	Critical
2-4	8	03/01/2024	12/01/2024	Critical
3-5	6	10/01/2024	18/01/2024	Critical
4-5	3	16/01/2024	18/01/2024	Critical
4-6	7	16/01/2024	24/01/2024	
5-7	9	19/01/2024	01/02/2024	Critical
6-7	4	25/01/2024	31/01/2024	
Project completion date: 01/02/2024				

Illustration 9

Determine the critical path and project duration of a project whose network diagram is given below; also, determine the EST, LST, EFT, LFT and all four float values for the same CPM project network.

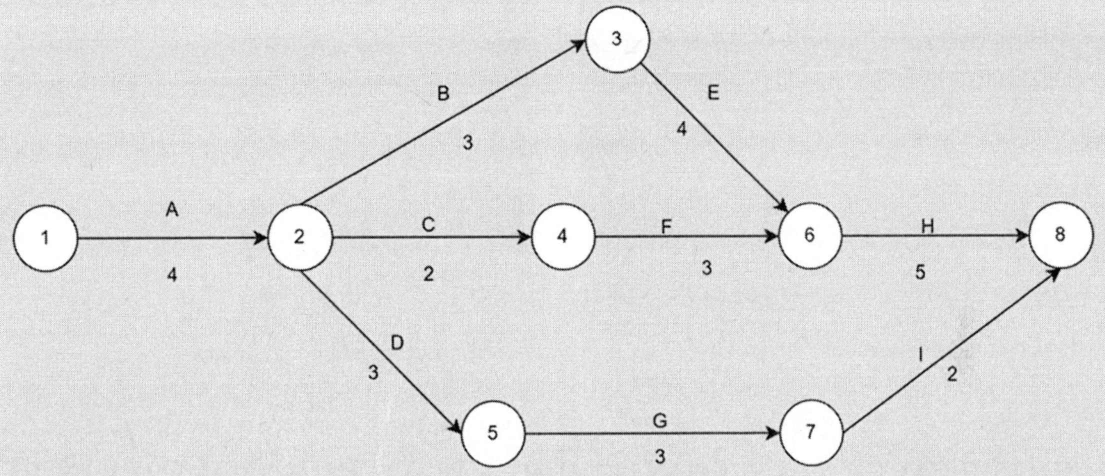

Solution:

Activity	i	j	Duration	EST	EFT	LST	LFT	Total float	Free float	Independent float
A	1	2	4	0	4	0	4	0	0	0
B	2	3	3	4	7	4	7	0	0	0
C	2	4	2	4	6	6	8	2	0	0
D	2	5	3	4	7	8	11	4	0	0
E	3	6	4	7	11	7	11	0	0	0
F	4	6	3	6	9	8	11	2	2	0
G	5	7	7	7	10	11	14	4	0	-4 =0
H	6	8	5	11	16	11	16	0	0	0
I	7	8	2	10	12	14	16	4	4	0

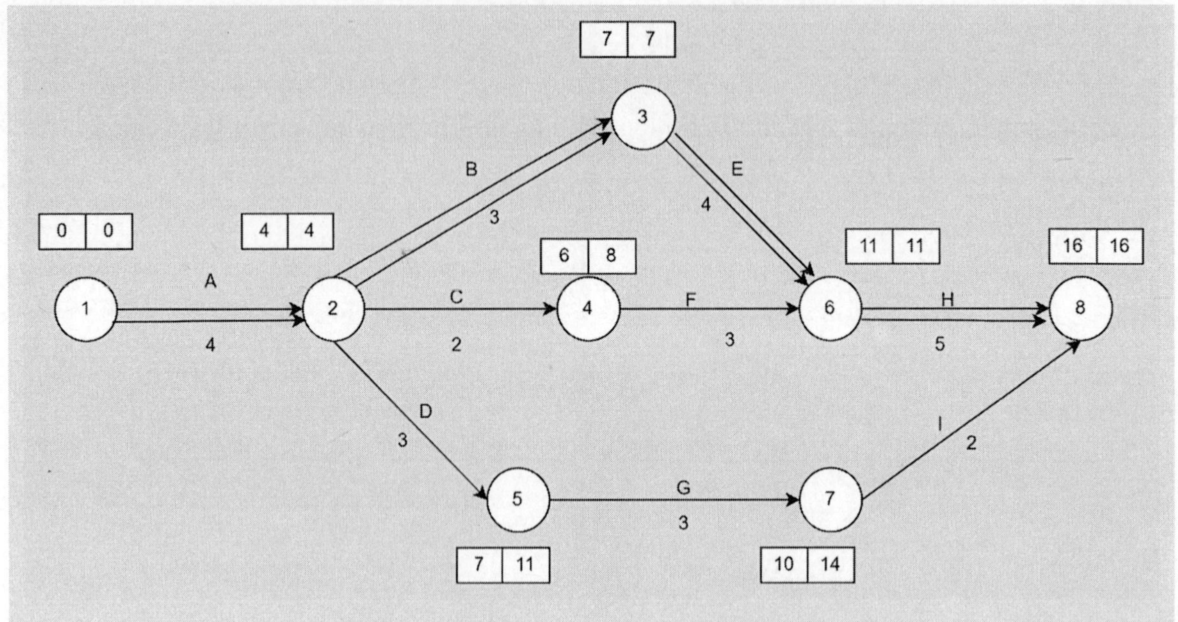

2.12 PROGRAM EVALUATION AND REVIEW TECHNIQUE (PERT)

Though the logic of the program evaluation and review technique is similar to that of CPM, it was developed separately and has varied uses in different sectors and circumstances. Although it acknowledges uncertainty in the time estimate of an activity, activities and their interdependencies are expected to be well-defined. Three durations are needed for each activity in PERT's analysis: the most likely, the optimistic (shortest), and the pessimistic (longest), considering uncertainty in activity durations. In reality, aside from what is thought to be the most likely estimate (t_m) for (completing) a task, a competent person, such as an engineer, is asked to provide two other time estimates: the pessimistic time estimate (t_p) and the optimistic time estimate (t_o). As its names suggest, the pessimistic time is the best estimate of the longest time needed to finish the task, while the optimistic time is the best estimate to finish the task in the shortest possible time. Optimistic time predicts the shortest time spent on the task, assuming every aspect proceeds according to plan. Due to the necessity of favourable conditions co-occurring, this time is typically small. Pessimistic time estimates the longest amount of time that can be used to complete the task. Therefore, it assumes the worst-case scenario to postpone this action. This typically offers a longer duration with a lower likelihood. Most-likely-time indicates how long it will take to complete the task under typical circumstances, considering every aspect that could influence it. The likelihood of this value happening is highest.

The PERT approach uses a beta distribution to link the relationship between the three timeframes. The optimistic (t_o) and pessimistic (t_p) values show the distribution's bounds. The tm shows the most-likely-time. The expected time (t_e) is calculated using the three-time estimates. This can be done by applying the formula given in Eq. 2.13.

$$te = \frac{(to + 4tm + tp)}{6} \quad \textbf{(2.13)}$$

Illustration 10

Determine the expected time for brick wall construction of a building construction project given that the activity of brick wall construction has an optimistic time, most likely time, and pessimistic time, which are 12, 20, and 28 days, respectively.

Solution:

We have an optimistic time (t_o) = 12 days

most likely time (t_m) = 20days, and Pessimistic time(t_p) = 28days

therefore, the expected time of brick wall construction (t_e) = $\frac{(12+ (4*19) +27)}{6}$

t_e = 20days

2.12.1 Variability of Activity Time

It's necessary to ascertain the average or projected amount of time needed for an activity, but it's also critical to assess the accuracy of these estimations. When dealing with a high variable time estimate, a wider range of estimates may yield a less dependable outcome than one with a narrower range.

The standard deviation (SD or σ) and variance (Var), defined in PERT, are calculated to quantify the uncertainty surrounding estimating an activity's duration. The formula for calculating the SD and Var are shown in Eq. 2.14 and 2.15.

$$\text{SD } (\sigma) = \frac{\text{tp} - \text{to}}{6} \quad \textbf{(2.14)}$$

$$\text{Var} = (\text{SD})^2 \tag{2.15}$$

According to the above formula in Eq. 2.14, the standard deviation equals one-sixth of the difference between the extreme time estimates. The distribution curve will be more widely distributed and have a larger value of (t_p-t_o), making the time estimations more uncertain. A large standard deviation indicates significant ambiguity around the activity hours. Put otherwise, there's a higher likelihood that the time needed to finish the task will differ significantly from the estimated amount of time.

As was previously said, the PERT approach assumes that t_m and t_p are random variables that follow the beta distribution. T_e is also regarded as a random variable determined by computing the weighted sum of t_o, t_m and t_p. Nonetheless, T_e's distribution is normal by the statistical "central limit" theorem.

A planner or project manager may find it helpful to derive various conclusions from the well-known behaviour of the normal distribution. One can, for instance, calculate the chance (index) that a project (or a significant phase within it) will be finished on time. Naturally, this is predicated on the idea that the project's other actions are statistically independent.

Assume that it is necessary to determine the likelihood of finishing the project within the allotted target duration, i.e., T_D days. Given the project's Te, it is now feasible to determine the difference between T_D and Te in standard deviation units. The normal distribution table is used to compute this. A ratio is known as the standardised deviation—or, more frequently, the standard deviation, Z—is determined to accept the table. The difference ratio between T_D and T_e to SD is Z, as given in Eq. 2.16.

$$Z = \frac{TD - Te}{\sigma} \tag{2.16}$$

2.12.2 Critical Path Analysis of PERT Network

As previously explained, the PERT network receives the same critical path calculation treatment as the CPM network upon converting the three-time estimations into an estimated mean time for each activity. The computation of event time, which is explained by, provides a systematic and scientific way to identify the critical path:

The Earliest Expected Occurrence Time (T_E): The calculation of T_E is the same as the calculation of EOT of the CPM network (Eq. 2.17).

$$(T_E)_j = (T_E)_i + t_{i\text{-}j} \tag{2.17}$$

The Latest Allowable Occurrence Time (T_L): The calculation of T_L is the same as the calculation of LOT of the CPM network (Eq. 2.18).

$$(T_L)_i = (T_L)_j - t_{i\text{-}j} \tag{2.18}$$

Schedule Completion Time or Target Duration (TD): Schedule completion time or target duration refers to the decision made regarding the project's completion after the PERT network is implemented. Generally, T_D refers to the allowable occurrence time of the project's final event (Eq. 2.19).

$$T_D = T_L \tag{2.19}$$

2.12.3 Slack

Slack in the Program Evaluation and Review Technique (PERT) is the time that may lapse between an event or activity and the project's completion date. Every event has a time box with two compartments; the value in the left compartment represents the event's TE value, while the value in the right compartment represents its TL value. Therefore, Slack(S) is calculated by using Eq. 2.20.

$$\text{Slack(S)} = (T_L - T_E) \tag{2.20}$$

2.12.4 Central Limit Theorem

Although it is not directly related to the Program Evaluation and Review Technique (PERT), the Central Limit Theorem (CLT) is a statistic. The Central Limit Theorem has consequences for probability distributions and statistical analysis, and it's crucial to remember that PERT employs a probabilistic technique to estimate project length. PERT tells us that the overall time distribution for the project will closely resemble a normal distribution curve if there are n activities distributed along a critical path, each with its beta distribution and expected mean time of T_{e1}, T_{e2}, ..., T_{en}, Standard deviation of σ_1, σ_2, ..., σ_n, and variance v_1, v_2, ..., v_n respectively. The normal distribution curve will have a mean expected time (T_{eT}), variance (v_T) and Standard deviation (σ_T) and can be given as:

$$T_{eT} \text{ (Expected meantime of the project)} = T_{e1} + T_{e2} + ... + T_{en}$$

$$v_T \text{ (Variance of the project)} = v_1 + v_2 + \ldots + v_n$$

$$\sigma_T \text{ (Standard deviation of the project)} = \sqrt{v_T} = \sqrt{\sigma^2_1 + \sigma^2_2 + \ldots\ldots + \sigma^2_n}$$

Determine the variation along each critical path in a PERT network if there are multiple critical paths, then choose the largest number for the intended use.

Illustration 11

Calculate the expected mean time of all activities and also calculate the slack of each event for the network diagram given below:

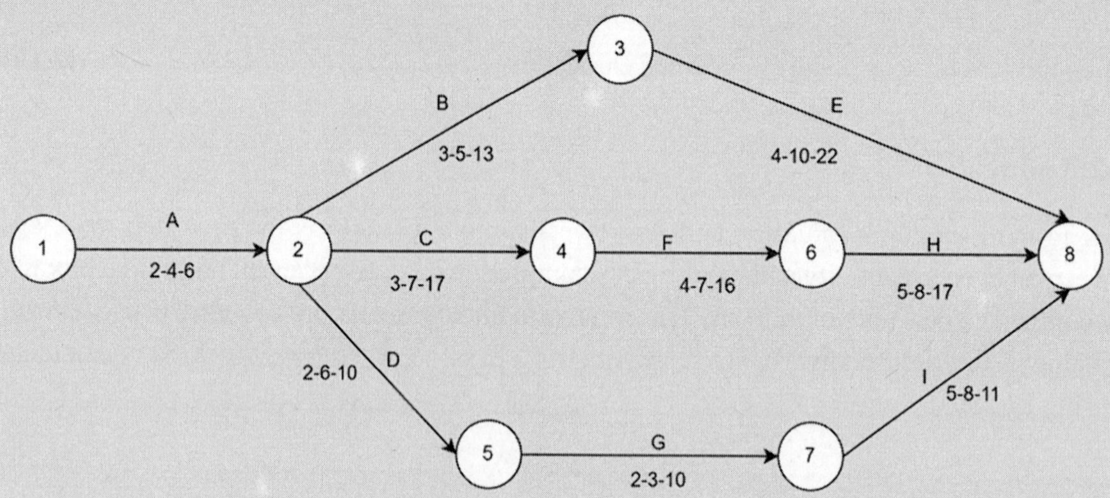

Solution: Forward and backward passes are carried out in the way described under the section on the network once the t_e's of all the activities have been calculated. All events have an early occurrence time (T_E) determined using the forward pass and a late occurrence time (TL) determined using the backward pass.

Expected meantime (t_e) can be calculated using the following:

$$te = \frac{(to + 4tm + tp)}{6}$$

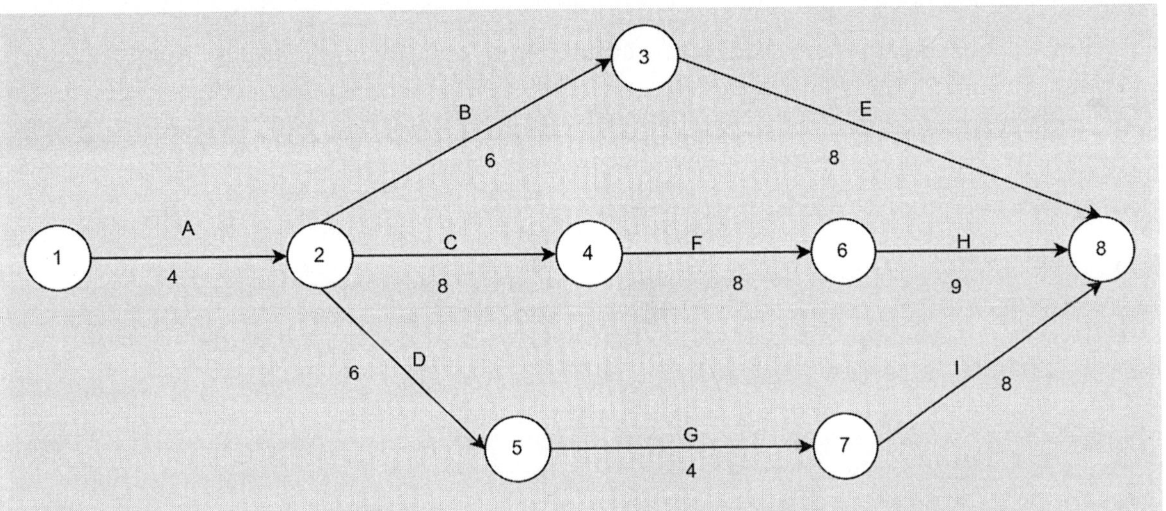

Events	Earliest Expected Occurrence Time (T_E) (days)	Latest Allowable Occurrence Time (T_L) (days)	Slack (S) = (T_L - T_E) (days)
1	0	29-29 =0	0
2	0+4 = 4	Min of (21-6, 12-8, 17-6) = Min of (15,4,11) = 4	0
3	4+6 = 10	29-8 = 21	11
4	4+8 = 12	20-8 = 12	0
5	4+6 = 10	21-4 = 17	7
6	12+8 = 20	29-9 = 20	0
7	10=4 = 14	29-8 = 21	7
8	Max. of (10+8, 20+9, 14+8) = Max of (18,29,22) = 29	29	0

Illustration 12

Calculate the Standard deviation and Variance of the project given in Illustration 11.

Solution: The standard deviation and variance can be calculated using the following equations:

$$SD\ (\sigma) = \frac{tp - to}{6}$$

$$Var = (SD)^2$$

Activity	t_o (days)	t_m (days)	t_p (days)	t_e (days)	σ (days)	Var(days)
A	2	4	6	4	0.67	0.44
B	3	5	13	6	1.67	2.78
C	3	7	17	8	2.33	5.44
D	2	6	8	6	1	1
E	4	10	22	8	3	9
F	4	7	16	8	2	4
G	2	3	10	4	1.33	1.78
H	5	8	17	9	2	4
I	5	8	11	8	1	1

Minimum slack value = 0

Therefore, All the events having zero slack are critical events

Critical path: **1-2-4-6-8**

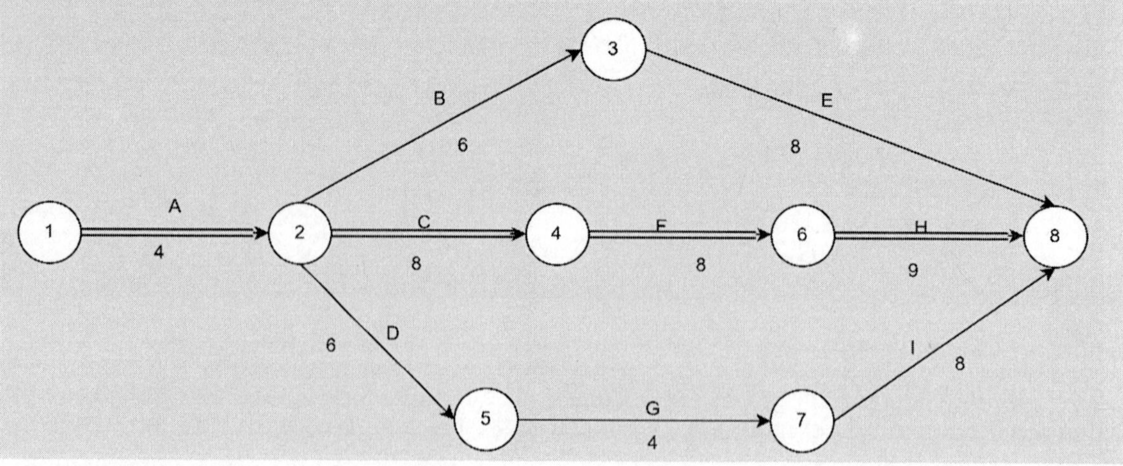

Illustration 13

Find the following information from the given data.

a) The expected time for project completion

b) Probability of completion of project in 41 days

c) Time duration that will provide an 89.4% probability of its completion in time

Activity	Estimated Activity Duration		
	T_o	T_m	T_p
1,2	2	8	14
1,6	3	5	13
2,3	6	15	30
2,4	2	5	8
3,5	4	11	18
4,5	2	3	16
6,7	4	6	26
5,8	2	4	6
7,8	3	22	29

Solution:

The following formula can calculate the expected mean time, standard deviation and variance of each activity-

$$te = \frac{(to + 4tm + tp)}{6}$$

$$\text{SD } (\sigma) = \frac{\text{tp} - \text{to}}{6}$$

$$\text{Var} = (\text{SD})^2$$

Activity	Estimated Activity Duration			t_e (days)	σ (days)	Var(days)
	T_o	T_m	T_p			
1,2	2	8	14	8	2	4
1,6	3	5	13	6	1.67	2.78
2,3	6	15	30	16	4	16
2,4	2	5	8	5	1	1
3,5	4	11	18	11	2.33	5.44
4,5	2	3	16	5	2.33	5.44
6,7	4	6	26	9	3.67	13.46
5,8	2	4	6	4	0.67	0.44
7,8	3	22	29	20	4.33	18.74

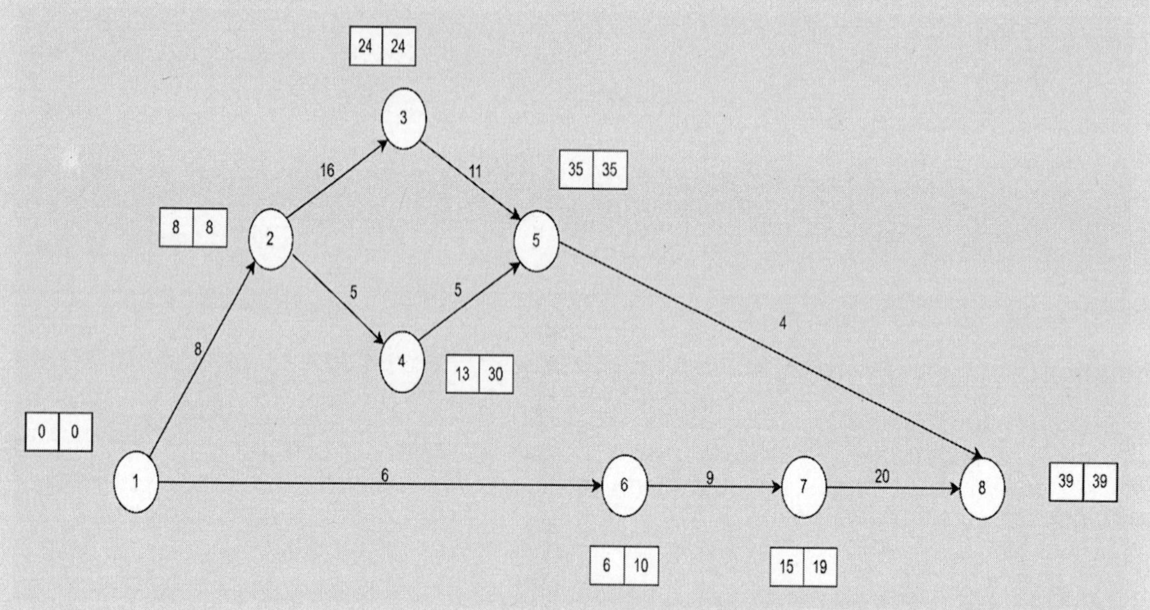

a) Expected time of completion of the project (T_{eT}) = 39 days

Since the project's scheduled completion time is not given, $T_L = T_E$ has been taken for the last event. So, T_D = 39days

Therefore, z = 0

So, the project will be completed with a 50% probability.

From the network diagram, we can observe that the critical path of the project is **1-2-3-5-8**

The variance of the project along the critical path (**v_T**) = $v_{1-2} + v_{2-3} + v_{3-5} + v_{5-8}$

$= 4+16+5.44+0.44$

$= 25.87$

Standard deviation of the project (**σ_T**) = $\sqrt{(\sigma^2_{1-2} + \sigma^2_{2-3} + \sigma^2_{3-5} + \sigma^2_{5-8})}$

$= \sqrt{(4+16+2.33^2+0.667^2)}$

$= 5.088$

b) Probability of completion in 41 days:

Normal deviate (z) corresponding to x= 41days

$$z = (x - T_{eT}) / \sigma_T$$

$$= (41-39)/ 5.088 = 0.39$$

Probability % corresponding to z = 0.39 (from probability distribution table)

$$p(z) = 65.17\%$$

c) For time duration that will provide an 89.4% probability of its completion in time:

$$p(z)= 0.894$$

by using cumulative probability distribution table z=1.25

$$z= (TD- T_{eT})/\sigma_T$$

$$1.25= (TD-39)/5.088$$

$$TD= 45.36 \text{ days}$$

So, in 45.36 days, the project has a chance of completion of 89.4%.

SUMMARY

The construction project planning chapter offers a comprehensive overview of the critical processes of effectively organising and preparing for construction projects. It delves into the systematic approach required to initiate, define, and develop project objectives, scope, and deliverables. Key components such as site analysis, feasibility studies, and risk assessments are explored to ensure that projects are well-conceived and viable from the outset. Moreover, the chapter highlights the importance of establishing clear project goals, timelines, and budgets supported by robust scheduling by creating WBS, CPM, and PERT networks. The chapter underscores the significance of meticulous project planning as the cornerstone of successful construction project execution.

EXERCISE

Make a few groups of students, each having five students. The students take on different roles in managing a construction project and assigning each group a unique construction project scenario (e.g., building a statue, constructing a dam, renovating the world's highest railway bridge). As the projects are unique, students need to conduct a PERT analysis. In the analysis:

a) Discuss the assumptions underlying PERT analysis and explain the process of determining three-time estimates for each activity.

b) Prepare a PERT network for the project, incorporating optimistic, pessimistic, and most likely time estimates for each activity. Compute slack values and identify critical paths.

c) Conduct a comprehensive project analysis, considering various scenarios and probabilities of completion within specified timeframes.

d) Calculate the probability of completion for the project based on PERT analysis results and discuss the implications for project management and scheduling decisions.

MULTIPLE CHOICE QUESTIONS

1. In which stage of project planning are project requirements and objectives clarified, and initial feasibility studies conducted?

   A) Pre-tender planning
   B) Pre-construction planning

C) Detailed construction planning
D) None of the above

2. What is the client's primary responsibility during the pre-construction planning stage?

A) Developing detailed construction schedules
B) Providing project funding and approvals
C) Hiring subcontractors
D) Managing construction activities

3. Which of the following is NOT typically included in a work breakdown structure (WBS)?

A) Cost estimates
B) Project objectives
C) Sequential tasks
D) Resource allocation

4. The concept of productivity in project planning refers to:

A) The number of tasks completed per day
B) The efficiency of resource utilisation
C) The complexity of project tasks
D) The duration of the project

5. Which planning technique is commonly used to visually represent the sequence of activities in a project?

A) Bar charts
B) Gantt charts
C) PERT analysis
D) Critical Path Method (CPM)

6. In a CPM network, what does float represent?

A) The time an activity can be delayed without delaying the project completion time
B) The duration of an activity
C) The earliest start time of an activity
D) The latest finish time of an activity

7. Which type of relationship in network terminology indicates that one activity cannot start until another activity has finished?
   A) Finish-to-start
   B) Start-to-start
   C) Finish-to-finish
   D) Start-to-finish

8. What is the primary purpose of creating a Gantt chart in project planning?
   A) To calculate float values
   B) To identify critical paths
   C) To visualise project schedules
   D) To perform risk analysis

9. In PERT analysis, what is the purpose of determining three time estimates for each activity?
   A) To calculate float values
   B) To identify critical paths
   C) To estimate activity durations
   D) To perform risk analysis

ANSWERS TO MULTIPLE CHOICE QUESTIONS

1	2	3	4	5	6	7	8	9
A	B	B	B	A	A	A	C	D

SHORT ANSWER TYPE QUESTIONS

1. What are the main elements of a construction planning procedure?
2. How is the scope of a construction project ascertained in the planning stage?
3. Could you explain the steps in creating a construction timeline, such as the important dependencies and milestones?
4. What are the main goals of pre-planning the construction projects?
5. What is a detailed construction plan, and what distinguishes it from pre-planning?

6. Explain the need for a Gantt chart and milestone chart.
7. What elements influence the efficiency of construction on a project site?
8. How can you best increase construction productivity using machinery and equipment?
9. How can you successfully regulate suppliers and subcontractors to guarantee that productivity goals are fulfilled?
10. What are the methods for locating and resolving obstacles or bottlenecks that reduce construction project productivity?
11. Write down a short note about the following terminologies:
    a. Predecessor activity
    b. Successor activity
    c. Dummy activity
12. Explain the difference between immediate predecessor and predecessor
13. Write down the various factors which can be seen as constraints or restrictions in any construction project.
14. Write a short note on the following: EST, EFT, LST, LFT and also make a relationship among them.
15. Write down the difference between CPM and PERT.
16. What are total and free float, and show their interrelation?

LONG ANSWER TYPE QUESTIONS

1. A project comprises eight events; their relationships are below; draw the network diagram.

Event	Immediate predecessor	Event	Immediate predecessor
10	-	50	30,40
20	10	60	50
30	10	70	50,60
40	20,30	80	40,70

2. Draw a network diagram for the conditions given below

   i) A and B start at the origin, ii) C follows A and B

3. Find the critical path and project duration of the given CPM project; calculate EST, EFT, LST, LFT and TF, FF, IF Int F in a tabular form.

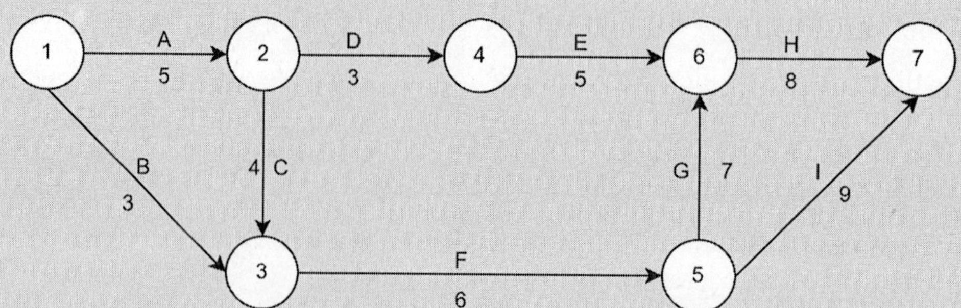

4. The network diagram of a particular project is given in the figure below; it determines the expected time of completion of each activity, the earliest expected event time and the latest allowable occurrence time for each event.

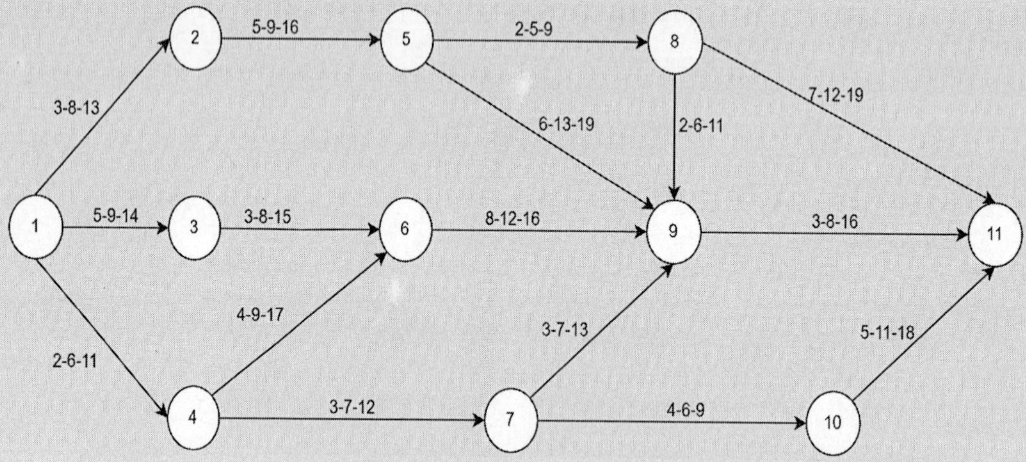

5. For the given PERT network diagram, determine

   a) the project's expected time, standard deviation, and variance and show the critical path.

   b) Find the probability of completion of the project in 36 days.

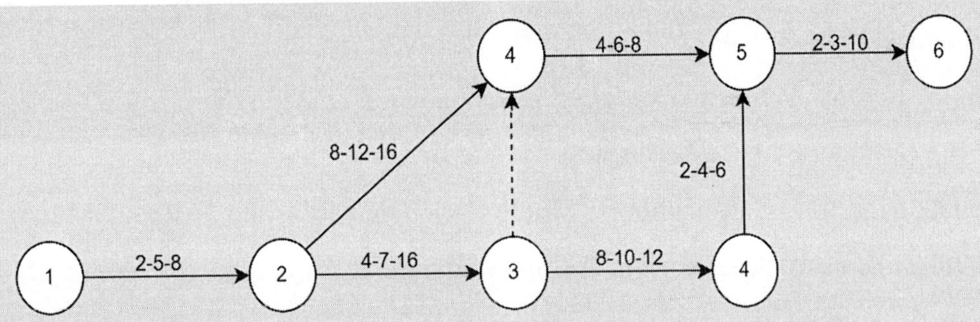

6. In the above question-
   a) Find the duration that will provide 89% of its completion in time.
   b) Find the minimum time range that will give a completion probability between 50% and 97%.

TUTORIAL

Develop a WBS for constructing the one-storeyed building; develop a bar chart for this building, including finishing activities, assuming reasonable activity durations.

KNOW MORE

For more information related to this topic scan the QR code.

OR

Type this link in your browser

https://nptel.ac.in/courses/105103093

BIBLIOGRAPHY

- Al-Gahtani, K. S., Al-Sulaihi, I. A., and Iqupal, A. (2016). Total float management: Computerized technique for construction delay analysis. *Canadian Journal of Civil*

Engineering, 43(5), 391-401.

- Hajdu, M. (1996). *Network scheduling techniques for construction project management* (Vol. 16). Springer Science & Business Media: Berlin.
- Karabulut, M. (2017). Application of Monte Carlo simulation and PERT/CPM techniques in planning of construction projects: A Case Study. *Periodicals of Engineering and Natural Sciences*, 5(3), 409-420.
- Lima, L., Trindade, E., Alencar, L., Alencar, M., and Silva, L. (2021). Sustainability in the construction industry: A systematic review of the literature. *Journal of Cleaner Production*, 289(1), 125730.
- Rolfsen, C. N., and Merschbrock, C. (2016). Acceptance of construction scheduling visualisations: bar charts, flowline charts, or perhaps BIM? *Procedia Engineering*, 164(1), 558-566.
- Siami-Irdemoosa, E., Dindarloo, S. R., and Sharifzadeh, M. (2015). Work breakdown structure (WBS) development for underground construction. *Automation in Construction*, 58(1), 85-94.

CONSTRUCTION METHODS BASICS

UNIT SPECIFICS

In the vast landscape of construction, understanding the fundamental methods is akin to grasping the building blocks of a complex structure. Whether erecting towering skyscrapers, intricate bridges, or humble homes, every construction project relies on basic principles and techniques. This chapter serves as a gateway into this world, offering an introductory exploration of construction methods. From traditional techniques passed down through generations to innovative approaches driven by technology, we delve into the essential concepts that underpin the construction process.

RATIONALE

Execution of vast varieties of construction activities requires different set of working methodologies.

PRE-REQUISITE

Nil

UNIT OUTCOMES

List of outcomes of this unit is as follows:

U3-O1: Understand conventional construction methods

U3-O2: Understand modular construction methods

U3-O3: Differentiate between types of formworks

Unit Outcomes	Expected Mapping with Course Outcomes (1 - Weak Correlation; 2- Medium correlation; 3- Strong Correlation)					
	CO-1	CO-2	CO-3	CO-4	CO-5	CO-6
U3-O1	3	2	3	3	3	1
U3-O2	3	2	3	3	3	1
U3-O3	3	3	2	1	1	1

3.1 TYPES OF FOUNDATIONS AND CONSTRUCTION

Foundations are an essential component of any structure. They cost about 5 to 10% of the total cost of the structure. Since the foundations are not visible, there is a general tendency not to take adequate care in the design and construction of the foundation. However, a foundation's failure reflects on the entire structure's safety and functionality. Thus, adequate care must be taken in the foundations' investigations, analysis, design, and construction. Two important aspects of a foundation are:

i. The loads from the structure are transferred to the ground safely.
ii. The foundation should not settle beyond limits, leading to impairment of the structure.

Foundations are of two types: shallow and deep. Shallow foundations are the foundations where the ground is excavated up to the desired foundation level (The foundation level is the level below the ground where the loads from the foundations are transferred to the ground), and then the foundations are constructed. Shallow foundations are also called Open foundations. In shallow foundations, the excavation depth is around 2 m to 10 m. Deep foundations transfer the foundation loads at greater depths beyond 10 m. Some pile foundations were constructed up to a depth of more than 100 m below the ground level. Deep foundations are more expensive than shallow foundations.

3.1.1 Shallow Foundations

Shallow Foundations can be individual column/pier footings or combined footings providing the foundation for more than one column/pier or raft foundation for all the columns or piers. The steps in the construction of shallow foundations are as follows:

i. Excavation: Excavation for the foundation is carried out using manual labour, excavators in soil, and blasting in hard rock. While excavating, the bottom width of the excavation shall provide extra width to cater for the width of the plain cement concrete levelling course, the width required for placing the formwork for casting the foundation, as shown in Fig. 3.1. The side slopes of the excavation shall be sufficiently flat so that the slopes do not collapse during the construction of the foundations. If the ground water table is above the founding level, the water shall be collected in a drainage pit and pumped out till the construction of the foundation is completed. It may be noted that payment for excavation is usually made for the shaded portion, corresponding to the width of the levelling course.

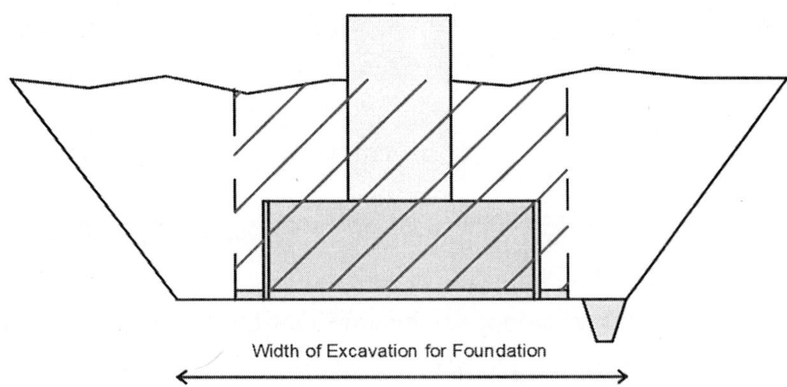

Fig. 3.1: Width of the foundation excavation

ii. After the excavation, the levelling course is laid, usually of M10 or M15 concrete of 100 mm to 150 mm thickness. The purpose of the levelling course is twofold. 1) Provide a level surface for constructing the foundation, and 2) prevent the foundation concrete from coming in direct contact with soil.

iii. The reinforcement is placed on the levelling course. Concrete cover blocks of concrete of the same grade as the foundation of the required thickness are used.

iv. Formwork/ shuttering is placed around the foundation after the reinforcement is fixed.

v. Concrete is placed from one edge of the foundation in layers of less than 500 mm thickness and compacted using needle vibrators.

vi. The formwork is removed after 24 hours of concreting, and the concrete is cured for 14 days.

vii. The foundation is backfilled to the ground level either by the excavated earth and compacted layers or lean concrete.

3.1.2 Deep Foundations

Typically, deep foundations are of two types: pile foundations and sound foundations. While pile foundations are used in the construction of buildings and bridges, sound foundations are typically used in the construction of bridges. Pile foundations are constructed with either driven piles or bored cast in-situ piles.

There is also a separate category of piles, like sheet piles, which are used during the construction stage and are meant to retain only the lateral earth pressure or water pressure during the construction stage. Similarly, compaction piles are driven into the loose ground to improve the bearing capacity of loose soils.

Construction of Driven Piles

i. Driven piles are made of hardwood, structural steel (H section or Tubular section), reinforced concrete, or prestressed concrete. Driven piles are used in soil strata. The piles are driven into the ground with the help of hammers. Suitable packing is placed between the pile head and hammer to prevent damage to the pile head.
ii. After the group of piles is installed, a pile cap is constructed, connecting all the piles in the group. Refer to Fig. 3.2 for understanding pile, pile cap, and column.

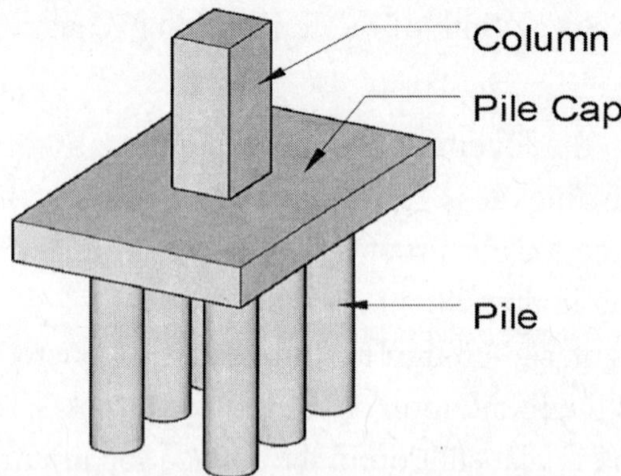

Fig. 3.2: Pile, pile cap, and column

Construction of Cast In-situ Piles

Cast In-situ piles are typically reinforced cement concrete and can be made in all soil and rock types. Construction involves boring a hole to the required depth, placing the reinforcement, and concretising. The boring process starts with driving a mild steel liner in the topsoil up to a depth of two to three meters. The hole is bored into the ground using a bailer and chisel operated with the help of a winch supported by a tripod, as shown in Fig. 3.3. Alternatively, the boring can be done by a hydraulic piling rig, as shown in Fig. 3.4. During the boring operations, the bore may collapse. The bore is stabilised using bentonite solution or polymeric gels.

After drilling the bore to the required depth, the prefabricated reinforcement cage is lowered into the bore. The pile is concreted with high-slump concrete using tremie pipes. In tremie pipe concreting, the concrete is placed below the already placed concrete. The piles are usually cast about 1 m above the pile cut-off level. After the concrete is set, the pile concrete is demolished up to the pile cut-off level. After the group of piles is installed, a pile cap is constructed, connecting all the piles in the group (as per Fig. 3.2).

Fig. 3.3: Bailer and chisel with tripod and winch

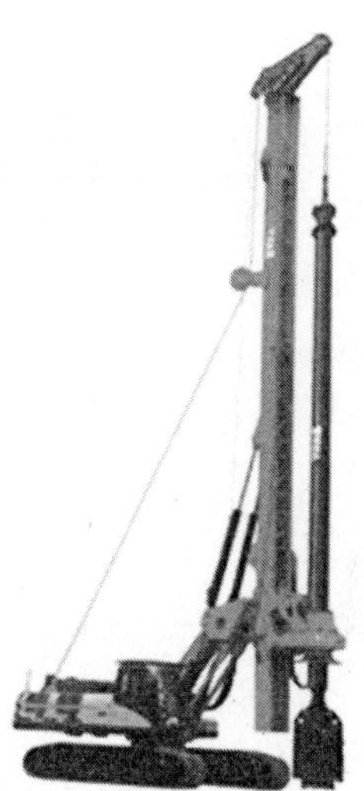

Fig. 3.4: hydraulic piling rig

Construction of Well Foundations

A well foundation is the most common choice for major bridges across rivers and large water bodies. A well foundation is most suitable where the foundation is required to resist large lateral forces and the river bed is prone to heavy scour during floods. The wells are typically circular or double-D shaped, as shown in Fig. 3.5. In addition, the components of a well foundation are shown in Fig. 3.6.

To start the construction of the well foundation, a temporary island is created with the help of coffer dams. The cutting edge is fabricated and placed at the required location. Well curb is cast in situ. Then, the soil within the hollow portion of the well is excavated. While the soil is excavated, the well sinks. While the well is sinking, the well steining is cast. The well sinks to greater depth under the increasing load of well steining. Once the well reaches the required depth, the bottom of the well is plugged with concrete. The well is filled with sand. The well cap is cast, leaving dowels for the pier construction.

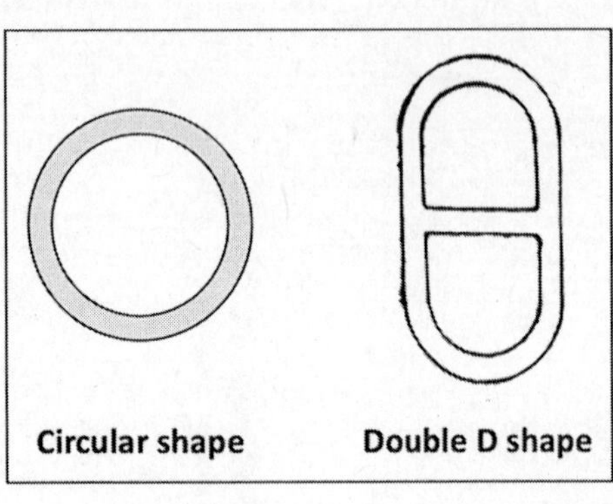

Fig. 3.5: Shapes of wells

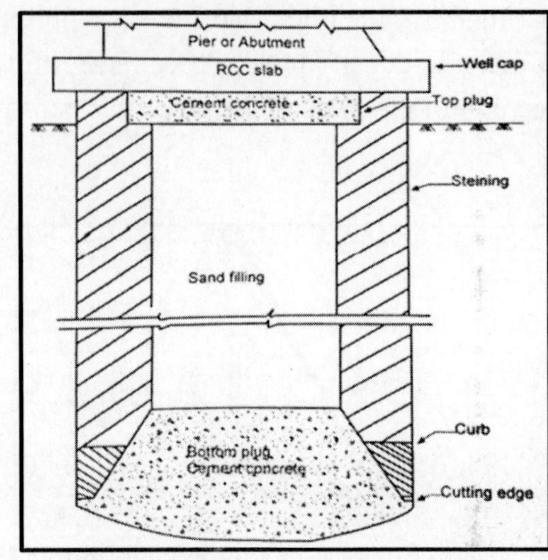

Fig. 3.6: Components of a well foundation

3.2 BASICS OF FORMWORK AND STAGING

Formwork is a temporary or permanent mould into which fresh concrete and reinforcement are placed to form a reinforced concrete element. The formwork system consists of two distinct components: forms and staging. The staging supports the forms. The photographs of the form for a concrete beam and staging for a building slab are shown in Fig. 3.7 and Fig. 3.8, respectively.

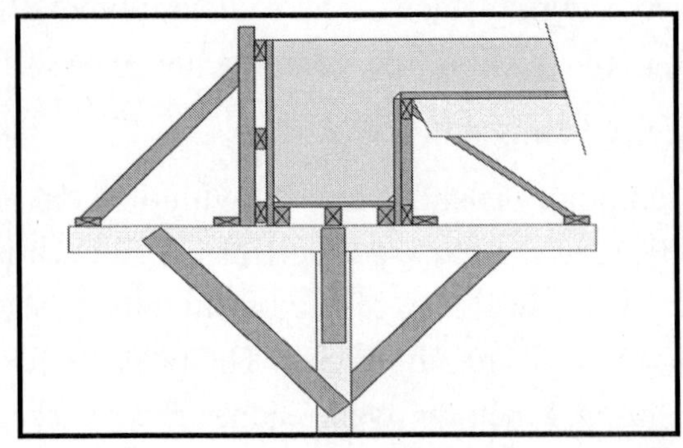

Fig. 3.7: Form for a beam

Fig. 3.8: Staging for slab

The formwork is of two types, viz., temporary and permanent. Temporary formwork is used only for the casting of concrete. Once the concrete is set, temporary formwork is removed.

Permanent formwork is also called left-in-place formwork. The formwork cannot be removed in specific structures like well foundations and, hence, left in place. Similarly, retrieving the formwork may not be economically feasible in viaducts. In such situations, alternative left-in-place formwork is used. An example of such an arrangement is a "Rolladeck" sheet made of corrugated galvanised iron, as shown in Fig. 3.9.

Fig. 3.9: Rolladeck left-in-place formwork

3.2.1 Types of Formwork Systems

Formwork systems are broadly categorised into traditional/conventional, modular/ engineered/ patented and site-specific systems.

Traditional/ Conventional formwork is built on site out of timber, plywood, or moisture-resistant particleboard. A photograph of the conventional formwork system is shown in Fig. 3.10. It is easy to produce but time-consuming for larger structures, and the plywood facing has a relatively short lifespan. The number of uses will be less. It is still used extensively where the labour costs are lower than those for procuring reusable formwork. It is also the most flexible type of formwork, so even where other systems are in use, complicated sections may use it.

Modular/ Patented/ Engineered Systems are built out of prefabricated modules with a metal frame (usually steel) and covered on the application (concrete) side with material having the wanted surface structure. Some engineered formwork system manufacturers are Doka, Peri, RMD Kwikform, Meva and Alsina. One of the engineered formwork systems is shown in Fig. 3.11.

The advantages of engineered formwork systems are as follows:

i. *High saving:* Recurring savings from the reuse of Formwork systems.

ii. *High Speed:* Dramatically increases the speed of construction due to ease of working. Means faster cycles and considerable savings in labour costs.

iii. *High safety:* Maintains international safety standards, with built-in features like guardrails, working platforms, etc., which are critical at great heights. Amenable to pumped concrete.

iv. *High accuracy:* This makes for high dimensional accuracy and accurate line, level, and plumb maintenance in structures.

v. *High-quality finish:* Smooth, even form finish greatly enhances aesthetics and soundness of structure.

Fig. 3.10: Traditional / conventional formwork system

Fig. 3.11: Engineered formwork system

Site-specific formwork systems are built from prefabricated modules with a metal frame and metal sheet or plywood. These types of shutters have two significant advantages of formwork systems when compared to traditional timber formwork, viz., speed of construction and lower life-cycle costs (barring major force, the frame is almost indestructible, while the covering if made of wood; may have to be replaced after a few uses). A site-specific formwork system is shown in Fig. 3.12.

3.2.2 Requirements of Formwork Systems

A formwork system can have functional, technical, time of removal and striping, and safety requirements. Each of these requirements is shown in the following subsections:

Fig. 3.12: Site-specific formwork system

Functional Requirements

i. Form sections should be of the size that can be lifted and transported easily from one job site to another.
ii. Formwork should be dismantled and moved as quickly as possible so that construction of the structure advances.
iii. Formwork units must be interchangeable so that they can be used to form different members.
iv. Formwork shall be designed to fit and fasten together reasonably quickly.
v. Forms should be simple to build.
vi. Formwork should be as lightweight as possible without any strength reduction.
vii. Forms should be made so workers can handle them without any safety issues, respecting the health, safety, and hygiene regulations.

Technical Requirements

i. Formwork should be of the desired shape and size and fit according to the drawings at the member's location in the structure.
ii. Formwork shall be carefully selected for the required finish surface and linings to produce the desired concrete surface.
iii. Formwork should withstand the pressure of fresh concrete and working loads and should not distort or deflect from its position during the concrete placing operation.
iv. Formwork should support the designed and other applied loads during construction.

v. The formwork must not damage the concrete or themselves during formwork removal.
vi. The panels of the formwork should be tightly connected to minimise gaps at the formwork connection and prevent leakage of cement paste.

Time for Removal / Stripping of Formwork as per IS:456

i. Vertical formwork of wall, column and beam – 16-24 hours
ii. Removal of props under-slab up to 4.5 meters – 7 days
iii. Removal of props under slab over 4.5 meters – 14 days
iv. Removal of props under arches and beams up to 6 meters – 14 days
v. Removal of props under arches and beams over 6 meters – 21 days

Safety Precautions

i. The material used for the construction of formwork must meet the specifications.
ii. Formwork is fixed firmly and properly
iii. Construction area must be protected.
iv. Formwork must be inspected before the concrete is poured.
v. Do not overload materials (for example, placing reinforcement at one location)
vi. Pay attention to Details.

3.3 BASICS OF SLIP FORMING FOR TALL STRUCTURES

Usually, when a pier or column is cast with conventional formwork systems, it is released in 2- 4 m lifts. Every lift of concreting involves the complete assembly of the formwork for concreting and disassembling it after the concreting. In the case of tall structures like chimneys, cooling towers, and bridge piers taller than 40 m, conventional formwork systems would consume a significant amount of time only in assembling and disassembling formwork. To save these activities, a slip formwork system has been developed.

In the slip form system, the forms move continuously as the concreting progresses, thereby saving time for assembly and disassembly of formwork. A photograph of a chimney cast with slip form is shown in Fig. 3.13.

Slip-form construction is a method in which concrete is poured into a continuously moving form. This method is also constantly called formed construction. The schematic layout of the slip form is shown in Fig. 3.14.

The slip-form panels are attached to a yoke frame continuously lifted using a hydraulic jack. Yoke frames also support the working platforms. The hydraulic jack takes the reaction from the climbing/jacking rod. The concrete meant for slip forms shall have the required workability for the ease of placing concrete and shall develop early strength so that slip forms can move quickly. The speed of the slip form is controlled by the setting time of the concrete. Typically, the speed would be 300 mm per hour. The slip-form system of a tall structure is in three different decks, as shown in Fig. 3.15. In the top deck, arrangements for placing the concrete are housed. The middle deck accommodates reinforcement-tying, concrete placement, and compaction arrangements. The bottom deck is usually employed for finishing the set concrete.

Fig. 3.13: Slip-form for a chimney under construction

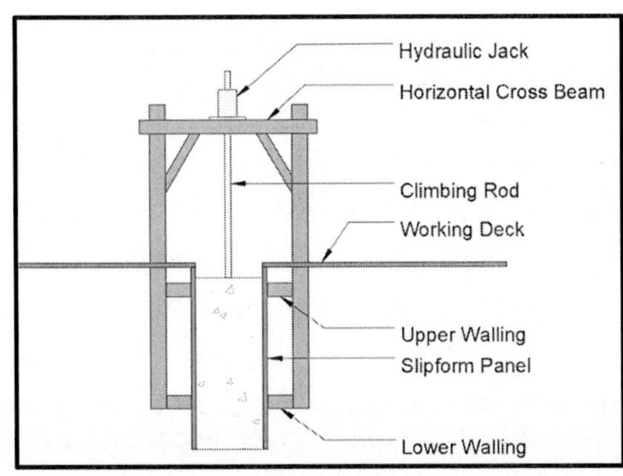

Fig. 3.14: Schematic layout of Slip-form

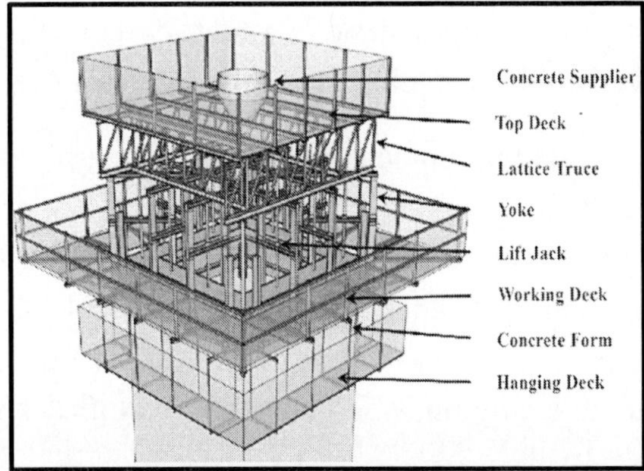

Fig. 3.15: Slip-form for tall Structures

In the case of tapered structures, like chimneys, the slip form can be used by adopting plates that slide against each other and provide the desired shape. The thickness can also be adjusted continuously or in steps. Slip-form is also used for long horizontal structures like concrete pavements and medians, as shown in Fig. 3.16. and Fig. 3.17.

Fig. 3.16: Slip-form paver for concrete pavements

Fig. 3.17: Slip-form for concrete medians

3.4 PRECAST CONCRETE CONSTRUCTION METHODS

Concrete structural components are broadly divided into cast in-situ concrete structures and precast concrete structures, depending on where the structure is being concretised. If the concreting is carried out at the final location of the structure, it is called cast in-situ concrete. If the concreting is done in a factory/ casting yard and the finished component is transported and erected in position, it is called precast concrete.

The concreting process involves setting up the formwork system, placing concrete, curing the concrete and waiting 7 to 14 days for the concrete to achieve the required strength to remove the formwork system. Precast concreting allows for all these activities to be parallel to the construction of other structural components, accelerating the construction time. The additional activities would be transportation and erecting the precast elements at the site. The precast beam and column, wall panel, and box girder segment are shown in Fig. 3.18, 3.19, and 3.20, respectively.

Fig. 3.18: Precast beam and column

Fig. 3.19: Precast I-girder for bridge

Fig. 3.20: Precast box segment

3.4.1 Advantages of Precast Concrete Construction

i. *Saving in time:* Since the precast elements can be cast simultaneously with other works, precast concrete construction saves time.

ii. *Superior quality:* The key factors that affect the quality of concrete are construction, such as mixing and curing, temperature of concrete, formwork system in general, etc. Since these factors are better controlled in a factory-type environment, the concrete quality would be superior to cast in-situ concrete. These factors can be monitored for pre-cast concrete. So, improved quality construction can be performed.

iii. *Durability:* Since precast concrete is of superior quality, the durability of the same is high. Hence, precast concrete elements have a longer life and require minimal maintenance.

iv. *Safety:* Since the concreting is carried out near ground level in a factory-type environment, the safety of operations is greatly enhanced in precast concreting.

v. *Cost-effective:* Since the precast construction process reduces time, it permits repetitive use of the formwork system and increases productivity, quality, and safety, thereby reducing costs.

vi. *Aesthetics:* As the structures are made of prefabricated concrete in a controlled factory environment, several combinations of colours and textures can be used. A wide range of shapes and sizes are available with smooth finishing; thus, the products' aesthetic value is increased.

3.4.2 Disadvantages of Precast Concrete Construction

i. *High capital investment:* Heavy and sophisticated machines are necessary to install a precast concrete plant, which requires a high capital investment. A large-scale precasting will only justify the financial viability of precast concrete construction.

ii. *Detailing of joints:* Joints between the precast elements are the most critical. Considerable attention needs to be paid to this aspect.

iii. *Transportation:* The transportation of precast elements adds to the cost. Transporting the elements correctly and with suitable packing is also essential so that the edges and joints are not damaged. In the case of transportation of long and wide bridge girders or segments within the city, selecting the route for transportation is essential.

iv. *Handling:* Proper care and precaution must be taken to handle precast concrete. Arrangements for lifting the elements using mobile towers or gantry cranes shall be made. The lifting position of the precast elements shall be decided at the design stage itself, and provision for lifting hooks shall be made.

v. *Requires precision work:* Working with precast elements requires precision work. Otherwise, the members may not fit properly, affecting the joint's overall performance and structure. Faulty joints lead to leakage from them. This problem is mitigated to some extent by adopting designed wet joints to be concreted at the site.

3.4.3 Precast Concrete Construction Process

i. *Rebar cage preparation:* The reinforcement cages are prefabricated. Most of the time, reinforcement coils are procured instead of separate bars. Thus, the wastage of reinforcement is practically nil.

ii. *Preparation of forms:* Formwork costs around 35% of the cost of concrete. In precast concrete, the moulds are made of steel and are used repetitively. The repetitive use reduces the formwork cost in the overall cost of concreting, leading to savings in the price. The rebar cages are placed in the forms.

iii. *Concreting:* Normally, precasting yards have automatic batching plants, ensuring proper concrete batching and mixing. The concrete is placed and compacted in the moulds. The concrete is then compacted using needles or form vibrators fixed to the forms.

iv. *Demoulding:* After the concrete achieves the desired strength, the precast element is moulded, i.e., released from the forms.

v. *Curing:* The concrete elements are cured using a membrane, immersed in a water tank, or steam curing.

vi. *Storage:* The precast elements are systematically stored in a stacking area. The elements that are cast early are taken out first. The layout of the stacking area follows the principle of "First come, last out." The stacking yard will have roads for the movement of cranes and trailers. A typical staking area is shown in Fig 3.21.

vii. *Transportation:* As and when required, the precast elements are transported to the erection site.

viii. *Erection:* The precast elements are erected in position using cranes.

ix. *Wet joints:* Wet joints are cast before further construction on the erected precast elements.

Fig. 3.21: Precast tunnel segment stacking yard

3.5 MODULAR CONSTRUCTION METHODS FOR REPETITIVE WORKS

Modularisation aims to transfer traditional in-situ construction work from the job site to a local or distinct fabrication yard. Modularisation is suited for repetitive tasks such as constructing high-rise residential buildings, office buildings, and hospital buildings. The modularisation method extends the precast concrete method to manufacture modules with specific features repeated throughout the building structure.

3.5.1 Purpose

The modularisation process offers significant benefits over traditional onsite construction, such as faster and safer manufacturing of construction elements. Panelised and volumetric construction, also known as modular construction, are the most efficient ways of prefabricated construction. The panelised system is a 2-dimensional system involving the individual walls and floors being built offsite. On the other hand, volumetric construction is the 3-D system where the entire unit or room is being constructed offsite. The finished building is built by stacking and adjoining factory-finished modules in volumetric construction. The building so constructed typically requires relatively little additional structure work.

3.5.2 Module

A module is a portion of a construction element that is completely fabricated, assembled, and tested at the fabrication yard away from the final placement site. The module's size and elements are decided so that utilisation and repeatability are maximised, and it is practical to transport it from the yard to the final site of placement.

3.5.3 Advantages and Opportunities

The adoption of modular construction for repetitive work provides several benefits:

i. Most of the construction can be carried out in a controlled environment away from the site. This assists in high-quality construction.

ii. Modularization helps standardise most of the construction process, thus reducing wastage, delays, and costs.

iii. Modularisation supports the simultaneous construction of different parts of the building. The work being carried out in parallel helps reduce the construction time further.

iv. The adoption of modularisation at the early stages of the project can assist in cost savings during the project's design phase.
v. Weather-related delays can be reduced by moving the construction off-site.

3.5.4 Disadvantages and Challenges

Modular construction's primary disadvantage is transporting the finished modular section. The transportation of the module might require a lot of planning and resources. Moreover, the transportation process might restrict the module size considered for construction.

3.5.5 Critical Success Factors for Modularisation

Factors that could determine the success of the modulation process include:

i. A detailed preliminary study of the transportation plan and constraints at an early stage can help the project team better plan and coordinate the modularisation process.
ii. The strategic alignment of stakeholders such as owners, consultants, designers, and contractors on important project features and elements (repeated throughout the construction) can establish a strong foundation for modular construction.
iii. A timely design can help ensure the modularisation process can proceed as planned.
iv. Recognition of cost savings while ensuring higher quality standards can auger the adoption of modular construction.

3.6 BASIC CONSTRUCTION METHODS FOR STEEL STRUCTURES

Steel structures are constructed with structural steel members made of rolled steel sections, fabricated sections, or a combination of both. The members are joined with either bolted, riveted, or welded connections. The riveted, bolted, and welded connections are shown in Fig. 3.22, 3.23, and 3.24, respectively.

There are two distinct stages in steel construction: fabrication and erection of steel members. Fabrication of steel members made of rolled steel sections is pretty simple. The rolled steel sections are I-sections, channel sections, angle sections, and plates. Typically, these sections are cut to size using oxy-acetylene torches or sawing machines and used to assemble the structure. These sections are occasionally joined by welding, bolting, or riveting. The fabrication of structural members out of plates and rolled sections is an involved process, as detailed below:

i. *Straightening of plates:* The plates are straightened using a machine.
ii. *Cutting of plates:* The plates are cut to the required size by shearing or using oxy-acetylene torches. In the case of heavy fabrication plants, the plates are cut using CNC (Computer Numerically Controlled) cutting machines, which can cut the plate to the desired shape. A typical CNC cutting machine is shown in Fig. 3.25.
iii. *Edge Preparation:* The edges of the cut plates are prepared by grinding depending on the welded, riveted, or bolted joint.
iv. *Drilling of holes:* The holes required in the plates are drilled using a drilling machine with a magnetic base. A typical drilling machine is shown in Fig. 3.26. CNC drilling machines are used in the case of heavy fabrication plants.
v. *Fit-up:* Fit-up is the proper alignment of the members and plates that need to be connected. The plates are fitted up sequentially and tack-welded so that the welding of the joint can be taken up. Sometimes, jigs are used for fit-up and welding. During fit, one of the aims is to have a down-hand welding position.\
vi. *Welding:* Welding of the joints is carried out using arc welding employing one of the processes – Shielded Metal Arc Welding (SMAW), Submerged Arc Welding (SAW), Gas Metal Arc Welding (GMAW), and Flux Core Arc Welding (FCAW).
vii. *Assembly of the member:* The entirely fabricated structure is assembled by systematically connecting the components as the drawing prescribes. Following the sequence is of utmost importance.
viii. *Corrosion Protection:* The fabricated members are treated with corrosion protection using different paint systems applicable to various corrosive environments.
ix. *Stacking of the members:* The members are carefully stacked on a level and hard-prepared ground.
x. *Transportation:* As and when required, the fabricated members are transported to the erection site.
xi. *Erection:* The fabricated members are erected in position using cranes.
xii. *Field joints:* The members are joined in the structure using field connections, typically bolted or riveted connections. For quality control reasons, field welding is usually discouraged.

3.7 BASICS OF CONSTRUCTION METHODS FOR BRIDGES

A bridge structure is broadly divided into substructure and superstructure. The substructure consists of foundations, abutments, a pier, and bearings. The superstructure consists of the deck structure, which directly supports the traffic on it. This section presents different methods of construction of the superstructure of bridges. Following are some of the methods for the construction of the superstructure:

i. In-situ construction using a ground-supported formwork system
ii. Girders erected with crane and the deck slab cast-in-situ
iii. Girders erected by launching and the deck slab cast-in-situ
iv. Full span erection of deck erected with crane
v. Full span erection of deck by launching
vi. Segmental construction of bridges
vii. Incremental launching of the bridge deck
viii. Cantilever method

In a bridge project, either a single method can be adopted, or a combination of two or more methods can be used. The choice of the process depends on the material of the superstructure, accessibility below the bridge, type of equipment available, etc.

Fig. 3.22: A riveted joint in a bridge

Fig. 3.23: A bolted joint in a bridge

Fig. 3.24: Welded joint

Fig. 3.25: CNC cutting machine

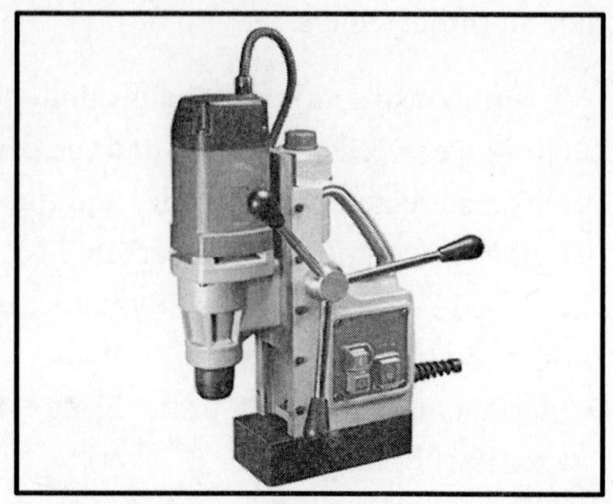

Fig. 3.26: Drilling machine with magnetic base

3.7.1 In-situ Construction using Ground-Supported Formwork System

This is a more traditional way of constructing bridges with solid slabs when the ground below is accessible, and the bridge deck height above ground is less than 10 m. The formwork is supported on the ground with staging. The deck is cast using in-situ concrete construction. This method is employed across small river streams, ordinarily dry during summer. Typical arrangements for construction with a ground-supported formwork system are shown in Fig. 3.27.

Fig. 3.27: In-situ construction using ground-supported formwork system

3.7.2 Girders Erected with Crane and the Deck Slab Cast-in-Situ

This method is adopted when the bridge deck comprises girders made of steel or precast concrete and the deck is made of in-situ concrete. The ground shall be accessible for the movement of cranes and trailers. This method is widely used in the construction of flyovers and elevated metro construction in urban areas and on existing highways. Fig. 3.28 shows the erection of girders on the piers. The deck slab can be cast in situ using left-in-place or temporary formwork. Fig. 3.29 shows the formwork for the casting of the deck.

Fig. 3.28: Erection of girders with crane

Fig. 3.29: Temporary formwork for the casting of deck slab

3.7.3 Girders Erected by Launching and the Deck Slab Cast-in-Situ

This method is adopted when the bridge deck comprises girders made of steel or precast concrete and the deck is made of in-situ concrete. The process is suitable when the ground is not accessible, as in the case of the construction of bridges across rivers where there is a perennial flow of water or across railways or highways where the services below cannot be blocked. The girders are launched using a launching girder. The girders are fed to the launching girder from one end. A launching girder is shown in Fig. 3.30.

3.7.4 Full Span Erection of Deck Erected with Cranes

This method is adopted when the bridge deck comprises a precast concrete box or U girder. The ground shall be accessible for the movement of cranes and trailers. This method is widely used in elevated metro construction in urban areas. In this method, the entire span of the superstructure is cast in a factory, transported to the site on trailers, and erected in position using high-capacity cranes. Usually, two cranes are used for erection. A full-span erection is shown in Fig. 3.31.

Fig. 3.30: Launching girder for girder erection

Fig. 3.31: Erection of full span by two cranes

3.7.5 Full Span Erection of Deck by Launching

This method is adopted when the bridge deck comprises a precast concrete box or U girder. The method is suitable when the ground is not accessible, as in the case of the construction of bridges across rivers where there is a perennial flow of water or across railways or highways where the services below cannot be blocked. This method is used in the Metro construction of the High-Speed Railway project between Mumbai and Ahmedabad. In this method, the entire span of the superstructure is cast in a factory and transported to the site on trailers to a convenient point. The girder is lifted and placed on trollies on the previously erected deck and transported to the location where the girder is launched into the position with the help of a launching girder, as shown in Fig. 3.32.

Fig. 3.32: Full span launching of girder

3.7.6 Precast Segmental Construction of Bridges

Precast segmental construction is a versatile method suitable for bridges of intricate geometry in horizontal and vertical planes. Segmental construction can be adopted in the span-by-span construction of bridge decks or by the balanced cantilever construction method. The span-by-span method is limited to spans up to 40 to 50 meters. In precast segmental construction, the bridge deck is cast in small segments of 2.0 m to 4.0 m in length. The segments are usually match-cast, so there is proper load transfer between segments. These segments are transported to the site by trailer on roads or by barges in case of rivers and marine conditions and lifted to position systematically using a launching girder, as shown in Fig. 3.33.

After all the span segments are aligned, prestressing cables are threaded into the segments, and the entire span is prestressed. Once prestressing is completed, the whole span of many segments behaves as a single unit. The span is lowered onto the bearings, as shown in Fig. 3.34.

Fig. 3.33: Lifting of precast segments

Fig. 3.34: Segmental span lowered onto the bearings

3.7.7 Incremental Launching of Bridge Deck

In the incremental launching, the deck is cast or fabricated incrementally in a casting yard/fabrication shop and pushed or pulled onto the completed piers. This method is employed when the ground below is not accessible. Typical arrangements for the incremental launching of girders are shown in Fig. 3.35

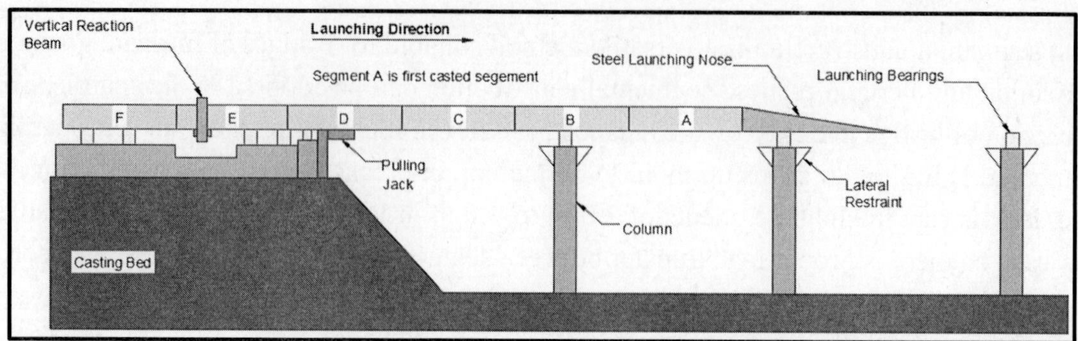

Fig. 3.35: Arrangements for incremental launching

The deck is cast on the casting bed behind the abutments in terms of short segments, viz., A, B, C, D, etc. Once segment A is cast, the same is attached to a launching nose and pulled or pushed onto the pier/column. The launching nose minimises the stresses in the deck while the deck is cantilevering out. After the launch of segment, A, space is created behind the abutment for the casting of segment B. The launching of the segment incrementally and casting of the segment continue till the complete deck is cast and launched.

3.7.8 Balanced Cantilever Method

The balanced cantilever method is suitable for spans from 50 m to 250 m. This construction method can use precast segments of 3 m to 4 m or cast in-situ concrete segments using cantilevers from travellers. The deck is erected/ released on either side of the pier, cantilevering on both sides, as shown in Fig. 3.36 and 3.37.

Fig. 3.36: Balanced cantilever construction using precast segments

Fig. 3.37: Balanced cantilever construction using cast in-situ segments

SUMMARY

The construction method basics chapter comprehensively introduces the foundational principles and techniques utilised in construction projects. It covers various topics, including the basics of formwork and staging, slabs, modular construction, slip form, and bridge construction methods. Readers gain insights into the various methodologies employed in construction, from traditional approaches to design-build and construction management. Emphasis is placed on on-site procedures, quality management, sustainability, and effective project management strategies to ensure successful execution. This chapter provides readers with a solid understanding of the fundamental concepts and practices essential for navigating the complexities of the construction methods used on construction sites.

EXERCISE

You are part of a team tasked with constructing a commercial steel-framed building in a seismic zone. In your construction plan:

a) Explain the key considerations in selecting and erecting steel structural components to withstand seismic forces.
b) Compare the construction methods for steel structures with conventional reinforced concrete structures in terms of speed, cost, and seismic resilience.
c) Evaluate the benefits and challenges of using precast concrete elements for specific building components, such as staircases and facades.

MULTIPLE CHOICE QUESTIONS

1. What is the primary purpose of formwork in construction?

   A) To provide structural support
   B) To create temporary moulds for concrete
   C) To reinforce concrete structures
   D) To facilitate site access

2. Which type of foundation is typically used for tall structures and heavy loads?

   A) Spread footing
   B) Mat foundation
   C) Pile foundation

D) Raft foundation

3. What is the purpose of staging in construction?

   A) To support temporary structures
   B) To provide access for workers
   C) To reinforce concrete slabs
   D) To create formwork moulds

4. Which construction method involves assembling standardised components off-site and transporting them to the construction site for assembly?

   A) Conventional construction
   B) Precast concrete construction
   C) Slip forming
   D) Steel structure construction

5. What is the primary advantage of modular construction methods?

   A) Reduced construction time
   B) Lower material costs
   C) Greater design flexibility
   D) Enhanced structural integrity

6. Slip forming is commonly used for constructing:

   A) Residential buildings
   B) Steel structures
   C) Tall structures
   D) Bridges

7. In steel structure construction, what is the purpose of bolting or welding steel components together?

   A) To provide temporary support
   B) To reinforce the structure
   C) To facilitate transportation
   D) To create a rigid frame

8. Which method is commonly used for constructing single-story buildings with repetitive floor plans?

A) Conventional framed structure
B) Precast concrete construction
C) Modular construction
D) Slip forming

9. What is the primary advantage of precast concrete construction methods?

A) Greater design flexibility
B) Faster construction speed
C) Lower material costs
D) Reduced environmental impact

10. What is NOT a common building material used in conventional walls and slab construction?

A) Reinforced concrete
B) Steel
C) Masonry
D) Wood

11. What type of foundation is suitable for soft soil conditions where load distribution is a concern?

A) Spread footing
B) Mat foundation
C) Pile foundation
D) Raft foundation

ANSWERS TO MULTIPLE CHOICE QUESTIONS

1	2	3	4	5	6	7	8	9	10	11
B	C	B	B	A	C	D	C	B	B	D

SHORT ANSWER TYPE QUESTIONS

1. What are the primary factors influencing the selection of construction methods for bridge projects?
2. Could you provide examples of temporary support systems used during bridge construction and explain their significance?
3. How do construction methods differ when building bridges, such as beam, arch, suspension, and cable-stayed bridges?
4. What types of structures are typically built using slip-form construction, and what are the key considerations when selecting this method?
5. How do engineers ensure the structural integrity and quality of slip-formed structures during construction?
6. How is precast concrete manufactured, and what are the advantages of using precast elements in construction?
7. What are the main components of a steel structure, and how are they assembled on-site?
8. What are the advantages of using deep foundations, and what are some common types of deep foundation systems?
9. Discuss the advantages and limitations of modular construction methods for repetitive work.
10. Describe the basic principles of formwork and staging in construction.

LONG ANSWER TYPE QUESTIONS

1. How do engineers determine the appropriate foundation type for a bridge project, and what are the common foundation construction methods used?
2. Can you explain the difference between conventional bridge construction methods and innovative techniques such as precast segmental construction?

3. How do modern technologies, such as Building Information Modelling (BIM) and drone surveys, influence bridge construction methods?
4. What are the main challenges of slip-form construction, and how can they be mitigated?
5. Investigate the construction methods used in historical and heritage preservation projects, considering material conservation and structural stability factors.
6. Analyse the safety considerations inherent in different construction methods, including fall protection, hazard mitigation, and worker training.
7. Evaluate the cost-effectiveness of various construction methods, considering factors such as initial investment, lifecycle costs, and long-term maintenance requirements.
8. Provide a detailed explanation of the construction process for a conventional framed structure with blockwork walls, highlighting the sequence of activities and key considerations.

TUTORIAL

Develop a CPM chart for a 5-span bridge on open foundations. Develop a comparative table for a 10-storeyed building constructed by at least three different methods, listing their pros and cons.

KNOW MORE

For more information related to this topic scan the QR code.

OR

Type this link in your browser

https://nptel.ac.in/courses/105104178

BIBLIOGRAPHY

- Bertram, N., Fuchs, S., Mischke, J., Palter, R., Strube, G., and Woetzel, J. (2019). Modular construction: From projects to products. *McKinsey & Company: Capital Projects & Infrastructure*, 1(1), 1-34.
- Ko, C. H., and Kuo, J. D. (2015). Making formwork construction lean. *Journal of civil Engineering and Management*, 21(4), 444-458.
- Lawson, M., Ogden, R., and Goodier, C. I. (2014). *Design in modular construction* (Vol. 476, p. 280). Boca Raton, CRC Press: Florida.
- Pan, N. F. (2008). Fuzzy AHP approach for selecting the suitable bridge construction method. *Automation in construction*, 17(8), 958-965.
- Terzioglu, T., Turkoglu, H., and Polat, G. (2022). Formwork systems selection criteria for building construction projects: A critical review of the literature. *Canadian Journal of Civil Engineering*, 49(4), 617-626.
- Zayed, T., Sharifi, M. R., Baciu, S., and Amer, M. (2008). Slip-form application to concrete structures. *Journal of Construction Engineering and Management*, 134(3), 157-168.

4 CONSTRUCTION EQUIPMENT BASICS

UNIT SPECIFICS

The construction industry is a vast arena where the productivity of construction equipment is crucial to completing complex projects. It becomes highly essential to select the right equipment for the right job. To choose the right equipment, the salient features of the equipment should be known to access the process. Efforts have been made in this chapter to discuss the wide variety of equipment that make up the core of modern construction methods.

RATIONALE

Based on the site conditions construction manager needs to alter construction equipment for achieving higher different productivity

PRE-REQUISITE

Basic mathematics

UNIT OUTCOMES

List of outcomes of this unit is as follows:

U4-O1: Difference in conventional and mechanised construction methods

U4-O2: Understand use of different construction equipment

U4-O3: Compute equipment productivity

Unit Outcomes	Expected Mapping with Course Outcomes *(1- Weak Correlation; 2- Medium correlation; 3- Strong Correlation)*					
	CO-1	CO-2	CO-3	CO-4	CO-5	CO-6
U4-O1	2	2	3	3	3	1
U4-O2	3	1	3	3	2	1
U4-O3	2	3	3	1	1	1

4.1 CONVENTIONAL CONSTRUCTION METHODS V/S MECHANIZED METHODS

The conflict between traditional construction methods and their mechanical equivalents has significantly reshaped the approaches used in creating structures in the constantly changing construction sector. This paragraph analyses the subtle distinctions between these two methods, exploring the historical dependence on traditional equipment compared to the revolutionary impact of contemporary technology. The conflict between traditional methods and the efficiency-boosting advantages of mechanised construction becomes increasingly apparent as the construction industry struggles to fulfil rising demand.

Construction projects are growing in complexity and demand, posing a risk of delays if traditional construction methods are employed. In response to the high costs associated with such delays, developers are increasingly embracing mechanisation. Construction machinery is utilised to enhance productivity, achieve cost-effectiveness, handle tasks impractical for manual labour alone, alleviate the physical strain of heavy manual work, maintain high output levels, and ensure the timely completion of projects. The construction industry has seen a significant shift towards mechanisation in recent years. This refers to the increasing use of machinery and technology to perform tasks traditionally done by manual labour. Mechanised construction can reduce manual work and improve working efficiency and quality. The mechanised equipment can also reduce human errors and lower construction risks.

4.2 ADVANTAGES OF MECHANISED CONSTRUCTION METHODS OVER CONVENTIONAL METHODS

The advantages offered by mechanised construction methods over conventional approaches are crucial and hence highlighted below:

4.2.1 Increase Productivity

Mechanised construction methods bring about a significant increase in productivity. The use of advanced machinery allows for quicker project completion times, enabling the meeting of tight deadlines and improving overall project timelines.

4.2.2 Efficiency

The precision and accuracy of mechanised construction equipment enhance efficiency. Tasks traditionally requiring considerable time can now be completed with greater speed, accuracy, and fewer losses, contributing to overall project efficiency.

4.2.3 Reduced Labour Resources

With the deployment of mechanised construction methods, there is a notable reduction in the need for manual labour. This addresses potential labour shortages and minimises labour-related costs, increasing cost-effectiveness.

4.2.4 Rugged Terrain

Mechanized methods excel in handling challenging terrains. Whether faced with uneven landscapes or harsh environmental conditions, advanced machinery can navigate and operate effectively, overcoming obstacles that may pose difficulties for conventional construction methods.

4.2.5 Improved Safety

Safety is paramount in any construction project. Mechanised construction methods prioritise safety by minimising human exposure to hazardous tasks. Automated processes and remote-controlled machinery contribute to a safer working environment, reducing the risk of accidents.

4.2.6 Less Wastage

Mechanised construction minimises material wastage through precise measurements and controlled processes. This aligns with sustainable practices and translates to cost savings by optimising the use of construction materials.

Try to find out!

Where Atal Setu sea bridge is located in India?

Name five construction equipment which have been used in construction of Atal Setu, India's longest sea bridge.

4.3 EARTHMOVING EQUIPMENT

The earthmoving equipment is used for various purposes on earth's surface, like excavation, digging, and compaction. The selection of earthmoving equipment depends on the following three criteria:

i. Purpose of application
ii. Type of soil
iii. Project size and scope

A brief description of various earthmoving equipment is discussed below:

4.3.1 Backhoe

This dual-purpose equipment is widely used in construction, excavation, landscaping, and utility work. The backhoe's primary function involves excavation tasks, such as digging trenches, foundations, and pits. Simultaneously, its front loader allows for the efficient movement and placement of materials like soil, gravel, or debris. The backhoe's compact size and manoeuvrability make it well-suited for various applications, including urban construction projects and tasks in confined spaces, showcasing its adaptability and efficiency in handling multiple earthmoving activities. Typically, the bucket capacity of the backhoe is 0.38 m^3 to 3.25 m^3. it is shown in Fig. 4.1.

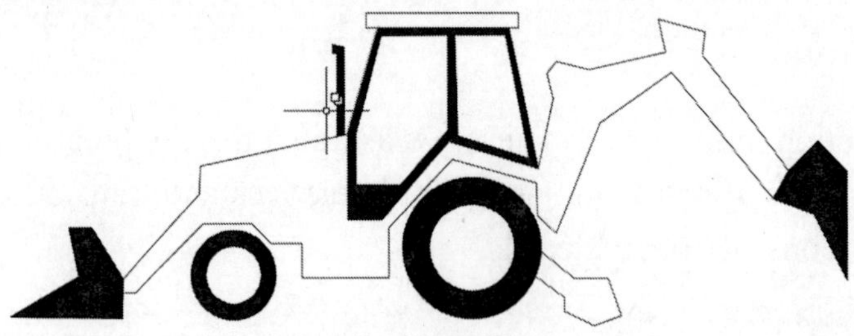

Fig. 4.1: Backhoe

4.3.2 Shovel

In construction, shovels are crucial for excavation and shaping terrain, aiding in transferring plants, rubbish, and soil from one place to another during construction. This equipment is helpful in excavating above its wheelbase (shown in Fig. 4.2). It is suitable for cutting and loading dry soil. The bucket capacity of the shovel is 0.38 m^3 to 3.25 m^3.

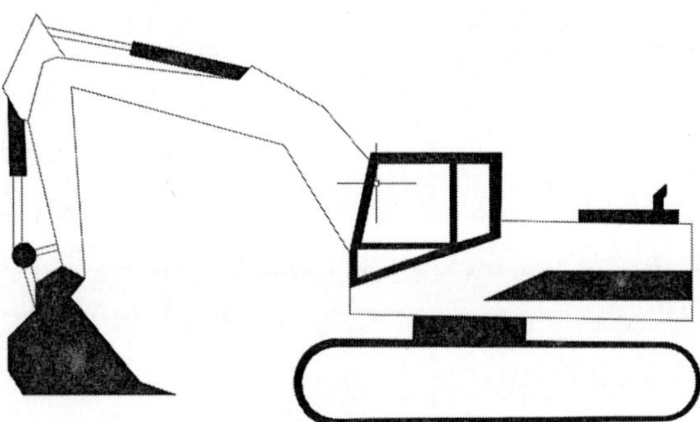

Fig. 4.2: Shovel

4.3.3 Dragline

A dragline is a specialised earthmoving machine known for its large bucket suspended from a long boom. It excels in the bulk excavation of loose soil below the wheelbase, making it ideal for deep and high-volume projects such as mining. With a capacity for selective excavation and the ability to work in various terrains, especially marshy lands, draglines offer cost-effective solutions, mainly when precise material removal or environmental considerations are crucial. Generally, canal, pit excavation, and desilting of ditches activities are performed using draglines. A typical dragline is shown in Fig. 4.3. The capacity of the dragline is 0.38 m^3 to 3.06 m^3.

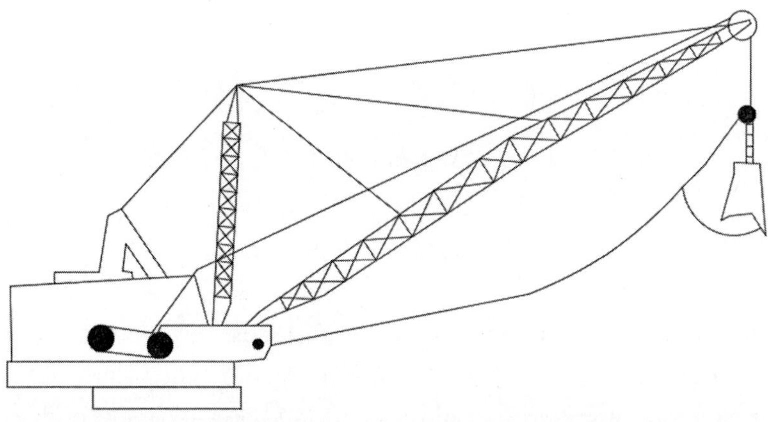

Fig. 4.3: Dragline

4.3.4 Clamshell

A clamshell is a type of earthmoving equipment characterised by a hinged, two-piece bucket that resembles a clamshell. It is commonly used for tasks that require precise digging and material handling. The two halves of the bucket can be opened and closed, allowing for efficient grabbing and lifting of materials such as soil, sand, or debris. Clamshells are often mounted on cranes or other lifting devices, making them versatile for various applications, including dredging, excavation in confined spaces, and loading materials onto trucks. Their design provides a controlled and effective means of picking up and transporting materials where other earthmoving equipment may be less suitable. Clamshells find their application in shafts, pits and wells. A typical clamshell is shown in Fig. 4.4. The bucket capacity of the clamshell is 0.38 m^3 to 0.36 m^3.

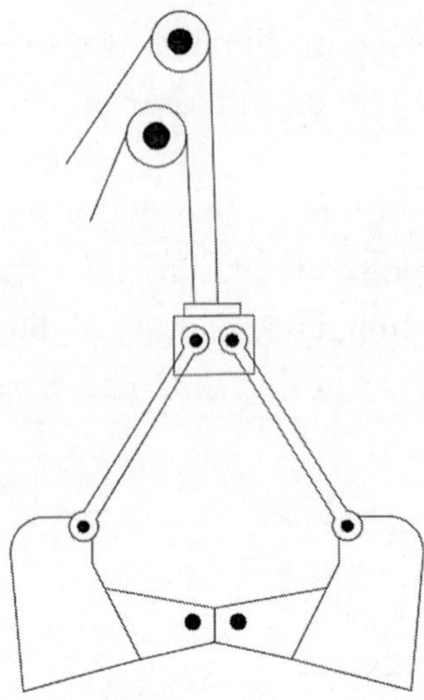

Fig. 4.4: Clamshell

4.3.5 Dozer

Bulldozers, commonly known as dozers, are robust earthmoving machines designed for clearing and grubbing sites, excavating earth surfaces, grading, road construction, and foundation preparation. A typical dozer is shown in Fig. 4.5. The broad metal blade at the front is extensively utilised in construction, mining, and land development endeavours. Dozers can also be wheel-mounted. The blade capacity of dozers is 1.14 m^3 to 6.11 m^3.

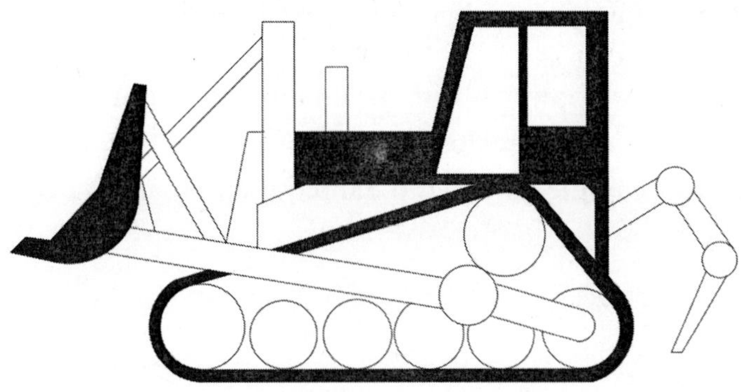

Fig. 4.5: Dozer

4.3.6 Roller Compactor

A roller compactor, often called a roller, is used for compacting various materials, especially soil, gravel and asphalt. A typical roller is shown in Fig. 4.6. It consists of one or more metal drums that exert pressure on the compact surface, reducing voids and enhancing the soil's density. Rollers are essential in road construction, building foundations, and other projects where proper compaction is critical for structural integrity. Roller compactors play a vital role in improving the soil's load-bearing capacity, preventing settlement, and ensuring the durability of constructed structures. A variety of roller compactors are available viz. a) Smooth-wheeled roller (capacity: 8t -10t), b) vibratory roller (capacity: 4t -17t), c) Pneumatic-tyre roller (11t-25t), and d) sheep foot roller (capacity: 2.5t -11.5t). Here, t = tonnes.

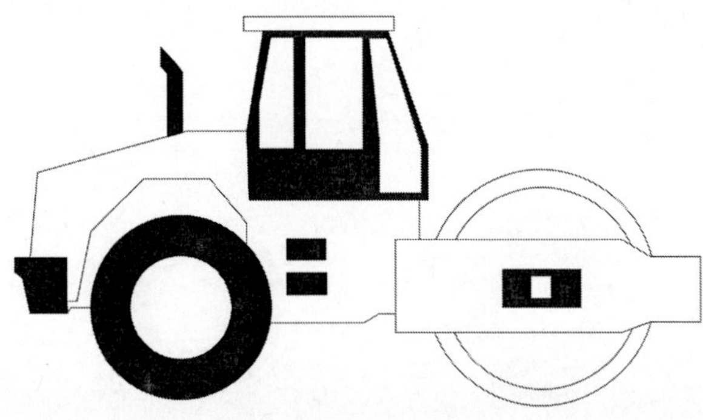

Fig. 4.6: Roller

4.3.7 Scraper

A scraper is specialised earthmoving equipment designed to efficiently move large quantities of soil, rock, or other materials over short to medium distances. It consists of a self-loading hopper and a cutting edge (as shown in Fig. 4.7), allowing it to cut into the earth, load the material, and transport it to a designated location. Scrapers are commonly used for site stripping, loading and dumping the material to the required point. The capacity of the scraper varies from 8 m^3 to 50 m^3.

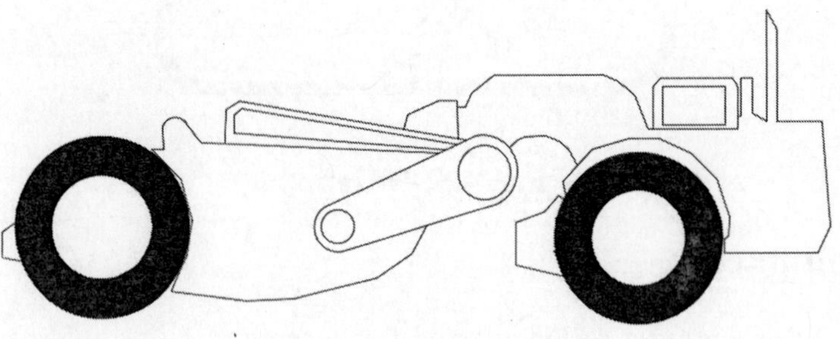

Fig. 4.7: Scrapper

4.3.8 Dumper

A dumper is designed for transporting and dumping various materials, such as soil, gravel, or construction debris. A typical dumper is shown in Fig. 4.8. It features a bed or container that can be hydraulically tilted to unload its contents. They are commonly used to transport bulk materials efficiently from excavation sites to disposal or stockpile areas. Dumpers come in different varieties, such as side tipping, front tipping, etc. The load capacity of a dumper is 1 t to about 80 t.

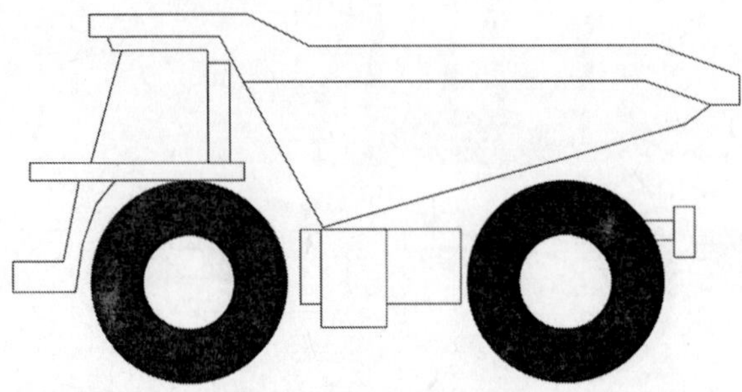

Fig. 4.8: Dumper

4.3.9 Grader

The primary functions of a grader include cutting, spreading, and levelling the ground, making it suitable for tasks such as creating even road surfaces, building embankments, and preparing the ground for construction projects. Graders are essential in achieving proper drainage, controlling slopes, and ensuring the overall quality and precision of the graded surface. It typically features a long blade that can be adjusted to different angles and positions, as shown in Fig. 4.9. Graders are equipped with wheels or blades known as a moldboard, which can be rotated to cut and redistribute soil or other materials.

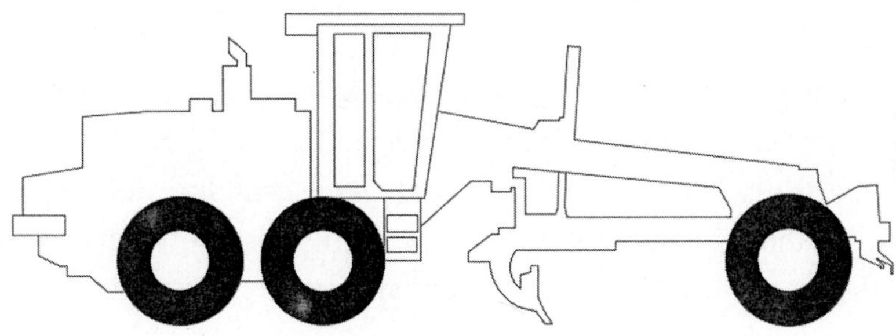

Fig. 4.9: Grader

4.4 DEWATERING EQUIPMENT

Dewatering equipment is essential for managing and controlling water in abundant water problems. It ensures that water is removed or appropriately controlled to improve project safety, stability, and overall effectiveness. There is a variety of equipment available for dewatering, which depends on a few crucial factors, like

i. Volume of water to be removed from soil or sludge
ii. The height of the lift
iii. Geological condition
iv. Corrosion potential of the dewatering equipment, etc.

Based on the above factors, the common dewatering equipment is centrifuge, vacuum filters, filter presses, and drying beds. These are explained in the following subsections.

4.4.1 Centrifuge

Centrifuges separate solids from liquids through sedimentation and centrifugal force. As the sludge accelerates through the ports in the conveyor shaft, it is subsequently distributed to the periphery of the spinning bowl. The high-speed rotation of the bowl effectively separates water from the solids. The separated solids are compacted against the bowl wall. Following this separation, the solids move on to the drying stage of the centrifuge. At the same time, the continuously separated liquid is discharged over the weir arrangements positioned along the sides of the bowl. Centrifuge has a wide application area, such as municipal sewage treatment, sludge dewatering, separating oil from unwanted impurities, etc.

4.4.2 Vacuum Filter

A vacuum filter is designed to generate a vacuum, facilitating water extraction from solids. The equipment typically features a drum immersed in sludge, with a filtering medium positioned across the drum. The arrangement of valves ensures that, during the drum's rotation, a vacuum is applied to the inner side of the filter medium. This rotational movement effectively draws water from the sludge. Some common area of application of vacuum filter are wastewater system, Sludge dewatering etc.

4.4.3 Filter Presses

A filter press is an equipment in sludge dewatering, operates by pressing the sludge between porous plates to force water out, effectively separating solids from liquids. As part of industrial wastewater treatment, it removes impurities and suspended solids. The filter press is a key player in industrial dewatering, alongside other techniques such as centrifuges and belt presses. Its application spans various industries, including mining, concrete washout recovery, food production, and waste handling, contributing to improved water quality. The equipment's efficiency lies in forming a filter cake during the filling cycle, releasing solids when the plates reach capacity. With advanced features like automatic plate shifters, filter presses offer continuous operation, making them suitable for demanding environments like mines and chemical plants. In contrast to settling ponds, filter presses provide a more efficient and sustainable solution for water treatment, ensuring a clean water return to the industrial processes.

4.4.4 Drying Bed

Drying beds are designed to dewater and dry sludge or biosolids efficiently. These beds feature a porous surface, often composed of sand or gravel, facilitating water drainage while supporting the sludge layer. As part of their operation, sludge is evenly spread across the bed, and through natural processes like evaporation and drainage, moisture content is significantly reduced over time. Underdrains beneath the bed surface collect drained water for appropriate disposal or treatment. They find widespread use in municipal wastewater treatment plants and offer applications in agriculture, where the dried sludge can be utilised as a beneficial soil conditioner or fertiliser. Drying beds are commonly used in small-scale wastewater treatment plants and agricultural applications.

4.5 CONCRETE MIXING

Concrete mixing is one of the common processes required on construction sites. Concrete mixtures are used for concrete mixing. Concrete mixers prepare a homogenous mix of cement, sand, aggregates, additives (if required) and water. Hand mixing may be adopted for handling a minimal quantity of work. Moreover, the selection of mixing equipment should be such that the aggregate should be uniformly coated with the finer particles. The portable or stationary mixer may be used based on the project's demand. Some commonly used mixers are discussed below:

4.5.1 Tilting Drum Mixer

A tilting drum mixer is a continuous concrete mixer utilised in construction projects for blending materials like cement and aggregates. Its distinctive feature lies in the design of the cylindrical drum, mounted on a central axis, allowing it to be tilted at various angles through hydraulic or manual mechanisms. Loading is facilitated through a top charging chute, and after the mixing process, the drum is tilted to discharge the thoroughly blended concrete through a bottom opening. These mixers, available in various sizes and often mobile, offer flexibility in handling different concrete mixes on construction sites, making them suitable for multiple projects, from small-scale residential buildings to significant infrastructure developments. Tilting drum mixers require less manual labour than non-tilting counterparts, as the mixed material can be quickly unloaded by tilting the drum, streamlining the process and enhancing overall efficiency in construction applications. As per IS 1791-1961, tilting mixers have been designated as 100T,140T, and 200T; T stands for tilting type, while the numeric associated with it specifies the volume of concrete mix in litres.

4.5.2 Non-tilting Drum Mixer

Unlike tilting drum mixers, these continuous-type mixers have a fixed drum that does not tilt for loading or unloading. Instead, materials are loaded into the drum through the open top, and the mixing process is achieved by rotating the drum in one direction. Once the mixing is complete, the mixer is typically equipped with mechanisms to discharge the mixed concrete through an opening at the bottom. In the case of the non-tilting type, the discharging time taken is longer; hence, the cycle time is longer. More cycle time implies less productivity (say up to 10 m3/hr), so it is not preferred in large-scale projects. As per IS 1791-1961, non-tilting mixers have been designated as 140NT, 200NT, 280NT, 400NT, and 800NT, where NT stands for non-tilting while the numeric associated with specifies the volume of concrete mix in litres.

4.5.3 Reversible Drum Mixer

Reversible drum mixers are also the most preferred in the construction industry. The spiral arrangement blades of the drum enable efficient mixing by rotating the drum in one direction and discharging the mixed material by reversing the rotation. RMC (ready mix concrete) transit mixer is an example of a reversible mixer. These can be free-fall mixtures or power mixtures.

The output of mixers can be calculated by Eq. 4.1.

$$Output \left({m^3}/{hr}\right) = production\ per\ cycle(m^3) \times no.of\ cycle\ per\ hour \left(\frac{1}{hr}\right) \times plant\ efficiency \tag{4.1}$$

Free fall type of mixer is capable of handling slump mix above 50 mm. However, power mixers are preferred for a more cohesive and stiffer mix. The chapter discusses two power mixers – pan-type concrete mixers and trough-type concrete mixers.

Pan-type concrete mixer

Distinguished by its shallow, pan-shaped mixing drum, this mixer employs a vertical central shaft with mixing blades or paddles attached. The materials are introduced into the pan, and the mixing process occurs as the paddles revolve around the central axis and are discharged through the trap at the base. Scrapper blades are so arranged inside the pan that they scrape the material that sticks to the pan during the blending. Pan mixers are advantageous for achieving a homogenous mix with a production rate of 4 to 100 m^3/hr.

Trough type of concrete mixer

Unlike pan concrete, the shaft is attached horizontally, and the paddles are spirally attached along the shaft. This arrangement is fitted in a trough-shaped drum, ensuring a more homogenous ingredient blending. The mixing time of this mixer is less; hence, increased productivity is achieved when compared to pan mixers. Trough concrete mixers are available in both single-shaft and twin-shafts.

Try to find out!

Can you name the type of concrete mixers shown below?

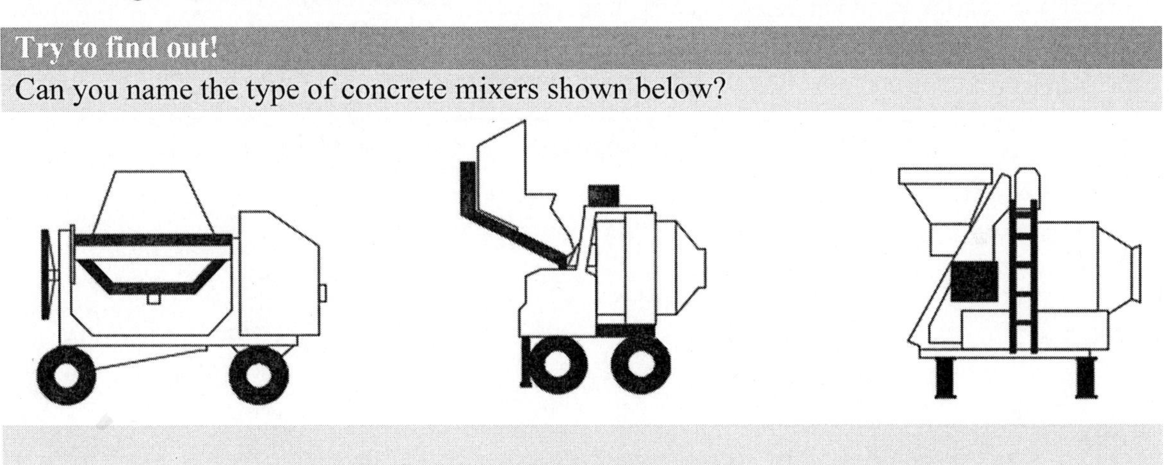

4.6 ON-SITE CONCRETE MIXING VS CENTRAL BATCH CONCRETE MIXING

On-site concrete mixing or job batch mixing means the concrete is prepared at the job site. This is preferred when the job site is inaccessible due to remoteness, rugged terrain, congested sites, etc. Delivering concrete on time using an RMC (ready mix concrete) transit mixer isn't easy. In this situation, raw materials (cement, aggregates, water, and additives) are brought to the construction site separately and mixed on-site in small batches as needed for specific tasks or sections of the project and transported using various equipment. Meanwhile, central batch concrete mixing involves preparing concrete at a central location, usually a concrete batch plant, before transporting it to the construction site. The central plant is equipped to handle the storage of raw materials in large volumes. Better quality control and higher productivity are advantages of a central batch mixing plant.

4.7 CONCRETE TRANSPORTATION AND PLACING

To select the equipment for transporting the mix, the mix's volume and the site where the mix is to be utilised must be ascertained. A wide variety of equipment handles low volumes of less than 1 m^3 to a high of 10 m^3 along horizontal and vertical directions. However, utmost care should be taken while selecting the transporting equipment so concrete segregation and setting can be avoided before placing. Different concrete transporting and placing equipment, along with their applications and capacity, are given in Table 4.1.

Table 4.1: Concrete transporting and placing equipment

Type of equipment	Application	Capacity	Remarks
Wheel burrow/power-driven buggies	Wheel burrows are preferred when the haul distance is less than 60 m. Power-driven buggies can be used up to 300 m	0.2 m^3 to 0.5 m^3	Generally, Hand buggies are two-wheeled, while wheel burrows are single-wheel
Concrete buckets	For transporting material in the vertical direction	Bucket size: 0.4 m^3 to 3 m^3	i. Need to be hoisted using cranes, towers or cableways ii. Chutes are used attached to buckets to avoid segregation of concrete
Belt conveyors	Preferred when haul distance is the large and economical placement of a large volume of concrete is required	Can deliver up to 115 m^3/hr	i. Capable of handling large volumes of material ii. The speed of the belt is maintained at 2-3 m/s iii. Width of the belt: 400mm-1000mm

			iv. More than 30^0 inclinations can lead to segregation
Concrete transit mixer	Enable the delivery of ready-mix concrete at remote location sites	Rotating drum capacity: 3 m^3/hr to 9 m^3/hr	i. Generally, wet concrete is transported in a rotating drum mixer attached to a truck ii. Slump loss during the travel time has to be ascertained to avoid setting before placing
Concrete pumps	Usually, mix with slump value 50-150 mm to be transported and placed on congested sites	In general, a truck-mounted pump = 120 m^3/hr up to a height of 40m	i. Minimum pipe diameter should be at least three times MSA (maximum size of aggregate) ii. Pumps may be truck mounted and boom facilitated iii. Double handling is unnecessary as the material can be transported directly from the mixer to the formwork via pipes

4.8 CRANES, HOISTS, AND OTHER EQUIPMENT

Cranes, in general, are hoisting equipment that primarily moves selectively or in combination with a) travelling, b) lifting/lowering, c) derrick, and d) slewing. In addition, hoisting equipment may be broadly classified into a) Tower cranes and b) mobile cranes.

4.8.1 Tower Cranes

These are lifting equipment that operate while remaining stationary or moving. Based on the motion, tower cranes may be distinguished as top-slewing and bottom-slewing cranes. Slewing motion enables the crane to shift the load line to revolve around the crane.

Top slewing cranes

In case of top-slewing motion, the jib, tower and cabin rotate. With a maximum capacity of 10,000 to 90,000 lbs, it facilitates lifting materials such as reinforcements to greater heights and a better working radius, especially at high-rise construction sites. A typical tower crane is shown in Fig. 4.10. The crane can also be mounted on the rail track for better reachability.

As in the Fig 4.10, jib is the horizontal arm, extending from the main body of the crane. This component rotates, facilitating lateral movement and supporting the lifting mechanism, allowing the crane to reach loads at different distances. Meanwhile, the tower component supports the jib and lifting mechanism. The cabin also called the operator's cab, is an enclosed compartment attached to the crane, usually positioned near the turntable or mast. It serves as the operational space for the crane operator, offering a vantage point to oversee activities and control the crane's movements.

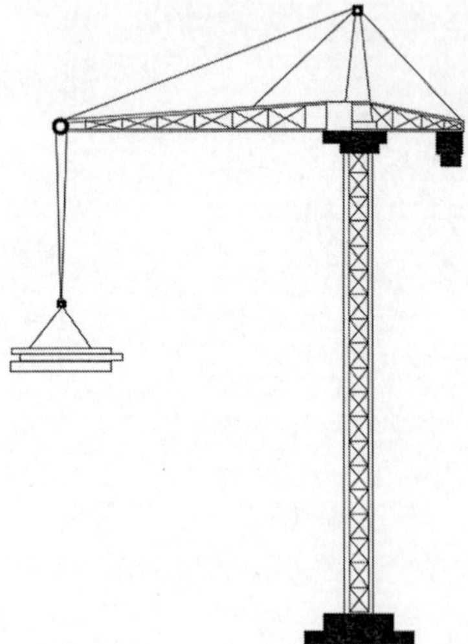

Fig. 4.10: Top Slewing Crane

Bottom slewing cranes

Bottom slewing cranes are suitable for low-rise construction sites (Fig. 4.11). A slewing ring at the base characterises them, and rotation of the tower and the jib occur relative to each other. The lifting capacity of bottom slewing cranes is much lower than that of top-slewing cranes, varying from 2,000 to 20,000 lbs, while the maximum load capacity at the end of the jib is 1000 to 7,000 lbs.

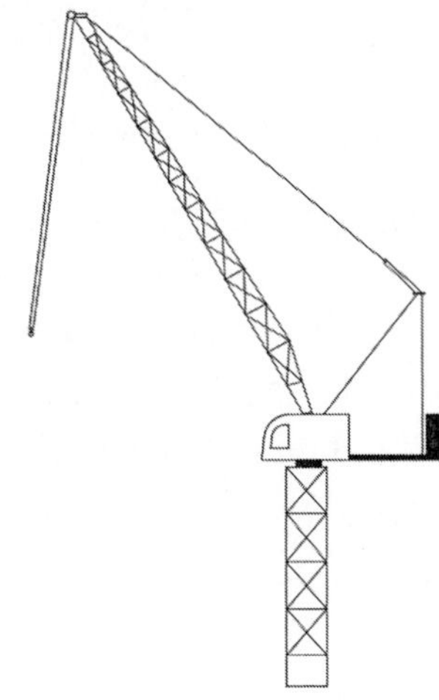

Fig. 4.11: Bottom Slewing Crane

4.8.2 Mobile Cranes

Unlike tower cranes, these types can manoeuvre around the sites to specific locations. Four types of mobile cranes are discussed here – truck, crawler, rough terrain, and all-terrain cranes.

Truck cranes

As in Fig. 4.12, the boom, engine, counter-weight and cabin are mounted on a special truck; hence, they are called truck cranes. Booms are available in lattice type or telescopic boom. With a maximum lifting capacity of 20 to 100 tons and a boom length of up to 120 ft, truck cranes are most suitable for short-term lifting operations for a shorter duration only.

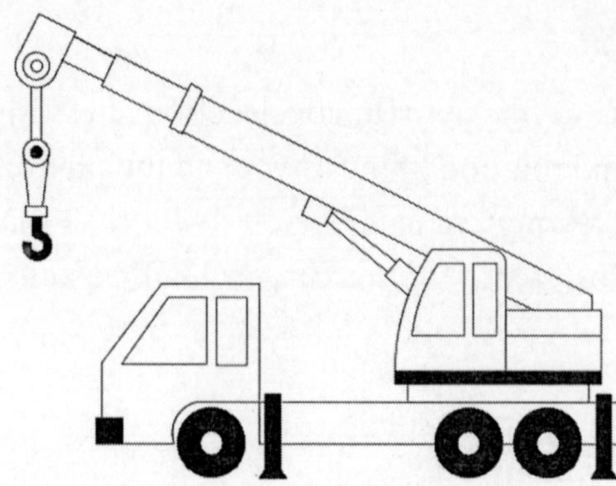

Fig. 4.12: Truck Cranes

Crawler cranes

It can travel to different locations within the site with better mobility. However, moving to another location may be mounted on a trailer if required. With a maximum lifting capacity (at minimum radius) of 25 tons to 120 tons and up to 160ft boom length, crawler cranes find their suitability in areas with restricted contact pressure, especially in the case of underground utilities. A typical crawler crane is shown in Fig. 4.13.

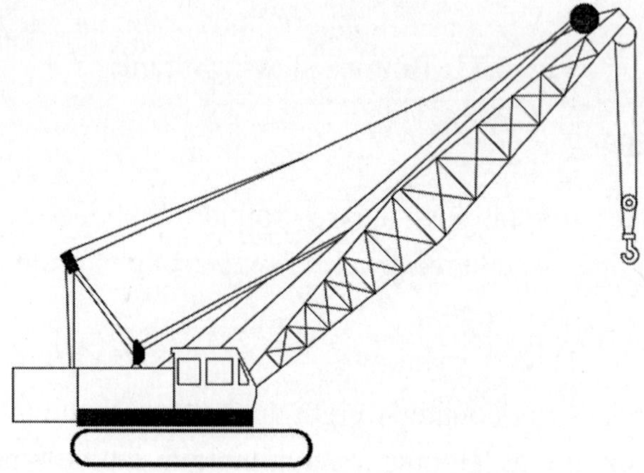

Fig. 4.13: Crawler crane

Rough terrain cranes

This category of cranes works best with tower cranes. Rough terrain cranes (Fig. 4.14) overcome the disadvantage of crawler cranes, the inability to relocate, as they can be used in rough terrain with frequent relocation. These cranes are also available in both lattice and telescopic boom types. The maximum lifting capacity (at minimum radius) is 10 to 100 tons, while the maximum boom radius is 70 to 140 ft.

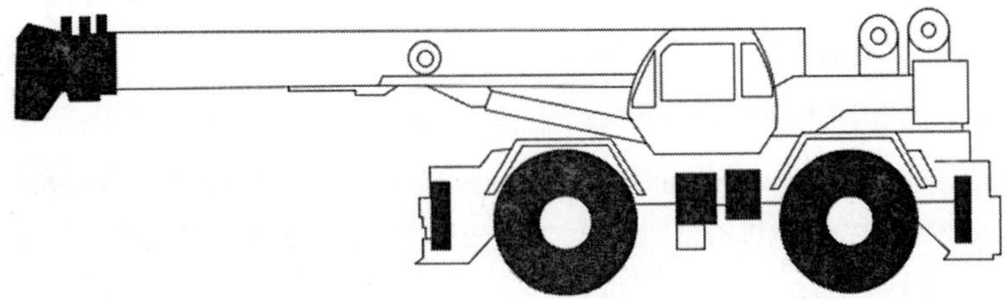

Fig. 4.14: Rough-terrain cranes

All-terrain cranes

This crane category comprises axel-drive, all-wheeled steering, crab steering, large tyres, and high ground clearance. This type of crane can manoeuvre through a variety of terrains. The maximum lifting capacity (at minimum radius) is 40 to 300 tons, while the maximum boom radius is 70 to 250 ft. A typical all-terrain crane is shown in Fig. 4.15.

Fig. 4.15: All-terrain crane

4.8.3 Equipment for Transportation of Materials

Transportation of aggregate, coal, etc., is generally done by trucks, tractors, etc. Such equipment may also be mounted on a trailer to increase productivity and mobility. Based on the dumping of the load, different types of trucks are discussed below:

Rear dump trucks

This heavy-duty truck category has a large cargo bed hinged at the back and is hydraulically mechanised so that the front end can be elevated and tilted at the rear end to allow the free flow of materials. Rear dump trucks are also capable of hauling large rocks. In cold weather, the truck is modified through strategically positioned ducts, which carry hot exhaust gases to facilitate a warm truck body and avoid freezing the material.

Bottom dump truck

The distinctive feature of a bottom dump truck is its ability to unload its cargo by opening a gate or doors on the bottom of the truck bed. Apart from transporting material, this truck category can also discharge the material in a controlled way while still in motion. However, it is not preferred for handling wet material or large rocks.

Side dump trucks

This truck category facilitates a dumping mechanism, i.e., a tilting facility from both sides. Also, side dump trucks' loading rate is higher than that of other equipment. Large rocks, earth, coal, and aggregate can be easily transported and dumped at specific locations.

4.9 EQUIPMENT PRODUCTIVITIES

Different approaches are employed to calculate the output of different equipment. In this section, the productivity of a few important equipment is illustrated.

4.9.1 Bulldozers

Ideally, the output measured in bulk volume of loose soil of dozers depends on the following factors:

i. Size of the bulldozer
ii. Haul distance
iii. Forward and backward speed of the dozer
iv. Blade factor
v. Type of soil
vi. Swell factor where, $swell\ factor = (loose\ volume)\ /\ (bank\ volume)$

The following equation (Eq. 4.2) can give the output of the dozer

$$Output\ Dozer\ of\ bulldozer\left(\frac{m3}{hr}\right) \tag{4.2}$$

$$= \frac{Theoretical\ capacity\ of\ the\ blade}{Swell\ factor} \times \frac{Operating\ time(\frac{min}{hr})}{cycle(trip)time\ (\text{min})}$$

Illustration 1

Calculate the output of a bulldozer handling clayey soil swell factor of 1.3 for a haul distance of 30m. The theoretical capacity of the blade is 4m^3 of loose soil volume. The operating time of the dozer per hour is 40 minutes. Also, the forward and backward speeds are 3kmph and 5.4 km, respectively.

Solution:

Cycle time (min) =

$$Hauling\ time\ in\ forward\ motion + Hauling\ time\ in\ backward\ motion$$

$$= \frac{30}{50} + \frac{30}{90} = 0.93 \text{ min}$$

Let us assume gear shifting time = 0.30

Overall Cycle time (min) = 0.93+0.3 = 1.23 min

Therefore,

$$Output\ of\ bulldozer\left(\frac{cum}{hr}\right) = \frac{3}{1.3} \times \frac{40}{1.23}$$

$$= 76 \text{ m}^3\text{/hr}$$

4.9.2 Power Shovel

The output(m^3/hr) of power shovel is given by

$$= \frac{Heaped\ bucket\ capacity}{1 + swell\ factor} \times \frac{operating\ time\ (\frac{sec}{hr})}{cycle\ time(sec)} \times efficiency$$

The output of the power shovel can also be calculated as

$$Output(\frac{cum}{hr}) = heap\ capacity\ of\ the\ bucket \times \frac{3600}{cycle\ time\ (sec)}$$

Illustration 2

Considering a swell percentage of 30%, calculate the output of a shovel to excavate earth material to handle a loose volume of 3 m^3. Assume a cycle time of 21 seconds.

Solution:

The heaped volume of the banked material per trip $= \frac{loose\ volume}{1+swell\ percent} = \frac{3}{1+0.3} = 2.3\ cum$

Let us assume the actual operational time be 50 min (considering equipment ideal time =10 min)

Therefore, no. of cycles per hour the shovel can be operated

$$= \frac{Actual\ operational\ tme}{cycle\ time} = \frac{50 \times 60}{21} = 143$$

cycles/hr

$$Now\ , Output\left(\frac{cum}{hr}\right) = heap\ capacity\ of\ the\ bucket \times no.of\frac{cycles}{hr}$$

=2.3 x 143 = 328 m^3/hr

4.9.3 Concrete Mixer

Illustration 3

Consider a concrete mixer of capacity of 250 litres and the total mixing time is 2 minutes per batch. Calculate the output of the mixer per hour. Also consider that time loss due to cleaning, labour rest time etc is 12 minutes.

Solution:

Capacity in cubic meters = 250 / 1000 = 0.25 m^3

Now, Mixing time = 2 minutes

Time loss due to cleaning, labour rest time, i.e., idle time for mixer = 12 minutes

∴ Time for which the mixer was operational = 48 minutes

∴ Number of batches of concrete mixing per hour = 48/2

= 24 batches

If the working hour is considered to be 8 hours per day,

Then, the output of the mixer per hour $= \frac{8 \times 24 \times 0.25}{24}$

$= 2 \text{ m}^3$

4.9.4 Dump Truck

To estimate the capacity of hauling unit like dump trucks, parameter such as pay load, cycle time may be ascertained. Payload is the maximum load (in tonnes or cum) that the truck may safely be hauled per cycle.

Illustration 4

Consider a construction project that requires transporting 5000 cubic meters of material over a lead distance of 8 kilometres using dump trucks. Each dump truck has a payload capacity of 15 cubic meters. The speeds during empty and loaded haul are 40 kmph and 20 kmph, respectively. The loading time for one dump truck is 0.5 hours. Calculate the estimated number of dump trucks needed for the task and the total time required for all trucks to complete the job. Assume the trucks unload at the destination point, and loading time is the only time spent at the loading site.

Solution:

Given data

Volume of material to be transported = 5000 m^3

Lead distance = 8 km

Speed during empty haul = 40 kmph

Speed during loaded haul = 20 kmph

Loading time of one dump truck = 0.5 hours

Payload capacity of each dump truck = 15 cubic meters

Now,

Volume Carried by One Truck} = 0.5×Payload Capacity,

(Considering the truck is loaded only half of its payload capacity)

∴Volume Carried by One Truck} $= \frac{15}{2} = 7.5\text{m}^3$

Now,

Number of Trucks = Total volume to be carried/Volume Carried by One Truck.

∴ Number of Trucks = 5000/7.5 = 667

Now, let's consider the time it takes for a truck to complete one cycle:

Time per Cycle = Loading time $+\frac{Lead\ distance}{speed\ during\ empty\ haul}+\frac{Lead\ distance}{speed\ during\ loaded\ haul}$

Time per Cycle = $0.5 + \frac{8}{40} + \frac{8}{20}$ =1hr 6 mins

The total time for all trucks to complete the job would be:

Total Time = 667 × 1.1 = 734.37 hrs i.e approximately 31 days

SUMMARY

The construction equipment chapter provides an essential overview of the diverse machinery and tools used in the construction industry. It covers equipment used for excavation, earthmoving, material handling, concrete production, and site preparation. The chapter emphasises the importance of selecting the right equipment for specific tasks based on project requirements, site conditions, and operational efficiency. Additionally, considerations regarding equipment maintenance, safety protocols, and operator training are highlighted to ensure optimal performance and mitigate risks on construction sites. By understanding the capabilities and limitations of various construction equipment, project managers and operators can make informed decisions to enhance productivity, minimise downtime, and promote a safe working environment throughout the construction process.

EXERCISE

You are tasked with managing the concrete operations for a high-rise building construction project. To ensure efficient concrete mixing, transporting, and placing:

a) Outline the equipment required for concrete mixing, including batch plants and transit mixers, and discuss their functions and advantages.

b) Describe the process of transporting concrete from the mixing plant to the construction site and explain the methods and equipment used, such as truck-mounted conveyors and pumps.

c) Discuss the importance of proper concrete placing techniques and equipment, including concrete pumps and placement booms, and their role in achieving quality and durability in concrete structures.

MULTIPLE CHOICE QUESTIONS

1. Which of the following is NOT a benefit of using mechanised construction methods over conventional methods?

   A) Increased productivity
   B) Higher safety standards
   C) Lower initial investment

D) Improved precision

2. Which equipment is commonly used to excavate and remove soil for earthmoving operations?

A) Concrete pump
B) Bulldozer
C) Concrete mixer
D) Tower crane

3. Which equipment transports mixed concrete from the batching plant to the construction site?

A) Bulldozer
B) Excavator
C) Transit mixer
D) Tower crane

4. What is the function of a concrete pump in construction?

A) Mixing concrete
B) Placing concrete
C) Transporting concrete
D) Compacting concrete

5. Which equipment is used vertically lifting and lowering materials at a construction site?

A) Bulldozer
B) Hoist
C) Excavator
D) Grader

6. What is the purpose of a tower crane on a construction site?

A) Transporting materials horizontally
B) Lifting and lowering heavy loads vertically
C) Excavating soil
D) Mixing concrete

7. Equipment productivity refers to:

   A) The efficiency of construction workers
   B) The output achieved by construction equipment in a given time
   C) The safety measures implemented on a construction site
   D) The cost-effectiveness of construction materials

8. Mechanized construction methods are advantageous over conventional methods mainly because they:

   A) Require less skilled labour
   B) Are less expensive
   C) Offer higher productivity and efficiency
   D) Have lower safety standards

9. Which equipment is commonly used to create level surfaces and slopes for earthmoving operations?

   A) Bulldozer
   B) Excavator
   C) Grader
   D) Dump truck

ANSWERS TO MULTIPLE CHOICE QUESTIONS

1	2	3	4	5	6	7	8	9
C	B	C	B	B	B	B	C	C

SHORT ANSWER TYPE QUESTIONS

1. What are the advantages of mechanised construction methods in developing countries like India?
2. A specific volume of concrete is to be mixed, transported and placed in a congested area in a city. Which equipment is preferred in this condition?
3. Discuss briefly the advantages of mobile cranes over tower cranes.
4. Enumerate the advantages and disadvantages of a dragline over a clamshell.

5. Discuss the factors the output of a bulldozer may depend upon.
6. Describe the primary function of a hoist in construction, and name one scenario where hoists are commonly used.
7. What equipment is typically used for transporting materials horizontally at a construction site, and how does it operate?
8. Define equipment productivity in construction and explain one-factor affecting equipment productivity on a construction site.
9. Discuss the importance of selecting the right equipment for construction projects, considering project scope, site conditions, and safety requirements.
10. Write short notes on
    a. Clamshell
    b. Dewatering equipment
    c. Dozer

LONG ANSWER TYPE QUESTIONS

1. Explain the importance of earthmoving equipment in construction projects and discuss the various types of equipment used for earthmoving operations. Provide examples of scenarios where specific earthmoving equipment would be utilised effectively.
2. Discuss the significance of dewatering in construction projects and describe the different techniques and equipment used. Provide examples of situations where dewatering is necessary and explain the potential consequences of inadequate dewatering.
3. Describe the concrete mixing, transporting, and placing process in construction projects, highlighting the equipment used for each stage. Discuss the factors that influence the selection of concrete equipment and the importance of proper concrete handling practices.

4. Evaluate the role of cranes in construction projects, including their various applications and types. Discuss the factors that influence the selection of cranes for specific projects and the safety considerations associated with crane operations.
5. A construction project requires excavating a trench with dimensions 50 meters long, 2 meters wide, and 3 meters deep. If an excavator has a bucket capacity of 0.5 cubic meters and can load a truck in 2 minutes, calculate the truckloads needed to remove the excavated soil.
6. A concrete batching plant produces 120 cubic meters of concrete per hour. If a construction project requires pouring 500 cubic meters of concrete, how many hours will it take for the batching plant to produce the necessary amount of concrete?
7. Consider an advanced concrete mixer with a capacity of 350 litres. The average mixing time per batch is 7 minutes, but it can vary randomly between 4 and 10 minutes. Time losses due to cleaning, labour rest, and equipment adjustments average 18 minutes per batch but can range from 12 to 25 minutes. Assuming a demanding workday of 9 hours, calculate the following:
   a) Calculate the potential range of mixing times per batch.
   b) Determine the volume of concrete mixed per batch, considering average and maximum mixing times.
   c) Calculate the potential output range of the concrete mixer per hour, considering the variable mixing times and unpredictable time losses.

TUTORIAL

Develop a Gantt Chart for constructing a two-storeyed precast framed structure, including open foundations and a list of equipment resources, assuming reasonable quantities and productivity. In addition, develop a bar chart for concreting 1500 sq. m of a 15 cm thick slab using various equipment for production to place concrete at 3 m height above ground level; show all equipment resources required, along with a site layout.

KNOW MORE

For more information related to this topic scan the QR code.

OR

Type this link in your browser

https://nptel.ac.in/courses/105103206

BIBLIOGRAPHY

- Alkass, S., and Harris, F. (1988). Expert system for earthmoving equipment selection in road construction. *Journal of Construction Engineering and Management*, 114(3), 426-440.
- Jha, K. N. (2015). *Construction project management: theory and practice*, Pearson India Education Service Pvt. Ltd: New Delhi.
- Kamali, M., and Hewage, K. (2017). Development of performance criteria for sustainability evaluation of modular versus conventional construction methods. *Journal of Cleaner Production*, 142(1), 3592-3606.
- Peurifoy, Robert L., Clifford J. Schexnayder, Robert L. Schmitt, and Aviad Shapira. (2018). *Construction Planning, Equipment, and Methods*, 9th ed., McGraw-Hill Education: New York.
- Piroozfar, P., Altan, H., and Popovic-Larsen, O. (2012). Design for sustainability: A comparative study of a customized modern method of construction versus conventional methods of construction. *Architectural Engineering and Design Management*, 8(1), 55-75.
- Shrivastava, U. K. (2000). *Construction planning and management*, 2nd Ed., Galgotia Publications Pvt. Ltd: New Delhi.

5 PLANNING AND ORGANISING CONSTRUCTION SITE AND RESOURCES

UNIT SPECIFICS

Effective planning and organisation are the bedrock of successful construction projects, ensuring smooth execution and optimal resource utilisation. This chapter delves into the intricacies of planning and organising construction sites and resources, which are essential pillars that underpin the construction process. From initial project conception to completion, meticulous planning sets the stage for efficient resource allocation, timely task execution, and project success. Through strategic coordination of workforce, materials, equipment, and schedules, construction professionals navigate the complexities of site management with finesse, maximising productivity while minimising disruptions. This chapter explores the fundamental principles and best practices that govern this critical aspect of construction management, guiding projects from blueprint to reality with precision and proficiency.

RATIONALE

To start, a construction manager must plan the layout of the construction site. It includes the location of the planning office, store worker housing, and training yard. In addition, managing workers, procuring materials, and hiring/renting equipment are also important aspects of managing a construction site. Further, a construction manager must be able to alter the construction schedule as per the availability of the resources.

PRE-REQUISITE

Basic mathematics

UNIT OUTCOMES

List of outcomes of this unit is as follows:

U5-O1: Understand a layout of a construction site

U5-O2: Use of different document and forms for construction

U5-O3: Managing construction workers

U5-O4: Understand material management and inventory control

U5-O5: Understand cash flow in a construction project

U5-O6: Update the project schedule as per the resource availability

Unit Outcomes	Expected Mapping with Course Outcomes (1- Weak Correlation; 2- Medium correlation; 3- Strong Correlation)					
	CO-1	CO-2	CO-3	CO-4	CO-5	CO-6
U5-O1	3	3	1	1	1	1
U5-O2	2	2	1	1	1	3
U5-O3	3	3	2	3	1	1
U5-O4	2	3	2	1	1	1
U5-O5	3	3	2	1	1	1
U5-O6	3	3	3	1	1	1

5.1 SITE PLANNING AND LAYOUT

Site planning is the art and science of arranging the uses of the various portions of the land for different allocated purposes. This involves selecting a site. The site is then analysed for the location of the construction facility in conjunction with vehicular and pedestrian circulation, necessary drainage and providing a good view. Based on a critical thinking process, the client's functional requirements are sought to be matched optimally with the existing site conditions.

5.1.1 Site Selection

There are two methods of selecting a site. In the first method, the alternative sites are considered within a general location, and a choice is made of the one that best meets the preliminary objectives of the project. In the second method, a client chooses the site location before planning the facility. The site should be selected using both methods based on a systematic analysis. The factors include natural, social, and aesthetic. The site should be chosen based on the following considerations:

Natural factors

i. Geological base and landform
ii. Topography-slopes, elevation, etc.
iii. Hydrography- streams, lakes etc.
iv. Soils - classification of types and uses
v. Vegetation
vi. Climatic factors include orientation, wind, humidity, etc.

Social factors

i. Existing land use – ownership of adjacent property, etc.
ii. Traffic -vehicular and pedestrian on and adjacent to the site
iii. Infrastructure

Aesthetic factors

i. Natural features
ii. Views, spaces, and sequences

5.1.2 Land Use and Circulation

The land use plan evolves from the analytical phase in three interrelated aspects: programme analysis, site analysis, and land use plan. The programme analysis shows a particular project's activities, linkages, and densities (in Town Planning, "density" means number of built-up units per unit area). The land use plan indicates how the programme requirements are optimally accommodated on the site. The land use plan thus integrates the project (which consists of buildings, movement of people, goods, water, communication networks, etc.) within the site. The type of construction also influences the land use plan. An alternative may be necessary if a plan is not economically feasible because of excessive site work. On the other hand, the type of construction may be a significant factor in determining a particular land use and may require a specific kind of site, which is flat, rolling or hilly.

Circulation systems are the nerves that connect all the elements on the site. Besides vehicular and pedestrian circulation systems, the site also requires utility and communication networks; after the overall importance of circulation is examined, patterns and criteria of arrangement and development should be pursued in depth.

Vehicular circulation patterns can be classified as grid, radial, linear, and curvilinear systems and variations of these. Similarly, the parking system should be planned. Provisions should be made for pedestrian (workers) circulation, including steps and stairs.

5.1.3 Site Drainage and Grading

A concept of design grading is essential in developing the physical form of the site. Positive drainage, a critical grading concept, allows stormwater runoff to flow away from the structures and activity areas. When water flows away from structures towards drainage, flooding is prevented.

Studying existing and proposed topography in model form can aid in designing the site's drainage system. Contours facilitate the visualisation of land in the third dimension. They show existing topography elevations and comprise a contour map to reveal site characteristics. For proper site planning, the characteristics of contours must be understood. The primary purpose of changing existing contours is to direct runoff water away from structures or activity areas and to adopt man-made structures for the existing topography. This process is called grading.

The grading plan is the most important study in the technical development of the site plan. The major consideration in a grading plan is to set trial or preliminary spot evaluations to achieve a positive drainage pattern. Before the grading study begins, the project's layout has already been drawn on the topographic map. This study may lead to changes in the placement of the building or circulation.

Controlling stormwater runoff is a major factor in preparing a grading plan. The principle of positive drainage is used to prevent problems caused by erosion or flooding. That is, diverting stormwater from a building or area and carrying it away from a site in a storm drainage system.

Surface drain lines are called storm sewers. Surface drainage can be provided by adjusting ground slopes to allow runoff stormwater and its interception at various intervals in catch basins. Drainage systems can be one of the higher-cost items in site development, and special assistance from a specialist engineer may be required.

The design of a drainage system is based on the amount of rainfall to be carried away at a given time. Runoff is that portion of precipitation that finds its way into natural or artificial channels either as surface flow during the storm or subsurface flow after the storm has subsided. Runoff is determined by calculating the volume of water discharged from a given watershed area and is measured in cubic meters of discharge per second. Runoff is affected by two factors: (1) intensity of a storm, amount of rainfall, and duration, and (2) watershed characteristics – porosity of soil, gradient or slope, and vegetative cover.

5.1.4 Site Investigation

The site investigation has to be carried out for the successful implementation of the project. This information generally comprises the following:

i. The nature and composition of the subsoil.
ii. Filling or natural strata of less strength and cohesion than the bulk of the subsoil.
iii. Variations in subsoil across the site due to natural fault lines or beds of material laid down by climatic conditions or natural features such as streams no longer exist.
iv. The level of the existing water table at the investigation date and the presence of any springs or movement in the groundwater flow.

Several methods may be utilised to determine the depth and composition of the subsoil of a building site – these range from the project's size or complexity to the financial resources available for the investigation.

For small residential or similar projects, it may be sufficient to determine the type of approximate bearing value of the subsoil by one of the following methods:

i. By digging several small holes about 600 mm deep around the approximate perimeter of the proposed building.
ii. Drilling several similar holes with a hand auger produces a hole about 150 mm in diameter and, when extracted, produces a cone or plug of the material through which the drill has passed.
iii. Driving a pointed steel crowbar into the ground and gauging the degree of resistance to the bar.

The best of these is probably using a hand auger to attract soil samples, followed by inserting a crowbar to estimate the resistance of the subsoil to penetration at foundation depth. More expensive methods may be used for relatively large projects.

i. The extraction of a series of trail holes about 1m square x 1.5 m deep. The depth should be at least 0.5 m below the proposed level of any foundations to ensure that the subsoil strata penetrated is continuous. Driving a crowbar into the bottom for a further 0.5 m confirms this continuity. This method is relatively inexpensive, with labour only being employed.
ii. Using a mechanical rig and drilling a hole either by percussion methods, which uses a chisel-pointed steel bit screwed to a steel rod, or by the use of a hollow tube that lifts a core of subsoil to the surface. These methods are used when the investigation is carried out at depths greater than at which trail holes are economical.
iii. By loading a reinforced concrete slab with increasing weight at 2-hour intervals and levelling up the upper surface with an optimal Level. From the settlement amount, the bearing value of the subsoil can be calculated based on the area of the slab.

5.1.5 Types of Sites

Before constructing any structure, there is a need to check the type of site. There can be typically three types of building sites:

i. Open fields where the topsoil has been cultivated for many years to a depth of about 300 mm.
ii. Jungle sites where a similar depth of topsoil can be expected.
iii. Reclaimed urban areas have been subjected to successive building and demolition for centuries.

A few problems are associated with the first type of site, subject to the bearing quality of the subsoil and the presence or otherwise of a high-water table. The second type of site poses more problems, where the whole root system must be removed, and trees must be cut down in proposed areas for buildings or roadworks. The excavations must be appropriately filled with hard soil in layers not exceeding 225 mm thick, well-watered, and consolidated by rolling or ramming.

The third type of site can pose many problems; the site has likely been filled in with hard soil, which is probably loosely compacted and can contain large voids. It is also possible that old foundations and floor slabs have been left in and need to be broken out. Drains and old service pipes can probably be found. All these problems must be fully considered, and steps must be taken to deal with them. Usually, it is necessary to take new foundations down to a level below that of any original work or filling.

5.2 SITE ORGANISATION

For the efficient execution of a project, some knowledge of organisation and administration is required. This section introduces the various aspects of site organisation. Good organisation reduces waste of time and materials, breakdowns of plants, and idleness of labour. It improves staff relations, the rate of progress, the general well-being, and the standing of the firm or organisation. Site engineers should aim for sound workmanship, construction speed, and low production cost. Materials ordered must be balanced against the plant or labour available. This applied particularly to concrete. Stockpiles must be reduced as the job nears its end. All trades, including the sub-contractors, are coordinated to ensure smooth operation without conflict of trades. All requirements are forecast in advance, and nothing is left to chance.

Before the site work begins, the site engineer makes a study of the following factors that have an important impact on the smooth execution of the project:

i. Adjacent buildings – may cause obstruction or affect access to the site.
ii. Ground surface – trees may have to be removed, and the ground must be cleared.
iii. Soil – based on the soil type, necessary actions must be taken.
iv. Site surrounded – whether fencing is required.
v. Access road – whether the temporary road should be built.
vi. Water supply – whether water is available for construction.
vii. Materials – whether construction materials are available locally.
viii. Labour – whether all the required types of labour are available locally.

ix. Amenities – whether the site is isolated, or all facilities are available nearby.
x. Electric power and transport – how the electric power can be available on site.

5.2.1 Site Accommodation

The site accommodation requirements can be classified into administrative offices for contractors and engineers-in-charge, retiring rooms for workers, stores for material storage, and, at remote sites, temporary housing accommodations for workers. The activities and the temporary nature of the site do not generally justify the provision of permanent buildings for staff accommodation or the storage of materials. It is, however, within the builder's interest to provide the best facilities that are economically possible for any particular contract; this should promote a good relationship between management and staff and reduce the loss of materials due to theft, accidental damage, and vandalism. Providing better facilities and amenities on a site for staff ultimately leads to higher productivity.

5.2.2 Development of Administrative Office

Site office space varies depending on the site's size and the nature of the work. As a rough guide, the site office of a construction unit employing 300 labourers needs a gross floor area of about 150 sq. m, while an operation using 1000 to 1500 labourers needs 200 to 300 sq. m.

The contractor's main office and the general storage buildings for site equipment should be located near the main entrance to the site. As all the materials being delivered to the site must be checked on arrival, the storekeeper's office must be at the main entrance. Care must be taken to avoid obstructing the entrance to the other vehicles while checking is carried out. For good communication, it is wise to establish the resident engineer's office close to the contractor's office. The subcontractor's office could also be in this location if the room allows it. This will lead to the economy providing such services as telephones, heating, lighting, cleaning, etc.

By following these points, an administration area is logically situated around the main entrance to the site, thereby decreasing the number of persons walking or driving around the construction areas. Where feasible, the contractor's and resident engineer's offices should be positioned to allow the overall view of the site from their windows, including the main entrance point.

The anticipated use of each accommodation unit will govern the construction and facilities required. Offices should contain artificial lighting, desks, worktops and chairs, cash chests, toilets, meals room, etc. Masonry walls are generally constructed with mud or lean lime mortar to facilitate easy dismantling. Timber huts are prefabricated for ease of dismantling and assembly to facilitate the reuse on other sites. Caravans and mobile cabins are made of ply-clad timber frames suitably insulated and decorated and are fully equipped with all necessary furniture, light, and HVAC units if necessary. Toilets have all necessary sanitary fittings and plumbing, which can be connected to site services or self-contained. While caravans can be towed, the cabins require special transporter trailers. The initial cost is higher than masonry and timber huts, but they can be installed faster.

5.2.3 Temporary Housing for Labourers

Workers from different districts and states are employed on-site because a sufficient local worker supply is not generally available within walking distance of the project. In that case, the site engineer must make provisions for the construction of workers housing.

A policy encouraging migrant workers to bring their families improves social relations between the camp and the neighbouring area during the construction work. Such a policy, however, may make the migrant workers more likely to settle in the project area after the construction work is completed. Unless the project location contributes to continuous construction activities, permanent settlement of the migrant workers could create conflicts with the local population. The site engineer should remember the following points when setting in labour camps:

i. Camps should be on a high, well-drained ground
ii. Camps should be within walking distance of the work site but well separated from it (minimum 200 m). Where the location of the work is likely to move more than 2 or 3 km during the season (For example, road/pipe/canal works), the camps must be planned to avoid unnecessarily long walks and to ensure that the periods when walking distance are most significant do not coincide with the times when the work is most difficult, such as during the heat of the summer.
iii. A minimum floor area of 5 sq. m per person should be allowed.
iv. Camps should be located away from villages to avoid clashes between workers and the local people. On irrigation projects that are expected to increase agriculture, there may be some value in setting camps to form the nuclei of new villages.

5.2.4 Temporary Services

The contractor must arrange temporary services such as telephones, electricity, and sanitation. Due to the contract, consideration must be given to diversifying existing service lines. It is usual for the engineer-in-charge to supply the contractor with detailed information to locate the services in question and contact the concerned departments, viz. telecommunication, water supply, sewage disposal, electricity authorities, etc. It is also necessary to arrange who will be responsible for diverting any services, i.e., the contractor or the authority concerned.

5.2.5 Storage for Materials

The objective of proper storage and stacking of materials is to prevent deterioration or intrusion of foreign matter and ensure the preservation of their quality and fitness for the work. The type of storage facilities required of any particular material depends upon durability requirements and vulnerability to damage or theft; the material mustn't deteriorate after being delivered to the site. As a general rule, positioning the storage of materials to avoid double handling and awkward access for delivery trucks is essential.

The materials shall be segregated according to type, size, and length and placed in neat, orderly piles that are safe from falling. If piles are high, they shall be stepped back at suitable intervals in height so as not to constitute a hazard to passersby. Efforts must be periodically taken to keep the stairways, passageways, and gang-ways free from obstructions by storing construction materials, tools, or rubbish. When the piles/stacks are closer to the passageway, warning signs must be kept in the daytime, and red lights must be on and around them at night. To facilitate inspection and removal of the materials, the piles must be arranged to allow a passageway not less than 1 m width between the piles or stacks. The materials shall be stored on well-drained, firm, and unyielding surfaces. Ensure the stacked material does not cause undue stress on walls or other structures. Since timber, coal, paint, and similar materials present fire hazards, to protect against fire, these materials are to be segregated from each other so that the fire spread can be minimised. When stacking materials is to be done on roadside berms in the street and other public places, permission should be sought from the local authority, and the remnants of the same should be removed after the construction is over to avoid any hazard to the public.

5.2.6 Storage for Equipment and Tools

The size and capacity of workshop facilities needed at the site depend not only upon the size of the project but also upon the distance from the nearest location where adequate commercial repair facilities are available. Where major maintenance and repair facilities are close, site maintenance involves much more than greasing, changing oil and filters, and repairing tyres. Such work requires a suitable building set with a concrete or brick floor. Major maintenance and some repairs must be carried out on-site on a large project in a remote area. Such work requires a frame for supporting lifting tackle to remove engines, an inspection pit, and machining, welding, and heat treatment facilities. The equipment storage ground needs a reasonably flat and well-drained ground. About 60 sq.m per item of equipment should be allowed, more if the shape or the sites make manoeuvring difficult. A convenient plot is 25 m wide, storing equipment in two rows, with manoeuvring space between. Space should also be provided for the reversing of towed vehicles.

5.3 WORKFORCE (MANPOWER)

Initially, the construction industry's use of human resource management (HRM) was limited to project management, where labour requirements were not considered. The construction sector has seen a significant expansion in the use of human resource management due to changes in the corporate environment, rising employee knowledge, and public and social activist interest. Like any other business, it now includes all human resource tasks. Being the most labour-intensive sector of the economy and the second biggest in the world, construction presents enormous opportunities for the development of human resources.

5.3.1 Planning

The integration of personnel policies, practices, and procedures to ensure the proper number and quality of workers in the appropriate positions at the correct times is known as workforce planning. It's a procedure that determines the amount of workers the sector needs, considering both present and future needs and ensuring the appropriate people are placed in the right places at the correct times.

One of the most important components of a construction company's success in achieving its corporate goals is the creation of its personnel strategy. The following are the goals of workforce planning:

i. To guarantee the best possible use of the available human resources
ii. To enhance the information, knowledge, skills, performance, capacity, and potential of the workforce that is already in place
iii. To guarantee increased output and performance

5.3.2 Staffing

Line functions report directly to upper management and are endowed with power and responsibility. Various operational departments, including those in charge of manufacturing and operations, sales and marketing, purchasing and materials, and accounting and finance, often handle line functions.

The roles that guide specialised matters and topics are known as staff functions. Human resources, research and development, quality control, etc. departments often handle staff functions. These departments serve in an advising role to support and improve the performance of various line departments. In the past, human resource management was only seen as a staff function in which line and operation managers, who are given direct responsibility, authority, and accountability for achieving results, receive the HR Manager's specialised services on various HR-related topics.

The categories for which recruiting is to be done determine the source of the hiring. The industry, whether a public or private enterprise, the location of the labour market, the level of expertise required of potential hires, the company's reputation, and other factors all affect the recruitment source. The following list includes a few of the most popular sources for hiring of workers:

i. At the site's gate
ii. Through unsolicited applications
iii. By way of recommendations from staff members, business partners, directors, and unions;
iv. Through job exchanges, welfare associations for the SC, ST, and OBC, Zila Sainik Board, the Directorate General of Resettlement of Ex-Servicemen, and non-governmental organisations that hire physically disabled people
v. By way of former workers required by law or other reasons
vi. Via interviews conducted in training centres
vii. Via associations of trade
viii. Via employment firms and management consultants
ix. By placing direct advertisements in trade publications, businesses, and newspapers

Induction and Training

Acclimating a new worker to the work, coworkers, and company is called induction. Organisation to organisation's induction procedure varies based on factors such as the company's human resource policy, the function the new hire has joined, how vital it is, etc.

A construction firm is made up of its workers and staff. The profitability and growth of the firm are determined by their talents, productivity, and work performance. The more successfully a corporation sells its goods or services, the better its workers are performing at what they do. Workers may improve and upgrade their abilities, serve better, be more productive, and reach their full potential for both their benefit and the company's benefit by receiving information, knowledge, skills, and behavioural inputs through training. It makes it easier for workers to change appropriately and helps them grasp their roles, responsibilities, and organisational culture.

Purpose of Training

Although it is difficult to dispute the benefits of training, companies and workers must be persuaded of its ability to improve workers' productivity. They might think investing in training is a waste of money and effort. They need to be convinced and shown the benefits of training. The best way to market training to workers is to emphasise its benefits to improved performance, job safety, increased motivation, and dedication, in addition to its ability to foster a positive workplace culture.

Types of Training Programs

Depending on the program's goal, there are several training courses. The training programs cover the whole spectrum of personnel, from entry-level labourers to managers and supervisors. The participants' level determines the program's contents, the training objectives, and the organisation's demands. Construction companies typically offer the following training programs:

i. Apprentice training: As required by the Apprentice Act of 1961, it is the legal responsibility of the firm to employ apprentices in the trades that are most common within the organisation.
ii. Programs for induction training – typically, one-day and seven-day induction training provided to the workers
iii. Programs for technical training – 30-day, 60-day, and 90-day training programs are available for construction workers

5.3.3 Organising

The term "organising" describes the interpersonal dynamics among members of an organisation. A big group of individuals must coordinate their operations to accomplish goals. The two fundamental organising components are assigning worker tasks and connecting the different organisational subsystems.

Dale (1967) described the following three basic steps which are involved in organising:

i. Every task that must be completed inside an organisation must be identified. It is essential. For instance, all activities required for manufacturing should be determined if it is a production organisation. If it is a service organisation, such as a hospital, a list of all the actions necessary to deliver the service should be included.

ii. The organisation's task must then be divided among its members after the tasks that must be completed are identified. It is important to remember that each person should be given tasks they can do. Workers' interests, abilities, and skills should align with their assigned tasks. Any departure from it might be detrimental to the company.

iii. The next stage after assigning tasks to different workers is to create systems for coordinating the efforts of all workers. Coordinating mechanisms aid in consistently guiding staff members towards their tasks and the organisation's objectives.

5.3.4 Motivation

Motivating construction workers is a crucial aspect of Human Resource Management (HRM) within the construction industry. Unlike many other sectors, construction work often involves physically demanding tasks, challenging environments, and potentially hazardous conditions. Therefore, fostering motivation among construction workers requires a nuanced approach that acknowledges these unique circumstances. Here are several strategies that HR professionals can employ to motivate construction workers:

i. *Recognition and appreciation:* Acknowledging construction workers' hard work and achievements through verbal praise, awards, or other forms of recognition can boost morale and motivation. Highlighting their contributions to the project's success fosters a sense of pride and ownership.

ii. *Clear communication:* Providing clear expectations, feedback, and information about project goals, timelines, and performance criteria helps construction workers understand their role in the larger context. Open lines of communication also allow workers to voice concerns or ideas, fostering a sense of involvement and empowerment.

iii. *Team-building activities:* Organizing team-building exercises, social events, or gatherings outside of work hours helps foster camaraderie and strengthen interpersonal relationships among construction workers. A cohesive team is more likely to collaborate effectively and support each other, improving morale and motivation.

iv. *Safe and healthy work environment:* Prioritizing worker safety and ensuring compliance with health and safety regulations are essential for maintaining motivation and productivity. Providing proper safety equipment, training on safe work practices, and addressing safety concerns promptly demonstrate the organisation's commitment to the well-being of its workers.

v. *Performance-based incentives:* Implementing performance-based incentives, such as bonuses, profit-sharing, or rewards for meeting project milestones, incentivises construction workers to strive for excellence and surpass performance expectations.

By implementing these strategies, HR professionals can effectively motivate construction workers, improving job satisfaction, productivity, and overall project success.

5.4 MATERIALS

Material management plays a pivotal role in the success and efficiency of construction projects. It encompasses the procurement, storage, transportation, and utilisation of materials for construction activities. Effective material management ensures that suitable materials are available at the right time, quantity, and location, minimising delays, reducing costs, and optimising project schedules.

All goods and services purchased or otherwise obtained from sources outside the organisation and utilised or processed to create finished goods for sale are collectively called "materials". Project materials can be broadly divided into revenue and capital items. While revenue items comprise non-capitalized goods like heavy equipment and tackles, small tools, consumables, electrical items, building materials, special/one-time items and spares, capital assets include plant and machinery, automobiles, office equipment, land and buildings.

First and foremost, efficient material management is crucial for maintaining project timelines. Delays in material procurement or shortages can disrupt construction activities, leading to costly delays and potential penalties. By carefully planning and coordinating material delivery schedules, construction companies can mitigate the risk of delays and keep projects on track.

Additionally, proper material management helps control costs and maximise profitability. Construction firms can reduce material costs and improve their bottom line by optimising inventory levels, minimising wastage, and negotiating favourable pricing with suppliers. Effective material management also minimises the risk of over-ordering or under-utilizing materials, reducing unnecessary expenses.

Moreover, material management is vital in ensuring quality and safety on construction sites. Construction companies can maintain high-quality standards and compliance with regulatory requirements by carefully inspecting incoming materials, monitoring storage conditions, and implementing quality control measures. Proper handling and storage of materials also reduce the risk of accidents and injuries on the job site, enhancing overall safety for workers and minimising liability for the company. Material planning is an essential component of comprehensive project planning and involves several key steps:

i. *Project analysis:* The first step in material planning is thoroughly analysing the project requirements, including the scope, schedule, budget, and specifications. Understanding the project's objectives, constraints, and critical path activities is crucial for determining material needs accurately.

ii. *Material identification and specification:* Based on the project analysis, construction professionals identify the types and specifications of materials needed for various aspects of the project, such as structural elements, finishes, mechanical systems, and equipment. This includes specifying the quality standards, sizes, grades, and other relevant characteristics of materials.

iii. *Quantity take-off:* Quantity take-off involves calculating the exact quantities of materials required for each component based on the project's design drawings, plans, and specifications. This process may involve manual measurements, computer-aided design (CAD) software, and estimating tools to generate accurate material quantities.

iv. *Material procurement planning:* Once the material quantities and specifications are determined, construction planners develop a procurement plan outlining when and how materials can be sourced, purchased, and delivered to the project site. This includes identifying suppliers, obtaining quotes, negotiating contracts, and establishing delivery schedules. The site planning engineer is responsible for this position. Any material acquisition usually starts with a need for it. It is advised that a specific engineer approves the material request to ensure efficient management of material acquisitions. In collaboration with the construction manager, the site-planning engineer drafts a buy request, and administrative staff purchase the material. The materials schedule ought to serve as the foundation for material requests. Identifying materials, estimating quantities, defining specifications, projecting requirements, and choosing the best sources for purchases are all included in materials planning.

v. *Inventory management:* Effective material planning also involves managing inventory levels to ensure that materials are available when needed without excess stockpiling or shortages. Construction companies may implement inventory control systems, just-in-time (JIT) delivery methods, or vendor-managed inventory (VMI) arrangements to optimise inventory levels and minimise carrying costs.

vi. *Logistics and transportation:* Coordinating the transportation and logistics of materials is essential for ensuring timely delivery to the construction site. Material planners consider transportation modes, routes, lead times, and handling requirements to minimise transportation costs and maximise efficiency.

vii. *Risk management:* Material planning also involves identifying and mitigating risks impacting materials' availability, quality, or cost. This may include supplier reliability, market fluctuations, currency exchange rates, weather-related disruptions, and regulatory compliance issues.

viii. *Communication and coordination:* Effective communication and coordination among project stakeholders, including architects, engineers, contractors, suppliers, and subcontractors, are critical for successful material planning. Regular meetings, progress reports, and collaboration tools facilitate seamless coordination and decision-making throughout the project lifecycle.

Material management is integral to the success of construction projects, impacting project timelines, costs, quality, safety, and sustainability. By adopting strategic approaches to procurement, storage, and utilisation of materials, construction companies can enhance efficiency, minimise risks, and achieve better project outcomes.

5.5 EQUIPMENT

Planning and organising equipment on construction sites are fundamental aspects of construction project management, crucial for ensuring efficient operations, optimal resource utilisation, and project success. Here are some basic concepts related to equipment management on construction sites:

i. *Equipment inventory and assessment:* Before planning, conducting a thorough inventory and assessment of all equipment required for the project is essential. This includes machinery, tools, vehicles, and any other specialised equipment needed for various tasks.

ii. *Equipment selection and procurement:* Based on project requirements, select appropriate equipment that meets specifications, capacity, and safety standards. Procure or rent equipment from reliable suppliers, focusing on quality, reliability, and cost-effectiveness.

iii. *Task analysis and equipment allocation:* Analyse project tasks and requirements to determine the type and quantity of equipment needed for each activity. Allocate equipment strategically to ensure timely availability and efficient utilisation throughout the project lifecycle.

iv. *Site layout and organisation:* Develop a plan that optimises space and facilitates the efficient movement of equipment, materials, and personnel. Organise equipment storage areas, staging areas, and traffic flow to minimise congestion and maximise productivity.

v. *Equipment maintenance and inspections:* Implement a proactive maintenance program to ensure equipment is well-maintained, safe, and operational. Conduct regular inspections, servicing, and repairs to prevent breakdowns, downtime, and delays.

vi. *Scheduling and coordination:* Develop a comprehensive equipment schedule aligned with project timelines and activities. Coordinate equipment usage with other project stakeholders, subcontractors, and suppliers to avoid conflicts and ensure smooth workflow.

vii. *Safety and compliance:* Prioritize safety by adhering to relevant regulations, standards, and best equipment operation and maintenance practices. Provide adequate training, supervision, and personal protective equipment (PPE) to personnel operating equipment on-site.

viii. *Resource optimisation and efficiency:* Continuously monitor equipment utilisation, downtime, and productivity metrics to identify opportunities for improvement. Implement strategies to optimise resource allocation, minimise idle time, and maximise equipment efficiency.

ix. *Contingency planning:* Anticipate potential risks and disruptions that may affect equipment availability or performance. Develop contingency plans and backup strategies to mitigate risks, such as equipment breakdowns, inclement weather, or supply chain disruptions.

x. *Documentation and record-keeping:* Maintain accurate records of equipment usage, maintenance activities, inspections, and repairs. Documentation helps track equipment performance, compliance, and costs, enabling informed decision-making and accountability.

Project managers can effectively manage resources, streamline operations, and enhance project efficiency and success by applying these basic planning concepts and organising equipment on construction sites.

5.6 DOCUMENTATION AT SITE

Documentation on construction sites encompasses a wide range of records and paperwork essential for project planning, execution, and management. These documents are the backbone of communication, compliance, and accountability throughout construction. At a construction site, you'll find various types of documentation, including project plans and specifications that outline the blueprints and materials required for construction. Contracts and agreements detail the scope of work, timelines, and payment terms between stakeholders. Permits and approvals obtained from regulatory authorities ensure compliance with local regulations. Safety documentation such as safety plans and hazard assessments prioritise worker safety. Daily logs and reports track progress, workforce, equipment usage, and any incidents encountered during construction. Change orders and variations authorise alterations to the original contract scope. Quality control and inspection reports monitor materials and workmanship standards. Submittals and shop drawings provide detailed layouts and dimensions for construction components. Progress payment requests facilitate payment based on completed milestones. As-built drawings and documentation reflect any changes made during construction. Closeout documentation includes operation manuals, warranties, and final inspections necessary for project completion. Communication records document correspondence and decisions among stakeholders. Environmental documentation ensures compliance with environmental regulations. Training and certification records track personnel qualifications. Financial records document project expenditures and financial performance. These documents provide construction site transparency, compliance, and efficiency, facilitating successful project delivery.

5.7 CASH FLOW

Any organisation participating in a project means getting and spending money at different times, and a cash-flow diagram depicts this influx and outflow of capital. Although in practice, this inflow and outflow do not always follow a pattern, it is sometimes assumed that all transactions (inwards or outwards) occur at the start or end of a specific period, which can be a week, a month, a quarter, or a year, to simplify analysis. In other words, if it is determined that all transactions in a month will be recorded as occurring on the final day of that month or the first day of the next month, any technique can be used as long as the system is followed consistently.

In a cash-flow diagram (see Fig. 5.1), time is typically drawn on the horizontal (X) axis in an appropriate scale regarding weeks, months, years, etc. At the same time, the Y-axis represents the amount involved in the transaction, with receipts and disbursements drawn on the positive and negative sides of the Y-axis. While the scale is maintained for the time axis, the depiction on the Y-axis is not always to scale; nonetheless, every effort should be taken to retain a sense of equilibrium. Thus, it is common practice to record the amount of each transaction after the arrow.

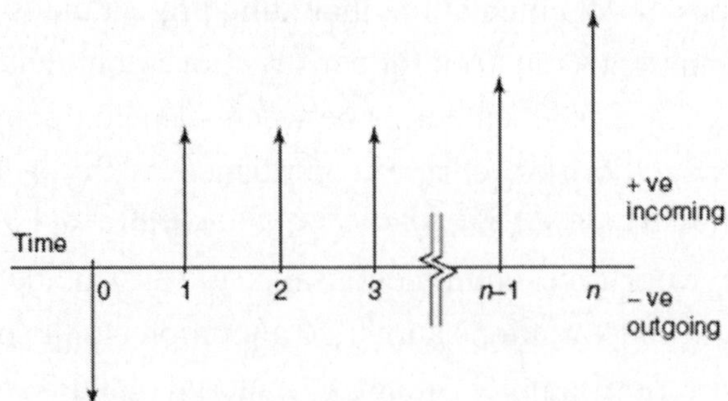

Fig. 5.1: Cash-flow diagram

5.7.1 Sources of Funds

Funding for construction projects can come from various sources, depending on factors such as the project's size, scope, location, and ownership structure. Here are some familiar sources of funds for construction projects:

Equity Financing

Equity financing involves raising capital by selling ownership stakes in the project to investors, such as individuals, private equity firms, or institutional investors. These investors become shareholders in the project and may receive dividends or a share of the profits upon completion.

Debt Financing

Debt financing involves borrowing money from lenders, such as banks, financial institutions, or bond investors, with the obligation to repay the borrowed amount plus interest over time. Construction loans, mortgages, and bonds are joint financing for construction projects.

Government Grants and Subsidies

Governments at the local, state, or national level may provide grants, subsidies, or tax incentives to support construction projects that serve public interests, such as infrastructure development, affordable housing, or renewable energy projects.

Public-Private Partnerships (PPPs)

PPPs involve collaboration between public sector entities and private sector investors to finance, develop, and operate construction projects. In PPPs, private sector partners may contribute funds, expertise, and resources in exchange for long-term contracts or revenue-sharing arrangements.

Construction Financing from Contractors or Developers

In some cases, contractors or developers may provide financing for construction projects using their funds or leveraging their relationships with lenders or investors. This arrangement, known as self-financing or developer financing, allows contractors or developers to retain greater control over the project and potentially earn higher returns.

Insurance Proceeds

Insurance policies, such as builder's risk insurance or property insurance, may cover construction-related risks, such as property damage, theft, or liability claims. Insurance proceeds can help offset construction costs and mitigate financial losses in unforeseen events or accidents.

Sale of Pre-sales of Units

Developers may pre-sell units or spaces to buyers or tenants before construction begins in residential or commercial development projects. Pre-sales generate upfront revenue that can be used to finance construction costs and secure additional funding from lenders or investors.

5.8 S-CURVES

The S-curve may be used to track the costs of a building project. The S-curve closely resembles the progress profile of a building project, which is marked by slow progress at the start, quick development in the middle, and slow progress again at the conclusion. A graph (S-curve) can track the anticipated invoiced (billed) amounts and the actual amount raised. A similar graph may be created for the amount intended to be spent against the amount paid.

Once the contracts have been granted, it is reasonably simple to determine the 'bill value' of each action using a comprehensive bar chart. By studying the nature of each action, one may predict how this value will be dispersed every month. These sums will then be added to get the estimated monthly value, presented on a graph as shown in Fig. 5.2. A second curve (a dotted line) may be drawn based on the job done.

Fig. 5.2 clearly shows that the amount that should have been billed on the monitoring day has not been done, which is why the second curve is below the first. This is an 'under-spend' problem. Similarly, the second curve is exhibiting a move to the right. This displays an 'overall delay', suggesting the project is running behind schedule. Thus, the financial value may be utilised as a single, broad indicator of a project's development.

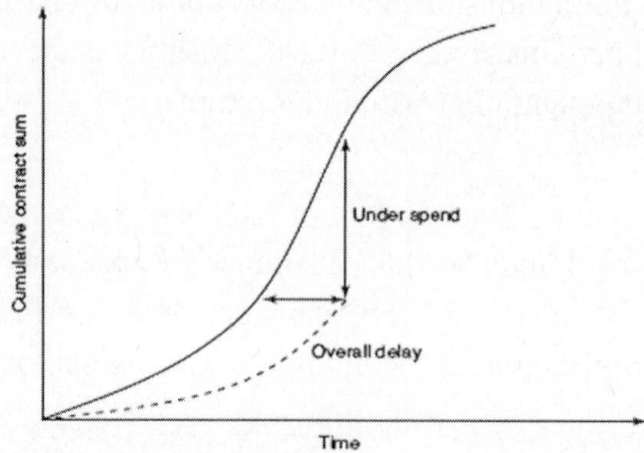

Fig. 5.2: S-curve showing planned and actual bill value

The continuous curves illustrated here can only be created if the value of the work done can be estimated in detail, as in the case of bill of quantities contracts. When contract payments are made via another technique, the project manager's ability to acquire a single and appropriate objective assessment of overall progress is limited.

5.9 EARNED VALUE

Earned value estimates a project's cost, schedule, and technical performance by comparing it to the intended or budgeted performance. It is considered that once the budget is created, it is more or less fixed.

The comparison is made using a common monetary word (rupees or dollars) or the number of work-hours, equipment hours, amount of material, and so on allotted to the activity. The concept of earned value is founded on the assumption that when tasks are performed, the value of the project's product improves. As a result, the accumulated value represents the project's actual development.

The earned value technique uses the ideas of work packages and earned value to assess a project's success. It informs us about the progress that must be made to stay on schedule and reveals if the resources being spent are proportionate with the budget. The earned value approach is also used to predict the future outcome of a project by extrapolating from the amount of work previously completed. It is feasible to anticipate the project's final cost and expected completion date. The predictions are also used to determine variations and trends. The project manager can take necessary action if any undesirable variations or destructive patterns exist. The terminologies of the Earned Value Method are as follows:

5.9.1 Budgeted Cost for Work Scheduled (BCWS)

This is the budget or plan for all work packages. The BCWS curve is created using the work breakdown structure (WBS), the project budget, and the master schedule. The cost of each work package is computed period by period, and the cumulative cost of work packages is displayed based on the expected completion dates provided in the master schedule.

5.9.2 Budgeted Cost of Work Performed (BCWP)

The earned value is the anticipated cost of the work assigned to accomplished activities. The BCWP is determined using the measured work completed and the budgeted expenditures. It is calculated with the help of Eq. 5.1.

$$\text{Earned value (BCWP)} = \text{Percentage completion of project x Project budget} \qquad \textbf{(5.1)}$$

5.9.3 Actual Cost of Work Performed (ACWP)

Work costs are attributed to completed activities. Precise measurements of finished work yield the ACWP curve. Invoices and time sheets are used to record actual expenses. This may appear tedious, but it can be completed quickly with proper preparation and organisation.

5.9.4 Variances

Using the data required to generate the S-curves, schedule and cost variances may be estimated in monetary terms (or in work-hour terms).

i. Schedule variance (SV) is the difference between the earned value and the anticipated budget, computed using Eq. 5.2.

$$SV = BCWP - BCWS \qquad \textbf{(5.2)}$$

ii. Cost variance (CV): It is the difference between the earned value and the actual cost of the activity. This is computed using Eq. 5.3.

$$CV = BCWP - ACWP \tag{5.3}$$

5.9.5 Schedule Performance Index (SPI)

Schedule performance index (SPI) determines if the project is on time. SPI is a ratio between earned value and budgeted value of completed works. If the earned value falls below the budgeted ($SPI < 1$), the project is considered 'behind schedule'. It is calculated by using Eq. 5.4.

$$SPI = BCWP/BCWS \tag{5.4}$$

5.9.6 Cost Performance Index (CPI)

The cost performance index (CPI) measures if the project is spending within its budget. The CPI is a ratio of earned value to the actual cost of finished work. If the accumulated value is lower than the actual cost ($CPI < 1$), it signals a 'cost overrun' problem. It can be calculated by using Eq. 5.5.

$$CPI = BCWP/ACWP \tag{5.5}$$

Estimate at Completion (EAC)

As previously explained, the earned value technique may predict the most likely path a project will take based on its present condition. This prediction aims to produce an accurate cost projection at the end of the project. One such forecasting metric is the 'estimate at completion' (EAC), defined as the actual cost to date plus an acceptable estimate of expenses for the remaining work. The EAC formulae involve various factors, including ACWP, BCWP, CPI, and BAC, all of which have been previously specified except 'budget at completion' (BAC). BAC is the sum of all budgets allotted to a project, always equal to the total BCWS. A typical Earned Value analysis curve is shown in Fig. 5.3.

Try to find out!

What do you mean by negative and positive cash flow in a construction project?

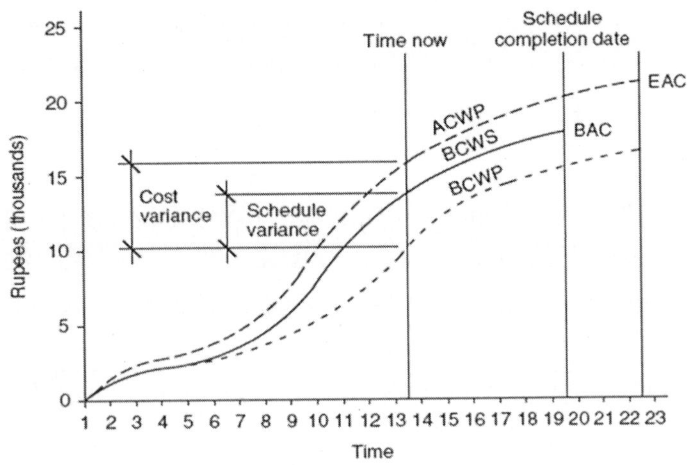

Fig. 5.3: The 3-S curve for the earned value method

5.10 RESOURCE SCHEDULING

When constructing the network diagram, we mainly emphasised technical limitations, such as the need for one action not to start until another is completed and the assumption that resources are infinite. Although many exceptional initiatives may experience these perfect circumstances, most real-life ventures have limitations on available resources. Activity start times in real-life contexts must account for both technological limitations, such as precedence relationships, and limits on the availability of resources. In other words, we have a certain number of resources available.

Following the completion of the network computations, it is essential to provide the results readily and comprehensibly to all individuals involved in the project. The results of network methodologies such as PERT, Critical Path Method, and Precedence Diagram are often shown using either a bar chart or a Gantt chart because of their apparent advantages.

5.10.1 Bar Chart

Bar charts, also known as Gantt charts, are widely used in resource scheduling within the construction industry. These visual tools give project managers a clear overview of project timelines, task dependencies, and resource allocation. In construction resource scheduling, bar charts are crucial in efficiently managing resources such as labour, equipment, and materials.

By representing tasks as horizontal bars along a timeline, bar charts enable project managers to visualise the sequence and duration of activities required to complete a construction project. This visualisation helps identify potential scheduling conflicts, optimise resource allocation, and ensure critical tasks are completed on time.

In resource scheduling, bar charts allow project managers to allocate resources to specific tasks based on their availability and requirements. For example, if a particular task requires specialised equipment or skilled labour, project managers can allocate resources accordingly by scheduling those resources during the appropriate timeframe on the bar chart. A typical bar chart is shown in Fig. 5.4. It can be seen from the figure that the resource (Labour) is allocated to each of the activities (bars). The red is critical activities, and the blue is non-critical activities.

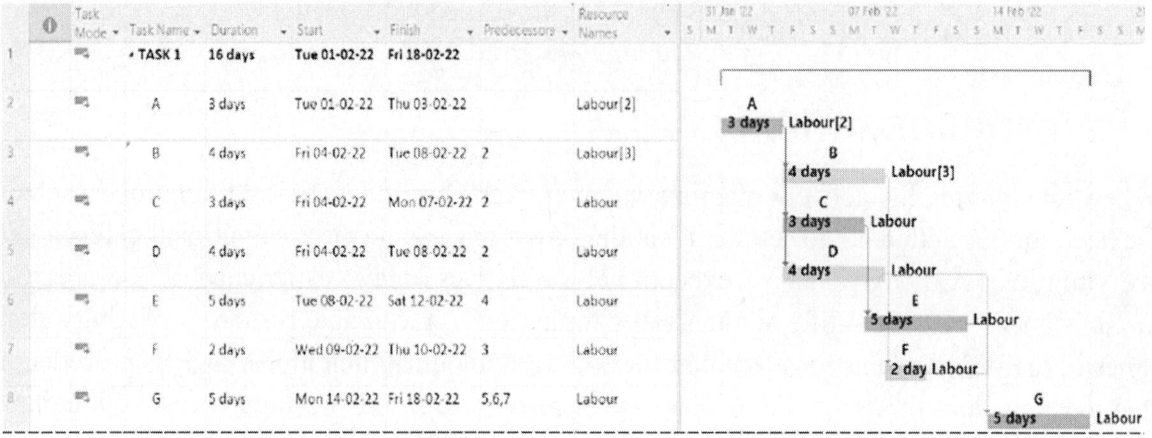

	Task Mode	Task Name	Duration	Start	Finish	Predecessors	Resource Names
1		TASK 1	16 days	Tue 01-02-22	Fri 18-02-22		
2		A	3 days	Tue 01-02-22	Thu 03-02-22		Labour[2]
3		B	4 days	Fri 04-02-22	Tue 08-02-22	2	Labour[3]
4		C	3 days	Fri 04-02-22	Mon 07-02-22	2	Labour
5		D	4 days	Fri 04-02-22	Tue 08-02-22	2	Labour
6		E	5 days	Tue 08-02-22	Sat 12-02-22	4	Labour
7		F	2 days	Wed 09-02-22	Thu 10-02-22	3	Labour
8		G	5 days	Mon 14-02-22	Fri 18-02-22	5,6,7	Labour

Fig. 5.4: A bar chart with the allocation of resources

5.10.2 Line of Balance Technique

A strategic scheduling methodology frequently used in project management, especially in sectors like construction where repetitive operations are the norm, is called the Line of Balance (LOB) technique. A linear graph is plotted to show the intended allocation of resources or effort over time. This methodology offers significant benefits for projects that involve recurring tasks or phases since it facilitates optimal resource allocation and workflow optimisation. For example, by depicting these operations as parallel segments on a timeline, the LOB approach enables project managers to expedite tasks such as laying foundations, erecting walls, and installing utilities in a construction project with several identical units.

Effective planning, monitoring, and schedule adjustment are made easier using the LOB approach, which maps out the project's timeline and resource requirements to ensure on-time project completion. We can consistently arrange all recurring components through meticulous design, optimising the efficiency of workers and machinery. Its systematic approach improves the effectiveness of project management by empowering teams to keep a balanced workflow and quickly identify and resolve any bottlenecks. A typical LOB graph is shown in Fig. 5.5. Activities A, B, and C are repetitive in a project. A gap between the two activities shows the available float.

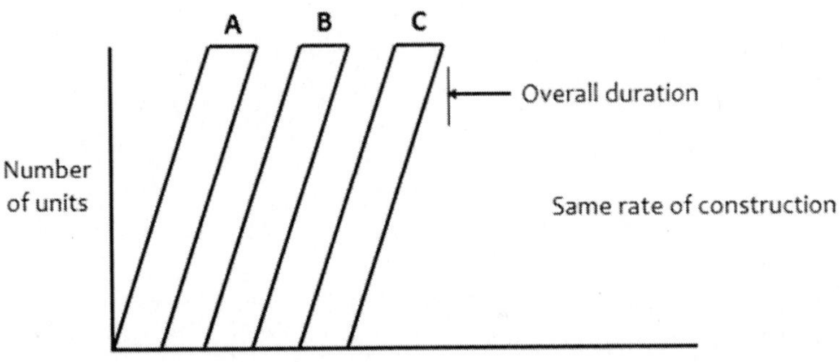

Fig. 5.5: Line of balance technique

5.11 RESOURCE ALLOCATION

Resource availability is limited in this context. To clarify, resources have a finite capacity. If it is not feasible to address the excessive allocation of resources on a given day, some tasks may need to be postponed. The primary goal is determining which operations may be delayed and to what extent, ultimately determining the minimum time required to finish the project while adhering to resource limitations.

5.11.1 Resource Constraint Condition

In construction project management, resource constraint condition refers to a situation where the availability of essential resources, such as labour, materials, equipment, or finances, is limited compared to the project's requirements or demands. This constraint can significantly impact project schedules, costs, and performance. The resource constraint conditions can affect delayed project timelines. Limited skilled labour or specialised equipment availability can delay project milestones and completion. For instance, a shortage of experienced plumbers may slow down the installation of plumbing systems, consequently delaying subsequent tasks.

Project managers can use a resource smoothing strategy to mitigate the impacts of resource constraint conditions in construction projects. Resource usage is redistributed in resource smoothening to balance workload peaks and valleys, reducing strain on limited resources.

5.11.2 Time Constraint Condition

In construction project management, time constraint conditions refer to situations where strict deadlines or time limitations are imposed on the project. Contractual agreements, client expectations, or external factors such as regulatory requirements or seasonal considerations often define these constraints. Time constraints are critical in shaping project schedules, resource allocation, and overall planning. Therefore, resource levelling is done to control time-constraint conditions. Resource levelling adjusts the project schedule to optimise available resources and minimise conflicts or bottlenecks.

5.11.3 Resource Levelling

The specified project duration acts as a constraint for resource levelling. Precisely, the project must be finished within a specific deadline. These heuristics aim to reduce the maximum number of resources needed at any time while allocating resources more consistently across different periods. These difficulties are referred to as time-limited/ time-constrained conditions. Resource loading or aggregation charts are used to evaluate resources. In resource levelling, one cannot increase the project's time but optimise resource usage as much as possible.

Try to find out!

Find out the projects where line of balance technique can be used?
Where will you prefer bar chart over network diagram?
List few construction projects which were constructed under time constrained condition?

Illustration 1

The network shown in Fig. 5.6 consists of 14 activities labelled A to N. The time of each activity is shown below the arrow, while the resource demand is displayed in the bracket next to the activity name. Say activity B will take three days to complete and demand two resource units. The network's critical route is 1-2-4-7-9-11-12, which comprises activities A, C, G, K, M, and N. Assume it is a time constraint condition, perform resource levelling

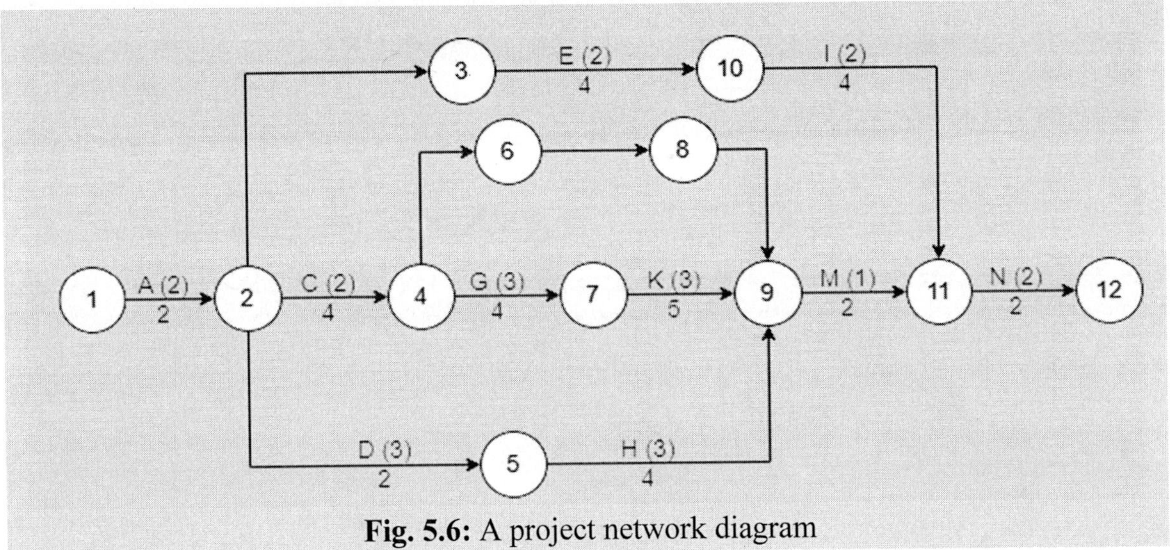

Fig. 5.6: A project network diagram

Solution:

Resource levelling may be accomplished by following these steps:

i. The project network is constructed using the data for each activity. As previously shown, the computation of event timings and activity times now includes the calculation of total float for each activity.

ii. The activities are arranged according to their earliest start date (Table 5.1). The resources needed for each activity daily are combined and shown in a chart known as a resource-aggregation or resource-loading chart. Fig. 5.7 shows the early-start resource aggregation chart. The project requires 103 work-days to finish, with the daily resource need ranging from a minimum of 2 to a maximum of 10.

Table 5.1: Resource-loading table based on early-start order

Activity	Early start	Duration (days)	Resources	1	2	3	4	5	6	7	8	9	10	11	12	13	14	15	16	17	18	19
1,2	0	2	2	2	2																	
2,4	2	4	2			2	2	2	2													
2,3	2	3	2			2	2	2														

2,5	2	2	3			3	3															
5,9	4	4	3					3	3	3	3											
3,10	5	4	2						2	2	2	2										
4,6	6	2	2							2	2											
4,7	6	4	3							3	3	3	3									
6,8	8	2	2									2	2									
10,11	9	3	2										2	2	2							
7,9	10	5	3											3	3	3	3	3				
8,9	10	3	4											4	4	4						
9,11	15	2	1																1	1		
11,12	17	2	2																		2	2
	Total			2	2	7	7	7	7	10	10	7	7	9	9	7	3	3	1	1	2	2

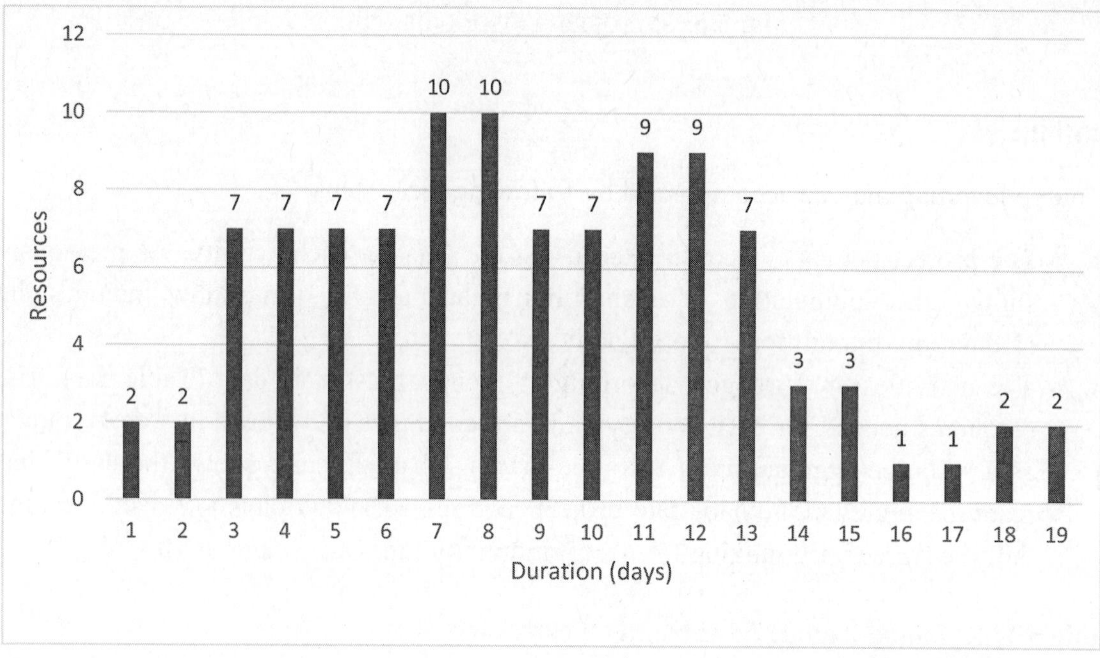

Fig. 5.7: Resource loading chart based on early start

iii. Now, the activities are arranged in a sequence based on their late start date (see Table 5.2). The latest start date of an activity may be determined by subtracting the length of the activity from the latest time of the completion event. The resource-loading chart in Fig. 5.8 is created by arranging the activities according to their latest start times in ascending order. The required resources range from a minimum of 2 to a maximum of 12.

Table 5.2: Resource-loading table based on late-start order

Activity	Late start	Duration (days)	Resources	1	2	3	4	5	6	7	8	9	10	11	12	13	14	15	16	17	18	19
1,2	0	2	2	2	2																	
2,4	2	4	2			2	2	2	2													
2,3	2	3	2			2	2	2														
2,5	2	2	3			3	3															
4,6	6	2	2							2	2											
4,7	6	4	3							3	3	3	3									
3,10	10	4	2											2	2	2	2					
6,8	10	2	2											2	2							
7,9	10	5	3											3	3	3	3	3				
5,9	11	4	3												3	3	3	3				
8,9	12	3	4													4	4	4				
10,11	14	3	2															2	2	2		
9,11	15	2	1																1	1		
11,12	17	2	2																		2	2
	Total			2	2	7	7	4	2	5	5	3	3	7	10	12	12	12	3	3	2	2

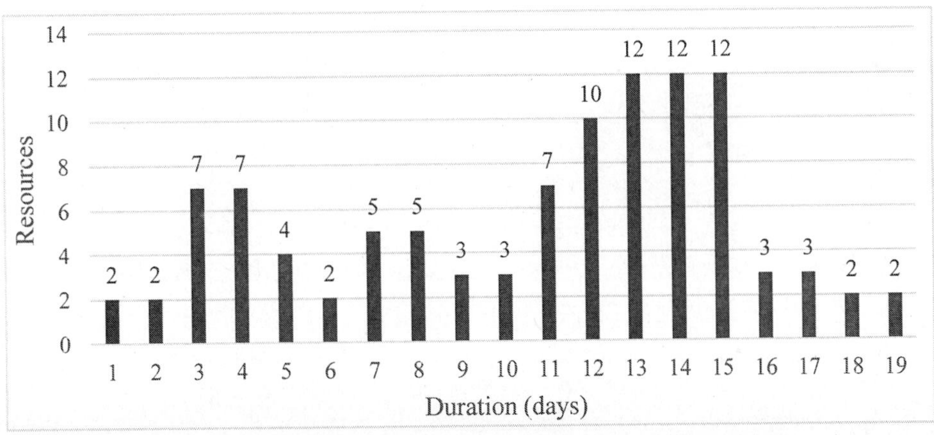

Fig. 5.8: Resource loading chart based on late-start

iv. A comparison is made between the two resource-loading charts derived from steps 2 and 3. The two charts depict the two most contrasting configurations of resource demands. Suppose there are fluctuations in the use pattern of a resource. In that case, the activities are adjusted by visual examination to determine an optimal resource need that falls within the range of these fluctuations. The primary objective is to maintain a consistent allocation of resources and minimise significant fluctuations in resource consumption. An example of a compromise approach is shown in Fig. 5.9 (also see Table 5.3). This has been derived by distributing the resources in the following way:

The non-critical activities (5,9) and (8,9) have adhered to the late start time.

The critical activities (1, 2), (2, 4), (4, 5), and (5, 6) have not been disrupted.

The adjustments above have successfully decreased the peak need from 12 to 10 while facilitating a progressive resource allocation adjustment.

Table 5.3: Resource loading table after levelling

Activity	Duration (days)	Resources	1	2	3	4	5	6	7	8	9	10	11	12	13	14	15	16	17	18	19
1,2	2	2	2	2																	
2,4	4	2			2	2	2	2													
2,3	3	2			2	2	2														
2,5	2	3			3	3															
5,9	4	3												3	3	3	3				
3,10	4	2						2	2	2	2										
4,6	2	2							2	2											
4,7	4	3							3	3	3	3									
6,8	2	2									2	2									
10,11	3	2										2	2	2							
7,9	5	3											3	3	3	3	3				
8,9	3	4													4	4	4				
9,11	2	1																1	1		
11,12	2	2																		2	2
	Total		2	2	7	7	4	4	7	7	7	7	5	8	10	10	10	1	1	2	2

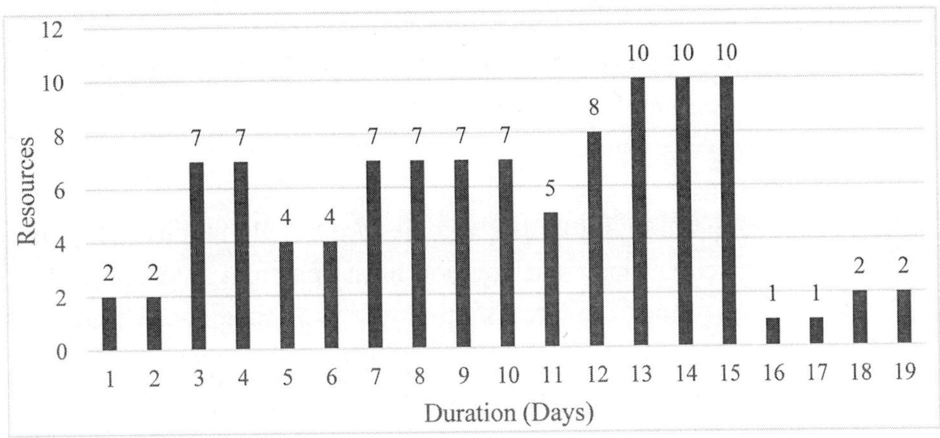

Fig. 5.9: Resource levelled chart (time constrained)

5.11.4 Resource Smoothing

As with resource levelling, in resource smoothing, we do resource optimisation. However, in resource smoothing, the availability of resources is a restriction rather than time (in the case of levelling). In other words, the resources have set boundaries. Therefore, resource smoothing is performed based on the same principles used in resource levelling. The fundamental goal here is to determine which tasks may be delayed and by how much and then arrive at the lowest feasible time to finish the project while meeting resource restrictions.

5.12 STANDARD GOOD PRACTICES IN CONSTRUCTION

5.12.1 Risk Management

Identifying, assessing, and mitigating potential risks is crucial for project success. This involves a proactive approach to anticipate and address uncertainties, minimising the impact on project timelines and budgets.

5.12.2 Value Management

Value management optimises project outcomes by balancing cost, quality, and functionality. It involves evaluating alternatives to enhance value without compromising project objectives.

5.12.3 Supply Chain Management

Managing the supply chain facilitates opportunities for reducing costs and increasing value. This enables the business to operate efficiently along the whole supply chain. As a result, supply chain management is becoming a crucial concern for several construction firms and clients. Operation and management procedures are two critical components of a good supply chain. The operational processes monitor how supplies are bought and transported to the job site, the chosen trade contractors, their participation in the planning and design process, and techniques for lowering invoicing and transaction costs. Management practices support collaborative approaches to keep the system functioning. It allows systems to provide appropriate support, incentives, and responsibility for supply chain partners.

5.12.4 Lean Construction

This method keeps the process that provides value while the process that adds cost is decreased or eliminated after an approach is analysed. Value is prioritised and allocated additional funds. Lean construction, then, is a method for controlling the production process. These are the five fundamental tenets of lean construction:

i. The value is stated from the client's viewpoint.
ii. Finding and incorporating the processes that provide value.
iii. Make the necessary changes when they are needed.
iv. Achieve excellence by constantly improving.
v. The value is stated from the client's viewpoint.
vi. Value is let to flow without interruption or bottlenecks.

5.12.5 Resource Management

Managing resources, including labour and equipment, is essential for project success. This includes proper allocation, monitoring, and optimisation of resources throughout the construction process.

5.12.6 Contractor Licensing and Insurance

Working only with licensed and insured contractors mitigates risks and ensures compliance with legal requirements. It provides financial protection and assurance of the contractor's qualifications.

SUMMARY

The chapter on planning and organising construction site and resources provides a comprehensive guide to efficiently managing project resources and orchestrating site activities. It outlines essential strategies for coordinating workforce, materials, equipment, and logistics to ensure seamless project execution. Emphasising the importance of meticulous planning, the chapter covers aspects such as site layout design, workflow optimisation, and resource scheduling to maximise productivity and minimise delays. Additionally, it addresses resource levelling and allocation to mitigate potential disruptions and maintain project timelines. By implementing effective organisational structures and communication protocols, construction teams can streamline operations, enhance collaboration, and deliver projects successfully while adhering to safety standards and regulatory requirements.

EXERCISE

As the project manager for a construction project, you need to plan and organise the workforce effectively. In your strategy:

a) Describe the workforce planning process, including forecasting labour requirements and recruiting skilled workers.

b) Explain how you would organise the workforce on the construction site to optimise productivity and ensure smooth operations.

c) Discuss the importance of motivation in enhancing workforce performance and morale and outline strategies for motivating construction workers.

MULTIPLE CHOICE QUESTIONS

1. What is the primary purpose of enabling structures at a construction site?

A) To provide temporary accommodation for workers
B) To support the construction process by facilitating access and utilities
C) To store construction materials and equipment
D) To serve as permanent structures after project completion

2. Which of the following is NOT a component of site layout planning?

A) Enabling structures

B) Equipment procurement
C) Access roads
D) Utilities placement

3. Documentation at a construction site primarily includes:

A) Architectural designs
B) Labor contracts
C) Invoices for materials
D) All of the above

4. Which concept is related to the efficient management of material resources in construction projects?

A) Equipment planning
B) Inventory control
C) Cash flow management
D) Earned value analysis

5. The basic concept of equipment planning involves:

A) Determining the number of equipment required for the project
B) Scheduling equipment maintenance
C) Selecting the most cost-effective equipment for the project
D) All of the above

6. Which of the following is a source of funds for construction projects?

A) Personal savings of the project manager
B) Bank loans
C) Donations from local charities
D) All of the above

7. S-curves are used in construction management primarily for:

A) Cash flow analysis
B) Material procurement
C) Equipment maintenance scheduling

D) Labour planning

8. What does "earned value" represent in construction project management?

A) The value of materials procured
B) The value of work actually performed
C) The total project budget
D) The cost of equipment rentals

9. Resource constraints and conflicts in construction management refer to:

A) The shortage of skilled labour
B) Disputes between contractors
C) Conflicts over equipment allocation
D) All of the above

10. What is a common good practice in construction project management?

A) Poor communication with stakeholders
B) Ignoring safety regulations
C) Proactive risk management
D) Overlooking environmental concerns

ANSWERS TO MULTIPLE CHOICE QUESTIONS

1	2	3	4	5	6	7	8	9	10
B	B	D	B	D	B	A	B	D	C

SHORT ANSWER TYPE QUESTIONS

1. What are the key factors when selecting a construction site?
2. How do you assess and manage risks associated with a construction site?
3. What steps are involved in developing a construction project plan?
4. How do you prioritise tasks and allocate resources effectively on a construction site?
5. What are the essential resources needed for a typical construction project?
6. How do you ensure compliance with regulations and permits on a construction site?

7. Can you describe scheduling activities on a construction site?
8. How do you handle unexpected delays or changes in a construction project?
9. What strategies do you employ to optimise productivity and efficiency on a construction site?
10. How do you manage and track materials and labour costs on a construction project?
11. What measures do you take to ensure safety and security on a construction site?
12. How do you document and report on-site activities and progress?

LONG ANSWER TYPE QUESTIONS

1. Explain the concept of cash flow in construction projects and discuss the sources of funds typically used to finance construction activities. Describe the challenges of managing cash flow on construction sites and strategies for optimising cash flow throughout the project lifecycle.
2. Discuss using histograms and S-curves in construction project management, including their applications for tracking project progress, resource allocation, and performance evaluation. Explain how earned value analysis assesses project performance and forecasts future outcomes.
3. Describe the resource scheduling process in construction projects using bar charts, line of balance technique, and resource levelling methods. Discuss the challenges associated with resource constraints and conflicts and strategies for mitigating these challenges.
4. Discuss common good practices in construction project planning and organising, including risk management, stakeholder communication, quality control, and environmental sustainability. Provide examples of how these practices are implemented on construction sites to achieve project objectives and deliver successful outcomes.
5. A construction project with a total budget of $5,000,000 is expected to last 18 months. If the project expenses are distributed evenly over the duration, calculate the monthly cash flow requirement.

6. A construction site has 30 workers available for a project. If the project requires 240 hours of labour per day and operates 6 days a week, calculate the days needed to complete the project.
7. A construction company has a fleet of 10 excavators and 15 dump trucks. If each excavator can load a truck in 20 minutes, calculate the time required for all excavators to load all trucks for a project requiring 300 truckloads of soil.
8. A construction project has a total duration of 24 months. The planned value (PV) of work scheduled to be completed by the end of the 12th month is $2,000,050, and the actual cost (AC) incurred by the end of the 12th month is $1,800,010. Calculate the earned value (EV) at the end of the 12th month and determine if the project is ahead or behind schedule.

TUTORIAL

To construct a typical 3-storeyed, framed structure with 400 sq. m area per floor, develop the histograms for the resources required, showing all intermediate calculations; draw S-curves for concrete placing and blockwork done over the period.

KNOW MORE

For more information related to this topic scan the QR code.

OR

Type this link in your browser

https://nptel.ac.in/courses/105106149

BIBLIOGRAPHY

- Abd, A. M., Hameed, A. H., and Nsaif, B. M. (2020). Documentation of construction project using integration of BIM and GIS technique. *Asian Journal of Civil Engineering*, 21(7), 1249-1257.
- Goedert, J. D., and Meadati, P. (2008). Integrating construction process documentation into building information modelling. *Journal of Construction Engineering and Management*, 134(7), 509-516.
- Heon Jun, D., and El-Rayes, K. (2011). Multiobjective optimisation of resource leveling and allocation during construction scheduling. *Journal of Construction Engineering and Management*, 137(12), 1080-1088.
- Howes, R. (2000). Improving the performance of Earned Value Analysis as a construction project management tool. *Engineering, Construction and Architectural Management,* 7(4), 399-411.
- Zhang, P., Li, N., Jiang, Z., Fang, D., and Anumba, C. J. (2019). An agent-based modelling approach for understanding the effect of worker-management interactions on construction workers' safety-related behaviours. *Automation in Construction*, 97(1), 29-43.

6 PROJECT MONITORING AND CONTROL

UNIT SPECIFICS

Regarding construction projects, effective monitoring and control systems are just as important as careful planning and execution. This chapter explores the vital aspects of monitoring and control in the construction industry, explaining the crucial procedures, instruments, and tactics used to guarantee that projects stay within budgets, schedules, safety, and quality requirements. This chapter offers a thorough framework for efficient monitoring and control, from resource management to progress tracking, ensuring optimum quality and safety on project sites.

RATIONALE

The success of construction projects not only depends upon timely completion, but quality and safety are also important.

PRE-REQUISITE

Nil

UNIT OUTCOMES

List of outcomes of this unit is as follows:

U6-O1: Update project plans

U6-O2: Understands modern project management systems

U6-O3: Ensure quality and safety in construction

Unit Outcomes	Expected Mapping with Course Outcomes (1- Weak Correlation; 2- Medium correlation; 3- Strong Correlation)					
	CO-1	CO-2	CO-3	CO-4	CO-5	CO-6
U6-O1	2	3	1	2	1	1
U6-O2	3	2	1	3	3	1
U6-O3	2	1	2	3	2	3

6.1 RECORD KEEPING

Maintaining records on construction sites is a vital component of project management to ensure that crucial information is organised, recorded, and available throughout a construction project. Maintaining accurate records is beneficial for several reasons, including accountability, quality assurance, legal compliance, and future reference. The following are record-keeping procedures that are frequently used on building sites:

i. *Project documentation management:* Establish a comprehensive project documentation management system. This includes contracts, permits, drawings, specifications, change orders, and correspondence. Implement a document control procedure to ensure the accuracy, accessibility, and version control of project documents.
ii. *Records of labour:* Including wage sheets, a record of the numbers of workers on site, total hours worked on a project, non-productive hours, and average hourly rate.
iii. *Daily construction logs:* Maintain daily construction logs to record activities, weather conditions, workforce attendance, equipment usage, and any significant events or incidents on the site. These logs provide a detailed chronology of project progress and can serve as valuable evidence in case of disputes or claims.
iv. *Submittals and RFIs (requests for information):* Track the submission and approval process of shop drawings, material samples, product data, and RFIs. Document any revisions, approvals, or rejections to ensure compliance with project specifications and contractual requirements.
v. *Quality control and inspections:* Document all quality control inspections, testing results, and non-conformance reports. Keep records of material certifications, inspection reports, and compliance documentation to verify that construction activities meet regulatory standards and project specifications.
vi. *Safety records:* Maintain records of safety meetings, toolbox talks, training sessions, and safety inspections. Document any safety incidents, near misses, accidents, investigation reports, and corrective actions taken to mitigate risks and ensure a safe working environment.
vii. *Progress reports:* Generate regular progress reports to track project milestones, schedule adherence, and budgetary expenditures. Include updates on work completed, work in progress, and any delays or deviations from the project plan. These reports facilitate communication with stakeholders and help identify potential issues early on.
viii. *As-Built drawings and documentation:* Update as-built drawings and documentation to reflect any modifications, deviations, or changes made during construction. These

records accurately represent the final built environment and are essential for future maintenance, renovations, or expansions.

ix. *Financial records and cost tracking:* Maintain detailed records of project expenses, including invoices, purchase orders, payment certificates, and change orders. Track costs against the budget to monitor financial performance and identify any variances or discrepancies that may require corrective action.

x. *Environmental compliance documentation:* Document compliance with environmental regulations, permits, and mitigation measures. Keep records of environmental assessments, monitoring reports, waste management plans, and any remediation efforts to minimise the project's environmental impact.

xi. *Closeout documentation:* Compile all necessary documentation for project closeout, including warranties, operation and maintenance manuals, record drawings, and final inspections. Ensure all contractual obligations are fulfilled, and all relevant records are transferred to the project owner or facility manager for ongoing maintenance and operations.

In addition to the aforementioned procedures, technical staff members on construction sites are required to maintain a diary in which they will document information about issued drawings, verified plans, verbal instructions given, comprehensive measurements of covered work, reasons and lengths of stoppages and changes in the rate of progress, details crucial to dispute resolution, deliveries of materials, transportation used, plant utilised, including the duration and reason of idle periods, and visitors' profile.

Keeping accurate records on building sites requires careful documentation and management of project-related data at different phases. Project teams may improve transparency, accountability, and efficiency by keeping correct and well-organized records, which eventually help to ensure the successful completion of construction projects.

6.2 PERIODIC PROGRESS REPORTS AND MEETINGS

Regular meetings and status reports are essential to efficient project management on construction sites. They help project stakeholders communicate, coordinate, and make decisions by updating everyone on progress, difficulties, and planned activities.

6.2.1 Purpose of Progress Reports and Meetings

Progress reports and meetings serve several purposes. A few of them are as follows:

i. *Communication:* Progress reports and meetings give project team members, clients, contractors, and other stakeholders a forum for sharing information, updates, and comments.

ii. *Coordination:* Progress reports and meetings support the synchronisation of tasks, the resolution of problems, and the alignment of efforts to guarantee the project's smooth and planned progress.

iii. *Making decisions:* Using up-to-date project data, performance indicators, risk assessments, progress reports, and meetings empowers stakeholders to make well-informed decisions.

iv. *Problem-solving:* By making it easier to recognise and address problems, disputes, and obstacles that arise during construction, progress reports and meetings help to avoid delays and overspending.

6.2.2 Frequency and Timing of Progress Reports and Meetings

Throughout a project, meetings and progress updates are usually held regularly. The frequency of these activities depends on the project's size, complexity, and development stage. Meetings are typically held every week, every two weeks, or every month, depending on the project's demands.

6.2.3 Content of Progress Reports

Progress reports typically include the following components:

i. *Introduction:* Summarise the project's goals, participants, significant checkpoints, and scope in the introduction.

ii. *Summary of progress:* A summary of the progress accomplished in a project since the last report should be included, emphasising accomplishments, significant milestones and difficulties faced.

iii. *Schedule performance:* Review the project schedule, compare the actual and projected progress, and note any deviations or variations from the schedule.

iv. *Cost performance:* Evaluate the project's financial performance by comparing actual and planned costs and addressing any cost patterns or variations.

v. *Quality and safety:* Assess the project's performance in terms of quality and safety, emphasising any problems with quality control, non-conformances, or safety occurrences.

vi. *Risk management:* It includes identifying and evaluating the main uncertainties and risks that could affect the project and developing plans to reduce those risks.

vii. *Next actions and suggestions:* List the scheduled tasks, goals, and suggestions for the next progress meeting.

6.2.4 Conducting Progress Meetings

Progress meetings should be well-organized, focused, and productive. Here are some key steps for conducting effective progress meetings:

i. *Preparation:* To ensure everyone is ready, create an agenda, compile pertinent information and reports, and provide resources ahead of time.
ii. *Facilitation:* Name a person to take charge of the meeting, steer the conversation in the right direction, and ensure that everything on the agenda is covered in the allotted time.
iii. *Participation:* Encourage everyone in attendance to participate actively by asking for suggestions, criticisms, and updates from all relevant stakeholders.
iv. *Problem-solving:* During the meeting, identify and discuss any problems, disputes, or difficulties that may arise during construction. Then, brainstorm solutions and assign tasks as necessary.
v. *Documentation:* Make sure that everyone is aware of their duties and deadlines by taking minutes of the meeting and recording decisions, action items, and follow-up tasks.

After the meeting, contact the relevant parties to ensure the action items are finished on schedule and the progress is monitored correctly until the next meeting. Hold people accountable for their commitments and take swift action to settle any outstanding concerns to avoid additional delays or complexities.

In conclusion, regular meetings and progress reports are crucial tools for tracking, controlling, and reporting the advancement of building projects. They contribute to project success by keeping stakeholders informed, involved, and aligned with project goals by offering a structured platform for discussion, decision-making, and problem-solving.

6.3 UPDATING OF PLANS

It is essential to update plans on construction sites to guarantee that the project proceeds according to schedule, meets all current specifications, and considers any modifications or difficulties that arise. Supervisors are primarily responsible for the typical progress-tracking procedures. Subsequently, to assess the progress made by that date, field engineers and superintendents examine these reports with as-planned drawings, project specifications, and construction details. After that, they review the construction schedule to determine what needs to be completed and when. This requires a substantial quantity of time and effort.

6.3.1 Purpose of Updating

On construction sites, plans are updated to guarantee that all parties involved have access to up-to-date, correct project information, promoting efficient coordination, communication, and decision-making. Updated plans ensure that construction operations align with project objectives and specifications by considering changes in the project scope, design revisions, regulatory requirements, and changing conditions. By updating their plans, construction teams may reduce risks, anticipate problems, and comply with applicable standards and requirements. Updated plans also facilitate accountability, documentation, and quality assurance efforts, which ultimately help construction projects be completed on time, under budget, and with acceptable quality standards.

Updating plans on construction sites has a strategic purpose that goes beyond simple documentation; it is essential to the project's success. Updated plans are necessary to ensure that construction projects are carried out effectively, safely, and in conformity with the highest quality and compliance standards. They promote communication, manage risks, and offer clarity and alignment.

6.3.2 Frequency of Updating Project Plans

The size and complexity of the project, the pace of development, and the extent of alterations or adjustments are some of the variables that determine how often and how construction sites update their plans. The following three factors affect the frequency of updating the project plans:

i. *Regular intervals:* Plans may be updated weekly, biweekly, or monthly, depending on the scope and schedule of the project. This regularity guarantees stakeholders access to the most recent information and that changes are swiftly recorded.
ii. *Events triggered:* Plans can also be modified in response to specific events or benchmarks, including design reviews, site visits, or modification orders. These trigger events force a thorough reassessment of the plans to make any required adjustments or changes.
iii. *Milestone accomplishments:* When major project milestones are reached, such as finishing a construction phase, installing important equipment/machines, or approving

key deliverables, updates to the plans may follow. These updates indicate development and guarantee that plans appropriately reflect the project's present status.

6.3.3 Methods of Updating Project Plans

To guarantee the precision, promptness, and accessibility of project information, updating plans on building sites is an essential component of project management. Construction teams may successfully manage plan updates and ensure all stakeholders operate from the most recent information by establishing transparent processes and using the right tools and technologies. This eventually contributes to the success of the construction project. The methods of updating the project plans are as follows:

i. *Manual revisions:* In traditional construction methods, plans are frequently changed manually by utilising drafting software or putting changes directly on paper drawings. Using this procedure, the current plans are marked up digitally or physically with annotations, modifications, or alterations.
ii. *Digital collaboration platforms:* Building Information Modelling, or BIM, programs and collaboration platforms are now widely used in building projects to manage and update plans due to the development of digital technology. These systems facilitate collaboration and expedite the revision process by enabling various stakeholders to access, review, and amend plans in real time.
iii. *Mobile applications:* Real-time plan changes and amendments are made more accessible on construction sites using tablets or cell phones to digitally access plans, annotate them, and communicate changes quickly to increase efficiency and accuracy.
iv. *Version control systems:* Version control systems manage different iterations of plans and ensure that all stakeholders work from the latest version. These systems track changes, document revisions, and maintain a history of plan updates, reducing the risk of errors or discrepancies caused by outdated information.

6.4 COMMON CAUSES OF TIME AND COST OVERRUNS

Common causes of time and cost overruns in construction projects are multifaceted, often stemming from various interconnected factors. Inadequate project planning and estimation, including inaccurate forecasting of resource requirements and project durations, can lead to initial budget and schedule shortcomings. Changes in project scope or design due to client requests or unforeseen circumstances frequently contribute to delays and additional expenses. Moreover, insufficient risk management practices, such as failure to anticipate potential disruptions or supply chain issues, can amplify project uncertainties. Ineffective communication and coordination among project stakeholders, including contractors, subcontractors, and suppliers, may delay decision-making and execution. External factors such as adverse weather conditions, regulatory delays, and economic fluctuations can also exacerbate time and cost overruns. Addressing these challenges requires proactive project management, robust risk mitigation strategies, transparent communication channels, and diligent monitoring and control throughout the construction process. A few of the Common causes of time and cost overruns are listed below:

i. *Change in the project scope:* Change orders are standard in building projects, often resulting in design alterations. As a result, it demands the additional allocation of resources, raising the project's cost and duration.
ii. *Poor site management:* Large-scale construction projects require enormous labour, equipment, and supplies. Controlling every resource to achieve the highest possible result becomes essential. However, if these things are not held on a project site, it may lead to a significant loss of working outcomes, which disrupts the project and adds to the costs.
iii. *Delays in progress payment:* The project management team frequently fails to make timely payments, which results in significant cost overruns. Projects are postponed, labour hours are wasted, and wages are not paid when payments are not made on time. The company's reputation with raw material distributors also deteriorates with late fees, and the raw materials get delivered late to the site.
iv. *Poor planning and scheduling:* Time and expense overruns result from inadequate layout and careless planning. These oversights can necessitate last-minute adjustments, significantly increasing project costs and delays.
v. *Inflation:* Increasing raw material prices impacts the project's total cost. The project may be delayed if the contractor or the owner cannot adapt to this economic shift.
vi. *Unqualified workforce:* The unskilled labour due to lack of knowledge, construction skills, lack of expertise, and absenteeism contributes to delaying the project.
vii. *Unforeseen site conditions:* Unexpected site features such as unstable soil, underground utilities, and hazardous contaminants can cause reconstruction and mitigation to take longer and cost more money.
viii. *Poor communication:* Every construction project involves numerous resources and several stakeholders. The continuous flow of such resources as people and materials needs a robust communication channel. Also, effective coordination amongst all interested parties is crucial for the project's success. Without this kind of collaboration

and communication, the project encounters unfavourable results that lengthen its timeline and raise the expense of starting over.

6.5 CORRECTIVE MEASURES TO AVOID COST AND TIME OVERRUN

The importance of corrective measures to avoid cost and time overruns in construction projects cannot be overstated. Implementing proactive strategies to address potential issues is crucial for maintaining project efficiency and profitability. By identifying and rectifying discrepancies early on, project managers can prevent minor setbacks from snowballing into major delays and cost escalations. Monitoring project progress against established benchmarks allows timely intervention and adjusting schedules, resource allocations, and budgets as needed. Moreover, fostering a culture of accountability and collaboration among project stakeholders encourages proactive problem-solving and decision-making, minimising the likelihood of future setbacks. Advanced project management tools and technologies, such as scheduling software and Building Information Modeling (BIM), can enhance project transparency and facilitate real-time data-driven decision-making. Ultimately, by prioritising proactive measures to mitigate risks and address challenges promptly, construction projects can achieve greater predictability, efficiency, and success. A few of the measures to avoid cost and time overrun are as follows:

i. *Provision of additional budget:* It may be possible to prevent cost and schedule overruns by initially overestimating and completing the project within the allocated budget. In that instance, further funds won't be needed and will contribute to strengthening the company's reputation.
ii. *Mandatory use of construction software:* The change order of a project may be previously visualised before being implemented onsite by using software that can save both time and money.
iii. *Accurate project planning:* The precious and detailed information can help deliver the project on time and within the budget.
iv. *Hiring a competent project manager:* The project manager's proficiency with project management tools and setting up a skilled team can improve the project's effectiveness and aid in controlling expenses. The tools can assist in maintaining a close watch on the project's resources, and a skilled team can help achieve the goals by using optimal resources, thus avoiding delays and overspending.

v. *Due diligence with vendors:* A careful investigation of the records of vendors hired for specific task completion or crucial raw material supply assures the project completion within the scheduled time and budget.

6.6 LEAN CONSTRUCTION

Lean construction is a methodology that revolutionises traditional construction practices by maximising value while minimising waste throughout the project lifecycle. Inspired by the principles of lean manufacturing, particularly Toyota's Toyota Production System (TPS), lean construction aims to optimise efficiency, productivity, and overall project outcomes. At its core, lean construction prioritises understanding and efficiently delivering the customer's value. This involves identifying and eliminating various forms of waste, such as overproduction, excess inventory, waiting times, defects, and underutilised talent. By reducing waste, resources are utilised more effectively, improving project timelines and cost-effectiveness.

One of the fundamental tenets of lean construction is continuous improvement, known as Kaizen, which encourages ongoing reflection, innovation, and refinement of processes. Collaboration and integration among all project stakeholders are also emphasised, fostering a culture of teamwork, open communication, and shared goals. Pull planning, a core practice in lean construction involves scheduling tasks based on project needs rather than arbitrary timelines, promoting greater adaptability and efficiency.

Another fundamental principle is just-in-time (JIT) delivery, which ensures that materials, equipment, and labour are provided precisely when and where they are needed, minimising storage costs and preventing overproduction. Lean construction also strongly emphasises respecting and empowering people at all levels of the organisation, recognising their contributions and fostering a supportive work environment.

Lean construction offers a systematic approach to optimising construction processes, enhancing project outcomes, and delivering greater customer value. While its implementation may require a shift in mindset and practices within the construction industry, the benefits of lean construction in terms of cost savings, quality improvement, and schedule adherence make it a compelling methodology for modern construction projects. Some fundamental principles and concepts of lean construction are given below:

i. *Value:* Lean construction starts with understanding what the customer values. This could be quality, functionality, cost-effectiveness, or timely delivery. The project team can focus on delivering what truly matters by identifying and prioritising value from the customer's perspective.

ii. *Identifying waste:* Lean construction emphasises identifying and eliminating waste. Waste can take many forms in construction, such as overproduction, excessive inventory, waiting times, unnecessary transportation, defects, and underutilised talent. By reducing or eliminating these wastes, resources are used more efficiently, and project timelines can be shortened.

iii. *Continuous improvement (Kaizen):* Lean construction promotes a culture of continuous improvement, where all project stakeholders are encouraged to seek better ways of doing things. This involves regular reflection on processes, identifying areas for improvement, implementing changes, and evaluating their effectiveness. Minor, incremental improvements over time can lead to significant advancements in efficiency and quality.

iv. *Collaboration and integration:* Lean construction emphasises collaboration and integration among project participants, including owners, designers, contractors, and subcontractors. By involving all stakeholders early in the project and fostering open communication, conflicts can be minimised, and decisions can be made more efficiently.

v. *Pull planning:* Rather than traditional push-based scheduling, lean construction employs pull planning techniques. This involves starting from the project's end goal and working backwards to determine the sequence of activities needed to achieve it. Pull planning fosters greater collaboration and flexibility, allowing teams to adapt to changes more effectively.

vi. *Just-in-time (JIT) delivery:* Just-in-Time principles involve delivering materials, equipment, and labour precisely when and where they are needed, thus reducing inventory and waste. This approach helps streamline workflows, minimise storage costs, and prevent overproduction.

vii. *Respect for people:* Lean construction emphasises respecting and empowering people at all levels of the organisation. This involves providing training and support, fostering a culture of trust and collaboration, and recognising the contributions of individuals and teams.

By adopting lean construction principles and practices, construction projects can achieve better cost, quality, safety, and schedule performance outcomes. However, implementing lean construction requires commitment, cooperation, and a willingness to challenge traditional practices in the construction industry.

Try to find out!

Suppose you need to construct your home what lean principles will you apply?

6.7 BUILDING INFORMATION MODELLING (BIM)

Computer technology is used in the construction industry using building information modelling (BIM). The BIM helps discard the use of drawings on paper for storing information. Instead, BIM stores, updates, and communicates information using comprehensive digital representations: the building information models. The setup and management of the construction process, the combination of models, the coordination of design operations, and the transfer of building information to the operator are all significantly enhanced by using BIM. By minimising the amount of human data entry and facilitating the repurposing of digital information, error-prone work is avoided, improving the productivity and quality of the project.

A BIM is an extensive digital depiction of a constructed facility with comprehensive information. It contains the three-dimensional geometry of the construction components in detail. It also includes non-physical elements like calendars, hierarchical project frameworks, and places and zones. Thus, producing digital building models and using, maintaining, and sharing them throughout the constructed facility's existence is collectively called "Building Information Modelling" (BIM).

The US National Building Information Modelling Standard defines BIM as "a digital representation of physical and functional characteristics of a facility. A BIM is a shared knowledge resource for information about a facility forming a reliable basis for decisions during its life cycle; it is defined as existing from earliest conception to demolition. A basic premise of BIM is a collaboration by different stakeholders at different phases of the life cycle of a facility to insert, extract, update or modify information in the BIM to support and reflect the roles of that stakeholder."

The importance of Building Information Modeling (BIM) in construction cannot be overstated in modern project management practices. BIM revolutionises the traditional approach to construction by enabling stakeholders to collaboratively design, visualise, simulate, and manage buildings and infrastructure projects throughout their lifecycle. By creating a digital representation of the project, BIM facilitates enhanced coordination and communication among architects, engineers, contractors, and other stakeholders, leading to improved project outcomes. Through BIM, stakeholders can detect and resolve design conflicts before construction commences, reducing rework and change orders during construction. BIM provides valuable insights into project performance, enabling informed decision-making, optimising resource utilisation, and minimising risks. BIM supports sustainability goals by facilitating energy analysis, material optimisation, and lifecycle assessment, contributing to more environmentally responsible construction practices. Overall, the adoption of BIM in construction not only enhances project efficiency and quality but also fosters innovation, collaboration, and sustainability across the industry.

6.8 INTRODUCTION TO QUALITY

The concept of quality in construction has evolved significantly over centuries, tracing its roots back to ancient civilisations. The journey of quality management began in medieval Europe with craftsmen organising into guilds, establishing the first formalised quality standards. These guilds enforced quality through inspection committees, using marks to signify workers' reputation and project excellence, a tradition that prevailed until the Industrial Revolution. Quality was predominantly a matter of craftsmanship, where skilled workers, like those in ancient India, focused on precision and durability in their structures, evidenced by marvels such as the Indus Valley Civilization. This era was marked by an intrinsic understanding of quality, where the workforce's skill directly influenced the robustness and longevity of constructions. However, there was little formalisation or documentation of quality standards, making quality a highly variable and personal attribute dependent on individual skills and integrity.

6.8.1 The Craftsmanship to Industrialization Evolution

The shift from craftsmanship to the factory system in the United States divided trades into specialised tasks, converting craftsmen to factory workers. Quality was maintained through skilled labour, supplemented by audits and inspections. The Industrial Revolution propelled this evolution; the craftsmanship model, dominant until the early 19th century, gave way to the factory system. This era introduced inspection to ensure quality, marking a shift from individual craftsmanship to mass production. With the advent of the Industrial Revolution and subsequent technological advancements, the notion of quality in construction began to evolve more rapidly, and the introduction of product inspection marked a shift towards systematic quality assurance.

6.8.2 Global Conflicts' Role in Enhancement of Quality

The difficulties of World War II in the United States highlighted quality as a paramount component, necessitating extensive inspection forces. The introduction of sampling inspection and statistical quality control (SQC) techniques during this period marked significant advancements in quality management. Following the necessity in the early 20th century, Walter Shewhart's emphasis on process control introduced a new dimension to quality management, focusing on the stability and control of processes, laying the groundwork for modern quality control tools like control charts. In the 20th century, we have witnessed a paradigm shift by introducing quality control (QC) and quality assurance (QA) concepts, instituting systematic quality methodologies and emphasising the reduction of variability in construction processes.

Post-World War II, Japan's embrace of total quality, influenced by American quality experts like Deming and Juran, shifted the focus from mere product inspection to improving organisational processes. This approach led to Japan's reputation for high-quality exports, prompting a re-evaluation in the United States towards total quality management (TQM). Total Quality Management emphasised statistics and organizational-wide approaches, leading to the adoption of ISO 9000 standards and the Malcolm Baldrige National Quality Award, underscoring a comprehensive approach to quality management.

6.8.3 Beyond Total Quality Management

The quality movement has matured in the 21st century, incorporating risk management and customer satisfaction into the ISO 9001 standards and expanding into sector-specific standards. Quality management extends beyond manufacturing, highlighting its evolution into a multifaceted and comprehensive discipline. The development of ISO standards and Total Quality Management (TQM) further revolutionised the field, making quality a comprehensive and holistic concept, integrating customer satisfaction, continuous improvement, and employee involvement. This transformation laid the foundation for modern quality management practices in construction, balancing the age-old emphasis on craftsmanship with systematic, process-driven approaches.

Further, the transition into the 21st century introduced a significant evolution with the advent of Quality 4.0, a term that marries traditional quality management with the digital revolution. This new phase integrates advanced digital technologies like AI, IoT, and big data analytics into quality management processes, offering unprecedented opportunities for predictive quality and real-time insights. Quality 4.0 represents the future of quality management, where the interconnectedness of digital tools and quality processes enhances operational efficiency and product excellence across industries.

6.9 ECONOMIC IMPLICATIONS OF QUALITY

While we understand what quality is and how it has evolved, it's also essential to explore why there was a need to enhance quality processes. Investing in quality can lead to cost savings in the long run by reducing maintenance needs and prolonging the lifespan of structures. On the other hand, poor quality can result in increased costs due to repairs, legal liabilities, and reputational damage. A study by the Chartered Institute of Building in 2015 stated that "the cost of poor quality in construction can amount to 5-10% of project cost".

The cost of non-quality construction is paramount, primarily because it directly impacts the structural integrity and safety of buildings and infrastructure. High-quality construction practices ensure that structures are built to last and conform to safety standards that protect the lives of occupants and the public. This is especially crucial in areas prone to natural disasters like earthquakes or floods, where the robustness of construction can be a matter of life and death. Moreover, good quality construction minimises the risk of costly defects and failures that can lead to accidents, thereby safeguarding the well-being of both construction workers during the construction phase and residents in the long term.

6.10 CONCEPT OF QUALITY

As we traverse the evolution of the quality era elucidated in the previous Sections of this Chapter, we begin with the concept of inspection. In this reactive process, products are examined post-production to weed out defects. This initial step represents the beginning of quality awareness, focusing on identifying failures rather than preventing them. Advancing from this rudimentary stage, we shifted to quality control, a more systematic approach that introduces standardised procedures and statistical techniques to reduce variability and improve product consistency. This phase marks a shift from detection to prevention. The progression continues with quality assurance, which expands the scope to encompass all systems related to the production process, integrating quality development, maintenance, and improvement into the organisational fabric. Finally, we arrive at quality management, a holistic and strategic framework that ingrains quality into the corporate culture, involving all employees and addressing customer satisfaction as a long-term objective. This culmination represents a comprehensive quality-era philosophy, transcending mere defect detection to a broad, proactive management strategy that seeks continuous improvement in all aspects of an organisation's operations. A schematic diagram of quality evolution is shown in Fig. 6.1.

6.10.1 Quality Assurance vs. Quality Control

Further, it is crucial to understand the clear difference between these two concepts from the beginning to understand the quality in general. Understanding the distinction between Quality Assurance (QA) and Quality Control (QC) is fundamental in construction. While these terms are often used interchangeably, they encompass different processes and objectives within the quality management spectrum.

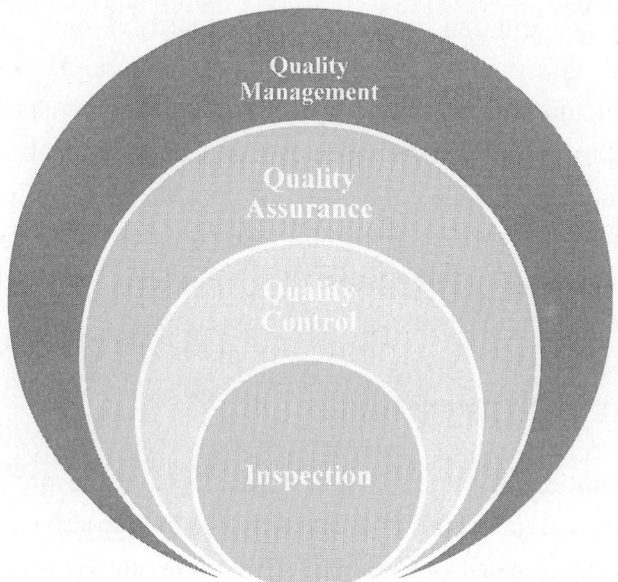

Fig. 6.1: Quality eras

Quality Assurance (QA) refers to the process-oriented activities designed to ensure that quality standards and operational requirements are being met in the construction process. QA focuses on developing and implementing processes that enhance quality and prevent defects. QA involves standardising processes and methodologies to achieve consistency in construction practices. An essential aspect of QA is the continuous improvement of processes, often through feedback loops and periodic reviews.

Quality Control, in contrast, is product-oriented. It involves the operational techniques and activities used to fulfil quality requirements for a product - in this case, the constructed structure. QC primarily focuses on identifying defects in the final product and implementing corrective actions. QC activities in construction include testing materials, workmanship inspection, and specifications compliance. QC ensures the construction project meets the specific quality standards established initially. The Table 6.1 shows the difference between quality assurance and control.

Table 6.1: Comparison between Quality Assurance and Quality Control

Characteristic	Quality Assurance (QA)	Quality Control (QC)
Definition (ISO 9000)	"A part of quality management focused on providing confidence that quality requirements will be fulfilled."	"A part of quality management focused on fulfilling quality requirements."
Objective	It prevents quality problems by focusing on the process used to make the product or deliver the service.	Identifies quality problems by inspecting the finished product or service.
Scope	Broad, involving all aspects of the product or service, from design to delivery.	Narrow focuses only on the finished product or service.
Responsibility	Involves the entire organisation, from top management to front-line employees.	Quality control inspectors or technicians.
Time of activity	Occurs during the development and production process of the product or service.	It occurs after the product or service has been completed.
Focus	Focuses on the prevention of defects or non-conformances with a focus on process (proactive process)	Focuses on the detection and correction of defects or non-conformances in the finished product (reactive process)
As a tool	Managerial tool	Corrective tool
Approach	Process-oriented; focuses on preventing defects by improving the processes.	Product-oriented: focuses on identifying defects in the final product.

Activities	It involves developing and implementing a QMS, defining standards, and setting quality objectives.	Involves inspections, testing, and measurements to ensure quality standards.
Feedback Mechanisms	Utilises feedback from QC to refine processes and policies.	Generates feedback through testing and inspections for QA to analyse.
Documentation	Establishes documentation requirements for quality processes, policies, and procedures.	Creates records of inspections, tests, and audits as evidence of quality performance.
Stakeholder Engagement	Sets expectations for quality and communication protocols among stakeholders.	Facilitates problem-solving and improvements through direct engagement in quality activities.
Quality Culture	Cultivates a quality culture by emphasising process improvement and preventive measures.	Reinforces a quality culture through adherence to standards and active participation in quality improvements.
Training and Development	Outlines the competencies and training programs required for quality management.	Offers practical training opportunities through involvement in quality activities.

In the Indian construction industry, the rigorous application of Quality Assurance (QA) and Quality Control (QC) practices has significantly contributed to the success of numerous projects, showcasing a commitment to excellence, safety, and sustainability. Among these, the Delhi Metro Rail Corporation (DMRC) project stands out as a benchmark for urban infrastructure development, where comprehensive QA and QC processes were integrated right from the design phase, complemented by regular audits, inspections, and a strong focus on workforce training to ensure high-quality workmanship. This meticulous approach to quality has been pivotal in the project's acclaim nationally and internationally.

Quality Assurance and Quality Control are essential and complementary aspects of quality management in construction. While QA focuses on process and preventive measures, QC emphasises product inspection and corrective actions. Understanding and implementing both QA and QC effectively ensures that construction projects meet the required quality standards from start to finish.

6.10.2 Cost of Quality

The cost of quality encompasses all expenses incurred throughout the lifespan of a construction project to prevent deviations from the owner's specified requirements. While some costs may not directly impact the project's overall budget, they can affect the consultant's ability to meet deadlines for design completion and ensure compliance with regulatory standards. Similarly, contractors face losses if their executed works are rejected by supervisors due to noncompliance, leading to material wastage, labour expenses, and project delays. To mitigate these risks, contractors must adhere to approved shop drawings, utilise endorsed materials, follow specified installation methods, conduct continuous inspections, employ skilled workers, maintain high standards of workmanship, and rectify any deficiencies promptly before seeking approval.

The cost of quality is divided into two parts. One is the cost of conformance, which refers to the expenses associated with ensuring that products or services meet quality standards and requirements. This includes expenses incurred to prevent defects, such as investment in quality control measures, employee training, and adherence to quality standards during production and the other, and the cost of non-conformance encompasses the expenses resulting from defects or failures to meet quality standards. These costs include rework, scrap, warranty claims, customer complaints, and lost sales opportunities due to poor quality.

6.11 QUALITY IN CONSTRUCTION AND CONSTRUCTED STRUCTURE

Having established an understanding of what quality entails and its significance, it's pivotal to explore the constituents of quality in construction at a granular level. However, before that, let us investigate how quality plays its role in construction. Quality is the cornerstone of trust and reliability in construction, providing peace of mind that structures will perform as intended under various environmental and usage conditions.

With safety, maintaining high quality in construction projects is integral for economic efficiency and sustainability. Quality construction practices lead to lower maintenance costs, longer lifespan of buildings, and enhanced energy efficiency, which collectively contribute to the economic viability of construction projects. Conversely, poor quality can result in frequent repairs, increased operational costs, and premature obsolescence, escalating the total cost of ownership.

Additionally, quality construction is increasingly intertwined with sustainable building practices. This involves using eco-friendly materials, efficient waste management and designs that minimise environmental impact. Implementing these practices aligns with global sustainability goals and responds to environmentally conscious consumers' growing demand for green buildings. Therefore, quality in construction is not just about building well but also about building responsibly for future generations.

6.11.1 Quality of Construction Component

Quality in construction is not a static goal but a continuous journey. It involves constant learning, adaptation, and improvement. In other words, quality in construction is a multifaceted concept with far-reaching implications. It encompasses safety, sustainability, economic considerations, and compliance with standards. As the construction industry continues to evolve, especially in rapidly developing economies like India, the focus on quality becomes increasingly critical. Focusing on critical areas such as materials, design, execution, management, workmanship, and compliance with standards offers a pathway to elevating quality to its zenith. Quality in construction is a complex and multi-dimensional concept, intricately woven with elements that enhance a building or infrastructure's structural integrity, safety, and durability. These components are the cornerstone for achieving excellence in construction, ensuring that projects meet and exceed the expected standards and requirements.

Materials

Materials used in construction lay the foundation for quality. The selection of appropriate, high-quality materials is critical to the durability and functionality of a structure. Materials must meet aesthetic requirements and possess physical and chemical properties suitable for specific construction needs. Using substandard materials can lead to a decline in building structural integrity and longevity.

Materials must withstand environmental factors and usage over time without significant deterioration, aligning with sustainability goals. Further, the consistency throughout the project ensures uniform excellence, from the foundation to the finishing touches. Selecting suppliers with proven records of delivering high-quality materials fosters robust relationships and a reliable supply chain. Together, these factors uphold construction quality, longevity, and performance while minimising environmental impact while construction materials are a concern.

Design, Planning, and Management

Design quality hinges on merging functionality with aesthetics to meet client expectations while ensuring safety and compliance with relevant codes and standards. Innovative design solutions enhance utility and performance, with material efficiency playing a key role in reducing waste and costs. A clear planning and management strategy is necessary to ensure the design quality. Planning and management of quality involves developing and implementing a Quality Management System (QMS) to oversee all quality aspects. Leadership and commitment at all levels foster a quality culture throughout the organisation. Continuous improvement strategies and effective risk management are integral, alongside clear and effective communication with all stakeholders about quality expectations and performance.

Execution and Workmanship

Execution of a construction project demands strict adherence to plans and specifications. Efficient use of resources—labour, materials, and machinery—reduces waste, while timely completion of projects avoids delays and extra costs. Implementing on-site quality control measures ensures issues are promptly identified and corrected, and high safety standards are maintained throughout the project lifecycle. Execution success relies on workmanship, which refers to the level of skill and quality applied in the construction process. Good workmanship is crucial in translating design concepts and quality materials into functional and aesthetically pleasing structures. To collect quality excellence from the workforce, the following aspects should be met:

i. *Skill and expertise:* The proficiency of the workforce, including their training and experience, plays a vital role in achieving construction quality. Not only that but optimised use of the right skills and expertise can lead to waste reduction and high productivity.
ii. *Quality work practices:* Promoting best practices and attention to detail among the workforce. Simultaneously, they provide ongoing supervision and training to maintain high standards of workmanship. Both site adequate supervision and quality control on the construction site ensure that workmanship adheres to the planned specifications and standards.
iii. *Technology integration:* Integrating modern technologies, like BIM and automated quality control systems, can significantly enhance the precision and consistency of workmanship. Where BIM offers a multidimensional view that enhances planning,

design, and construction management, automated quality control systems streamline the inspection process, enabling real-time monitoring and adjustments.

iv. *Accountability for quality and safety:* Holding individuals and teams accountable for the quality of their work is essential. Individuals must take pride in their workmanship, fostering a sense of ownership over the quality of work produced. This approach not only elevates the standard of the project but also cultivates a culture of excellence and responsibility within the team. Furthermore, it also adheres that the execution brings forth the highest safety standards.

Compliance with Standards

Compliance with established construction standards is a critical component of quality. These standards provide guidelines and benchmarks to achieve and deliver quality projects. It is essential to look for local, national, and international compliance to implement the best practice for an individual project.

i. *National and international standards:* Following standards set by the Bureau of Indian Standards or international bodies like ISO ensures that construction practices meet essential quality and safety thresholds. Considering national and international standards, it also implies that construction must be done under the best possible practices. Also, it is necessary to keep abreast of changes in laws and standards to opt for the newest listed compliance that bestows the highest construction quality.

ii. *Building codes and regulations:* Each location's construction method changes due to geography, climate, resource availability, etc. It becomes necessary to comply with local/national building codes and regulations to ensure that construction practices adhere to the minimum required standards for the safety and functionality of individual construction.

iii. *Certification and audits:* It is crucial to do time-to-time audits and get certified for what has been done. This reduces the chance of mistakes and rectifies them as soon as possible, if there are any. Regular audits and certification processes, such as ISO 9001 and other compliance and standards for quality management systems, help maintain consistent quality standards in construction projects.

iv. *Documentation and record keeping:* Just getting checked is not enough to sustain in the long run. To make any practice sustainable, it's essential to maintain detailed records of compliance efforts and quality control measures. Ultimately, these records will serve as guidelines and give a detailed SoP for dos and don'ts for future projects.

The quality in construction is not just about individual components but about how they interact. The compatibility of materials with the design, the skill level required for specific construction techniques, and the adherence of these elements to standards and regulations are all part of a complex interplay that defines quality in construction. The quality of a constructed structure is a cumulative outcome of meticulous planning, selection of appropriate materials, skilled workmanship, and adherence to standards and best practices at every stage of construction. Each phase contributes significantly to the structure's overall quality, safety, and functionality, from the foundation to the finishing touches. As the construction industry continues to evolve, these quality aspects become ever more critical in meeting the challenges and demands of modern construction.

6.11.2 Quality of Constructed Structure

After understanding the concept of quality in construction, discussing its application in actual structures will be more meaningful. Quality of constructed structure explores how quality manifests at different stages of construction, from foundation to finishing. Let's learn relevant examples and cases to understand the importance of quality at different stages of construction.

Foundation and substructure

You can't build a great building on a weak foundation. The quality of a structure's foundation and substructure is critical for its overall stability and durability. The foundation must be designed and constructed to bear the structure's load adequately. We all know the world's tallest building, Burj Khalifa in Dubai. To stand successfully in the world, it exemplifies quality in foundation construction. It features a deep foundation with 192 piles, each 1.5 meters in diameter, extending 50 meters below the surface. That is why this foundation can support the enormous load of the 828-meter-tall building.

Further, soil analysis and material selection are crucial in foundation or substructure work. Quality in this stage also involves meticulous soil analysis and selection of appropriate materials, ensuring that the foundation can withstand environmental stresses. This critical phase requires a detailed examination of soil properties to determine its bearing capacity, permeability, and potential for settlement. This ensures the chosen foundation type is optimally designed to support the structure under various environmental stresses. Moreover, carefully selecting high-quality materials resistant to corrosion, moisture, and other environmental factors is paramount in constructing a foundation that provides robust support and enhances the longevity and integrity of the entire structure.

Structural frame and load-bearing elements

The quality of the structural frame and load-bearing elements that are beams, columns, or walls is paramount for the safety and integrity of a building. Ensuring the excellence of these components involves two key aspects: the use of high-performance materials and the adoption of prefabrication and erection techniques. High-performance materials, such as advanced construction materials and concrete composites, are essential for constructing a robust structural frame that can endure environmental pressures, seismic activities, and the daily load demands of the building. These materials are selected for their superior strength, durability, and resistance to degradation, contributing to the overall resilience of the structure.

Further, the structural frame's quality depends on the precision in the fabrication and erection process, if methods allow. For example, Taipei 101 in Taiwan used a mega-column structure, requiring precise engineering and construction techniques to ensure stability against natural disasters like earthquakes and typhoons. Together, the strategic use of high-performance materials and the efficiency of prefabrication and erection techniques ensure that the structural frame and load-bearing elements of a building meet the highest standards of quality and safety.

Building envelopes and exteriors

The building envelope, including walls, windows, and roofs, also plays a crucial role in the overall quality of a structure, impacting everything from aesthetics to energy efficiency. Proper waterproofing and insulation are also vital for the longevity and comfort of a building, emphasising the need for quality in these aspects. High-quality construction in this stage involves using materials and designs that enhance thermal performance and sustainability. The Gherkin in London is a notable example, with its energy-efficient glass facade and aerodynamic shape. Similarly, Cybertecture Egg Mumbai utilises an innovative façade system that maximises natural light while minimising heat gain, significantly reducing energy consumption. Its unique egg-shaped design minimises the surface area exposed to the sun, further enhancing its thermal performance. The building also incorporates rainwater harvesting, solar photovoltaic panels, and an automated building management system, making it a paragon of sustainable architecture in India's booming construction landscape.

Interior finishing and services

The interior finishing and services are essential for its functionality and occupant comfort. It investigates the quality of Mechanical, Electrical, and Plumbing (MEP) Systems and fittings and finishes afterwards. The installation of MEP systems must adhere to high standards of quality to ensure efficient and safe operation. The quality of interior finishes, including flooring, paint, and fixtures, significantly impacts the building's overall aesthetic and functional quality. All these are incomplete without adherence to construction standards and best practices in all stages of construction. As mentioned in the previous sections, complying with local, national, and international building codes is critical to ensure safety and functionality. Also, implementing rigorous quality control processes and assurance measures throughout the construction process is key to achieving the desired quality in the final structure.

6.12 QUALITY CONTROL TOOLS

Quality control stands as a testament to the meticulous quality of process management. Control charts are a fundamental statistical tool for quality control, used to monitor, control, and improve processes over time. They serve as sentinels of the process, monitoring stability and predicting potential deviations. The commonly used control charts are as follows:

i. The check sheet is a simple yet effective form for collecting and analysing data.
ii. The flowchart is the cartographer's tool, mapping the process and identifying junctures where quality could falter.
iii. The cause-and-effect diagram, often known as the fishbone diagram, allows teams to dissect problems to their roots, fostering a culture of deep understanding. Causes in a typical fishbone diagram are usually grouped into categories, the main ones of which are The 6 Ms (men/people, machines, methods, materials, measures, and mother nature), 4 Ps (places, procedures, people, politics) and 4 Ss (surroundings, suppliers, systems, skills).
iv. The Pareto chart prioritises issues, teaching us that a few vital factors are often responsible for most problems. It is based on the 80-20 rule given by Vilfredo Pareto.
v. Histograms are used to investigate a visual summary of variation in data. Histograms display frequency distribution or process consistency. In other words, it shows how often a defect occurs across the range of the data.
vi. The scatter diagram uncovers relationships between variables; it acts as a detective who finds clues in the data patterns.
vii. The run chart tracks data over time, offering insights into trends and patterns.

These classical tools form the cornerstone of quality control, enabling practitioners to sculpt excellence from the raw production of marble. Each tool represents a unique perspective and capability, contributing to the holistic approach required for effective quality management.

6.13 ROLE OF INSPECTION

A thorough quality inspection involves measuring, examining, testing, or gauging various project attributes. Once done, the results are compared with specified requirements to ensure conformity. Building on the quality control tools, this part discusses how inspections enforce and verify the standards and procedures outlined in manuals and checklists. Inspections are a critical component in the construction quality control process. They implement and verify the adherence to the standards and guidelines, ensuring that every aspect of a construction project meets the required quality benchmarks.

Inspections in construction are carried out to assess the quality and safety of the work. They help identify issues and non-compliances early, preventing costly rework and ensuring the project's success. Inspections verify that construction practices adhere to local, national, and international standards and project-specific requirements. Regular inspections help in the early detection of defects or issues, allowing for timely corrections. Apart from quality, safety inspections are vital for identifying potential hazards and ensuring the well-being of workers and future occupants.

6.13.1 Method of Inspections in Construction

i. *Visual inspection:* Examining materials, workmanship, and finishes without specialised equipment, identifying surface defects, and overall compliance with specifications.
ii. *Mechanical and laboratory testing:* Testing material properties using tensile, compression, and flexural tests. Assessing concrete slump, air content, and strength.
iii. *Non-destructive testing (NDT):* Applying techniques like Ground Penetrating Radar (GPR), ultrasonic testing, and radiography and detecting internal flaws or discrepancies without damaging the construction materials.
iv. *Checklists and inspection sheets:* Utilizing standardised forms to meet consistent inspection criteria. Record findings and ensure traceability of the inspection process.
v. *Third-party inspection:* Engage external experts for unbiased quality assessment and provide certifications and independent verification of standards.

Apart from the stated methods, modern technology, such as drones, laser scanning, and Building Information Modelling (BIM), is increasingly being used to enhance the accuracy and efficiency of inspections. Third-party inspectors play an unbiased role in ensuring the quality and compliance of construction projects. They also ensure that internal quality control processes are being correctly implemented. Table 6.2 gives some essential construction elements and their corresponding inspection items.

Table 6.2: Construction element with its inspection items

Sl. No.	Category	Inspection items
1	Concrete	Inspection of mix design, batching, pouring, curing, and formwork
2	Masonry	Quality assessment of bricks, blocks, and mortar Alignment, levelling, and joint consistency
3	Metals	Verification of structural steel, welding, and corrosion protection
4	Wood and plastic composites	Inspection for defects and compliance with structural design requirements
5	Thermal and moisture protection	Waterproofing and insulation checks
6	Openings	Inspection of doors, windows, and glazing Operation tests and safety checks
7	Finishes	Inspection of painting, coating, and flooring Surface preparation and final appearance
8	Fire suppression	Inspection of sprinkler systems and fireproofing materials Verification of system design and installation
9	HVAC	Inspection of heating, ventilation, and air conditioning systems Performance testing and energy efficiency
10	Electrical	Inspection of wiring, circuit breakers, and fixtures Safety checks and functionality tests
11	Electronic safety and security	Inspection of alarms, surveillance, and access control systems Verification of system integration and functionality
12	Utilities	Inspection of water, gas, sewer, and electrical utilities installations Verification of connections and functionality Compliance with local utility and public work standards

6.13.2 Benefits of Inspection

Inspection is the master key for quality construction. The benefits of quality inspection include but are not limited to the following:

i. *Enhanced quality:* Quality inspections ensure that construction meets predefined standards, resulting in higher quality outcomes. That also prevents structural failures and accidents, leading to long-term durability and reduced maintenance costs.
ii. *Compliance assurance:* Inspections verify that products adhere to regulatory requirements and industry standards, reducing the risk of non-compliance issues. Also, compliance with quality standards through inspections can provide legal protection against liability claims and lawsuits.
iii. *Cost reduction:* By identifying defects early in the construction process, inspections help prevent costly rework and enhance efficiency, long-term durability and reduced maintenance costs.
iv. *Client satisfaction:* Consistently constructing high-quality projects improves client satisfaction and fosters long-term harmonious relationships.
v. Process improvement: Insights gained from inspections can inform process improvements, increasing efficiency and productivity.
vi. *Risk mitigation:* Inspections help identify potential risks and hazards, allowing for timely corrective actions to mitigate the risks.
vii. *Brand protection:* Maintaining quality standards through inspections protects the reputation and integrity of the brand of a company/ project in the market.
viii. *Continuous improvement culture:* Quality inspections promote a culture of continuous improvement by encouraging feedback and corrective actions to drive ongoing quality enhancement efforts.

6.14 USE OF MANUALS AND CHECKLISTS IN QUALITY CONTROL

Let us look at some of them in detail to understand better the tools, how they work, and their implications. Manual and checklists are some of the oldest, simplest, and most effective tools. The use of these dramatically enhances quality control in construction. These tools help standardise processes, ensure compliance with regulations and standards, and maintain consistent project quality. This Section dives deep into how manuals and checklists are utilised in the construction industry for quality control.

6.14.1 Quality Control Manuals

In the construction industry, Quality Control Manuals are vital documents that encapsulate the specific quality practices, guidelines, and standards to be adhered to during a construction project. These manuals are the bedrock for ensuring that every aspect of the project, from the initial ground-breaking to the final touches, aligns with the agreed-upon quality criteria and regulatory requirements. Quality control manuals in the construction industry typically encompass a comprehensive range of topics to address all quality aspects. These manuals include the following key points, among others:

i. *Quality objectives:* Clear articulation of the quality goals for the project.

ii. *Regulatory compliance:* Guidelines to adhere to local, state, and federal building codes and regulations related to the project.

iii. *Material procurement:* Procedures for sourcing, receiving, and storing materials to ensure they meet quality standards and set quality goals.

iv. *Workmanship standards:* Specify the criteria and benchmarks for the skills and techniques required by the workers.

v. *Inspection and testing procedures:* Detailed processes for ongoing inspections and testing at various stages of construction.

vi. *Documentation:* Requirements for record-keeping, including reports, inspection logs, test results and other relevant information.

vii. *Non-conformance management:* Steps to handle deviations from the quality plan, including corrective actions and preventative measures.

viii. *Quality assurance roles and responsibilities:* Definitions of team members' roles in maintaining quality, including training requirements.

ix. *Communication protocols:* Systems for internal and external communications regarding quality issues.

x. *Continuous improvement:* Mechanisms for feedback and processes for ongoing quality improvement.

xi. *Safety risk management:* Protocols to ensure the safety of workers in compliance with OSHA standards and other safety regulations. Further, identification, assessment, and management of potential risks affecting quality.

xii. *Environmental management:* Considerations for environmental impacts and sustainability practices in construction processes.

xiii. *Subcontractor and supplier management:* Guidelines for managing the quality of all subcontracted work and supplied materials and products.

xiv. *Quality audits:* Schedule and procedures for internal and external quality audits and inspections.

xv. *Customer satisfaction:* Processes to ensure the end product meets or exceeds client expectations, including handling customer feedback.

As we understand, manuals serve as tools for quality control, and the points above act as a roadmap for establishing a robust quality control system. They provide a structured approach to achieving high-quality outcomes in construction projects. The manual is a living document, subject to updates and improvements as projects evolve and new insights are gained. By exploring real-world applications and examples, students can better understand how quality control manuals are translated into day-to-day operations, ensuring that the construction industry can deliver safe, durable projects and meet the client's specifications and the highest industry standards.

6.14.2 Construction Checklists

A construction quality control checklist is a powerful tool to ensure that every aspect of a construction project adheres to predefined standards. Utilising different checklists throughout construction phases helps maintain quality assurance and manage the details that can affect the outcome. Construction projects have several activities, and to maintain quality standards, we need to check each step and activity. The important checklist is as follows to be account during construction:

i. *Pre-construction checklist:* This checklist is used before construction begins. It includes verifying permits, reviewing plans and specifications, and confirming the availability of materials and resources. For example, the checklist can contain broadly approved project scope and specifications, review and verify design drawings, obtain and verify all necessary permits and insurance, and pre-site safety assessment.

ii. *Site work checklist:* Focuses on the initial stages of construction, ensuring site clearance, grading, and excavation are conducted according to specifications. This checklist will be a tick to start the work in a well-managed site.

iii. *Concrete work checklist:* This checklist ensures that all steps related to concrete work, from mixing to curing, comply with quality standards. A few of the elements are – verifying the mix design complies with specifications, inspecting formwork for accuracy and stability, confirming steel reinforcement placement, checking concrete placement and finishing, and confirming the curing process and duration.

iv. *Masonry checklist:* Validates the quality of materials, mortar mixing, and the alignment and placement of bricks or blocks.

v. *Steel structure checklist:* Used for construction projects to ensure the correct handling, fabrication, and erection of steel components.

vi. *Finishing work checklist:* Encompasses inspections for painting, tiling, carpentry, and fixtures installation, ensuring finishes meet design requirements. Some elements are – inspecting surface preparation for painting, confirming paint type and colour against specifications, checking the quality of tile work, grout, and sealing, and verifying the installation of fixtures and hardware.

vii. *Safety compliance checklist:* Ensuring all safety protocols are followed and the site adheres to regulations is essential.

viii. *Post-construction checklist:* Includes final inspections, review, and preparation for handover to the client by ensuring that all project aspects meet the required quality standards.

Checklists are utilised at specific intervals and project milestones to verify that work has been completed correctly and to the required standards. They serve as a reference for inspections, ensuring consistency in quality control efforts. They promote accountability among workers and subcontractors and provide a paper trail that can be audited anytime. Each checklist acts as a step-by-step guide to ensure every detail is noticed, from the groundwork to the final touches that culminate in project delivery.

6.15 BASICS OF STATISTICAL QUALITY CONTROL

Now that we understand the practical aspects of quality control, introducing statistical methods will add depth, showing how quality is measured and maintained quantitatively. Statistical Quality Control (SQC) comprises various quality control tools that ensure construction quality. It involves using statistical methods to monitor and control the quality of materials and workmanship. It uses statistical techniques to analyse and improve processes, detect defects, and ensure that products meet quality standards.

We need SQC because of the variability in construction processes. It is a critical factor that significantly impacts quality control within the industry. The inherent uncertainty in construction arises from many sources: the uniqueness of each project, the fluctuating nature of work environments, and the diverse range of materials and human factors involved. Each project presents its challenges, from site-specific conditions to the bespoke design elements that resist standardisation. Furthermore, the dynamic weather conditions and varying skill levels of the workforce contribute to the inconsistency of outputs. The supply chain also introduces variability, with material properties differing between batches and deliveries. These variability elements necessitate robust, adaptable, responsive quality control systems. To mitigate the risks associated with variability, the construction industry leans on advanced planning, comprehensive process design, and continuous improvement strategies underpinned by empirical studies and theoretical research that inform best practices. Standardisation of procedures where possible, combined with a flexible approach to problem-solving, allows for maintaining quality standards while accommodating the unique aspects of each construction project. SQC helps in understanding and reducing this variability to improve quality.

6.15.1 Histogram

A histogram is a graphical representation of the distribution of a dataset. It helps visualise the data's central tendency, dispersion, and shape. In SQC, histograms are often used to examine the distribution of quality characteristics such as dimensions, weights, or defect counts. A well-centred and symmetric histogram indicates the process is under control, while deviations from the expected distribution may indicate process problems.

6.15.2 Control Charts

Control charts are one of the fundamental tools in SQC. They are graphical tools used to monitor the stability of a process over time. There are different types of control charts, but the most commonly used are the X-bar and R chart. The X-bar chart monitors the central tendency of a process, while the R-chart monitors the process variability. These charts have centre lines representing the process mean and control limits indicating the acceptable variation. Observations within the control limits suggest that the process is in control, while those outside the limits indicate potential issues.

6.15.3 Pareto Chart

It is a bar graph that ranks categories in descending order of frequency or impact. It helps identify the most significant factors contributing to defects or quality issues. In SQC, Pareto charts are often used to prioritise improvement efforts by focusing on the vital few factors that account for the majority of problems.

6.15.4 Scatter Diagram

A scatter diagram is a graphical tool to examine the relationship between two variables. In SQC, scatter diagrams can help identify potential correlations or patterns between process variables and quality characteristics. Understanding these relationships can aid in process optimisation and quality improvement efforts.

6.16 SAFETY, HEALTH, AND ENVIRONMENT ON PROJECT SITES

The construction industry is a vital sector contributing significantly to a nation's economic growth. The construction sector builds skyscrapers and improves infrastructure, boosting the economy and enhancing people's quality of life. However, the Occupational Safety and Health Administration (OSHA) in 2018 deemed the construction industry high-risk for its workers. The occupational injuries and worker accidents rate in construction sites is the highest compared to all other workplaces.

6.16.1 Definition of Accidents

Accidents are unforeseen and unintended occurrences that occur abruptly and can cause harm, injury, or loss. In the construction industry, accidents can refer to incidents resulting in property damage or personal injury.

6.16.2 Causes of Accidents

The construction site is full of hazardous conditions and prone to accidents. There are numerous causes of accidents, some of which are stated below:

i. *Monetary incentives:* Some companies pressure workers to meet milestones and avoid fines. This leads to working long hours or cutting corners on safety, increasing the risk of accidents of workers.
ii. *Faulty equipment:* The workers are put in danger by using faulty equipment that has not been adequately maintained. To save money, the companies avoid repairing or replacing the equipment, which leads to severe accidents and injuries.
iii. *Repetitive motion:* Repeated movements performed by workers over a prolonged period can lead to muscular fatigue. Tasks that are repetitive and require high vigilance but low neuromuscular work can induce a sense of effort and fatigue. Furthermore, cognitive factors and mental stress can contribute to the development of muscular fatigue.
iv. *Poor site conditions:* If the project environment lacks proper lighting control, it increases the risk of accidents and injuries.
v. *Contract anomalies:* The risk of accidents and injuries increases if a contract lacks clear safety conditions and operation procedures.

vi. *Lack of expertise, knowledge, and training:* Unskilled labourers who lack knowledge and training on personal protective equipment and safe working procedures are more susceptible to accidents and injuries on construction sites.

vii. *Irregular investigation:* Improper auditing system by the management drives the contractor to spend less on safety-related equipment and violates various safety-related laws.

viii. *Acts of God:* Various acts that can cause casualties on sites are rain, flooding, wind, earthquake, landslides, etc. For example, under heavy rain, scaffold workers can lose their balance and step or slide off the plank, resulting in a fall.

ix. *Inadequate coordination and communication:* Ineffective coordination and communication result in conflict, increased stress at work, and time and cost overrun.

x. *Demolition:* Explosives are frequently used in construction site demolitions, which puts workers in immediate danger if proper safety is not considered.

xi. *Fires and explosions:* Numerous conditions on the construction site, like Chemical and gas leaks, equipment malfunctions, electrical issues, and improper handling of flammable materials, can result in fires and explosive accidents.

6.16.3 Effects of Accidents

One accident can stop the whole site for several days. The effects of an accident are not just confined to workers, but clients, contractors, the government, and all the other stakeholders suffering. The following are the expected effects of an accident in the construction sector:

i. *Time loss of project execution:* In case of an accident of a worker on site, a detailed accident investigation leads to project delay.

ii. *The firm's reputation:* The frequent reports of mishaps on the site damage the company's reputation, eventually lowering sales for that company.

iii. *Psychology of co-workers:* The workers' morale and confidence are lower due to accidents involving co-workers onsite.

iv. *Emotional burden:* Dependency on the worker's wages owing to an accident may cause emotional strain on the household's independence and negatively affect the family's social relationships.

v. *Future cost:* The cost of recruiting a new worker and the additional cost of training him increase the overall expenses of the project.

vi. *Undue legal overheads:* The management is legally responsible for paying the workers' compensation insurance due to an onsite accident. In case of dissatisfaction with the remuneration amount, the worker may go to court, ultimately resulting in higher legal expenses due to the cost of legal representation and protracted court cases.

vii. *Worker's layover:* The frequent injuries at construction sites drive workers away from seeking employment at other construction sites.

viii. *Loss of profits:* The project's total profit is lost due to rising worker medical costs following an accident, replacing or repairing damaged equipment during the incident, and higher supervision costs (to prevent mishaps in the future).

6.16.4 Preventive Measures

As we have learned about the consequences of an accident, it is essential to prevent them on construction sites. The following are the measures used on construction sites to avoid accidents:

i. *Safety training:* Regular training to workers regarding safety awareness at construction sites can help to reduce injuries and fatalities on the construction site.

ii. *Safety gear:* An in-depth knowledge of personal protective equipment (PPE) lowers exposure to risks that result in significant illnesses and injuries on construction sites.

iii. *Safety inspection:* Onsite injuries can be avoided with a comprehensive safety check by the safety auditors. The auditor assesses the safety policies and practices and suggests further improvement.

iv. *Adoption of new technologies:* Modern technologies, such as virtual reality (VR), building information modelling (BIM), and others, might lessen the possibility of any accident or fatality occurring at the site as these technologies are efficient and successful in identifying locations prone to accidents.

v. *Regular meetings:* It is possible to reduce the number of accidents and fatalities on construction sites by deploying the toolbox meeting with workers and interacting with them regularly about their concerns about safety onsite.

6.16.5 Costs of Accidents

It is essential to evaluate the cost of accidents to allocate the safety budget of the construction project. The cost of accidents is a crucial tool for assessing the monetary value of safety investments in a project. Heinrich (1931) studied the cost of accidents and analysed its direct and indirect costs. He termed direct cost as the money the insurance company refunds and vice-versa. By developing the iceberg metaphor, he further differentiated between the two costs – direct and indirect costs. The part of the iceberg above sea level defines the visible or direct cost, while the lower part outlines the hidden or indirect cost. As the lower portion of the iceberg is not visible and difficult to estimate, so is the indirect cost of the cost of accidents. The visual or direct cost includes medical expenses, indemnity, legal overheads, insurance premiums, and workers' compensation payout. On the other hand, the hidden or indirect cost consists of hiring and training a new worker, costs due to project delays, expenditures on emergency supplies, costs of repairing the tools and equipment, legal expenses, etc. The visible/ hidden and direct/ indirect costs charts are shown in Fig 6.2 and 6.3.

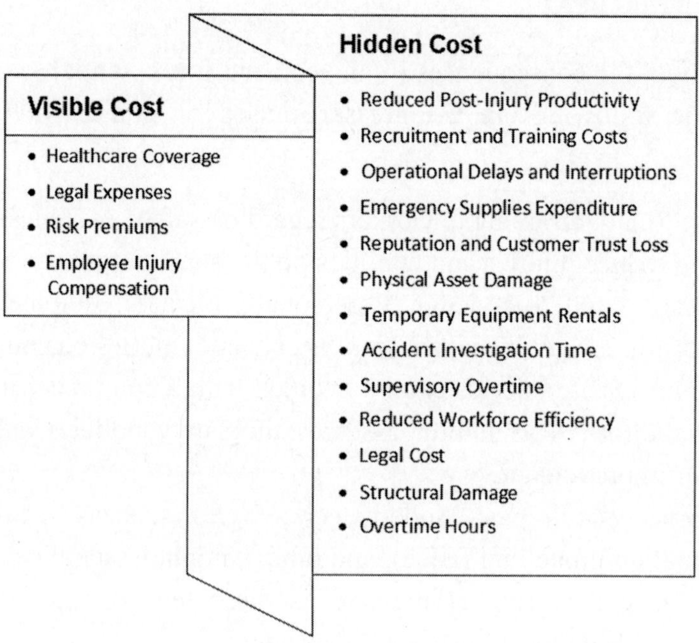

Fig. 6.2: Visible and hidden accident costs

6.17 OCCUPATIONAL HEALTH PROBLEMS IN CONSTRUCTION

Occupational health problems in construction are a significant concern due to the nature of the work involved, which often exposes workers to various hazards. Here's a theoretical overview of some common occupational health problems in construction:

i. *Heat stress:* The workers are exposed to heat for prolonged hours as they work on construction sites open to the atmosphere. Heat stress includes heat stroke, exhaustion, fainting, cramps, and rash.

ii. *Eye strain:* Workers are susceptible to vision issues due to inadequate night-time lighting and dust on construction sites.
iii. *Lung irritation:* Construction workers are exposed to airborne pollutants like dust, fumes, and asbestos, exposure to which increases workers' risk of respiratory issues during tasks on site.
iv. *Skin diseases:* Construction workers handle cement, which has constituents that produce irritant contact dermatitis and corrosive effects (from alkaline ingredients, such as lime), leading to allergic contact dermatitis (from ingredients, such as chromium).
v. *Hearing disorder:* The noise from jackhammers, chipping hammers, or similar machines used in construction can cause permanent occupational hearing loss due to their constant high-decibel sounds.

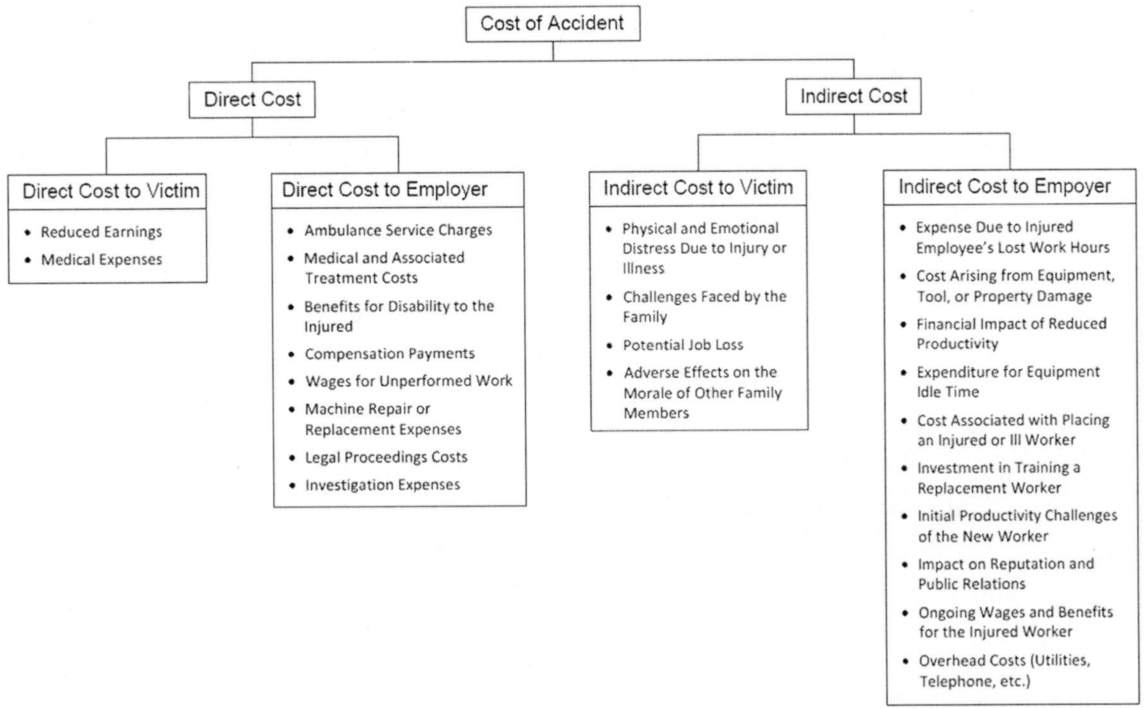

Fig. 6.3: Direct and indirect accident costs

Addressing these concerns requires a comprehensive approach that involves implementing safety regulations and protocols and fostering a culture of safety awareness among construction workers and employers. Regular training, hazard assessments, and continuous improvement in safety practices are essential elements of promoting occupational health in the construction industry.

6.18 ORGANISING FOR SAFETY AND HEALTH

Organising safety and health in any workplace, including construction sites, is paramount to ensure the well-being of workers and the success of projects. Here's how organisations can effectively organise for safety and health:

i. *Establish a safety culture:* Cultivate a culture where safety and health are prioritised at all levels of the organisation. This includes promoting open communication, encouraging reporting of hazards and near-misses, and recognising and rewarding safe behaviours.
ii. *Designate responsibilities:* Clearly define roles and responsibilities for safety and health within the organisation. Assign dedicated personnel, such as safety officers or committees, to oversee safety programs, conduct inspections, and provide training.
iii. *Develop safety policies and procedures:* Develop comprehensive safety policies and procedures tailored to construction activities' specific hazards and risks. Ensure these policies are communicated effectively to all employees and subcontractors and regularly reviewed and updated as needed.
iv. *Provide training and education:* Offer regular safety training and education programs to all workers, including new hires and subcontractors, covering topics such as hazard recognition, personal protective equipment (PPE) use, emergency procedures, and safe work practices.
v. *Implement hazard identification and risk assessment:* Conduct thorough hazard identification and risk assessments for all construction activities and environments. Regularly monitor and evaluate workplace conditions and processes to identify emerging risks and implement appropriate control measures.
vi. *Enforce safety standards:* Enforce compliance with safety standards, regulations, and best practices through consistent monitoring, audits, and inspections. Implement disciplinary measures when necessary to address non-compliance and reinforce the importance of safety.
vii. *Provide resources and support:* Allocate sufficient resources, including funding, time, and equipment, to support safety and health initiatives. Provide access to necessary safety equipment, tools, and resources to enable workers to perform their tasks safely.

viii. *Promote worker involvement and participation:* Encourage active involvement and participation of workers in safety and health initiatives. Solicit input from employees on safety concerns, involve them in safety committees or meetings, and empower them to take ownership of safety in their work areas.

ix. *Establish emergency preparedness plans:* Develop and regularly review emergency preparedness plans, including procedures for responding to accidents, injuries, and other emergencies. Conduct drills and exercises to ensure that all workers are familiar with emergency protocols and know how to respond effectively.

x. *Continuous improvement:* Foster a culture of continuous improvement by regularly evaluating the effectiveness of safety and health programs, soliciting worker feedback, analysing incident data, and implementing corrective actions to prevent recurrence and enhance safety performance.

By organising effectively for safety and health, construction organisations can create safer work environments, reduce the risk of accidents and injuries, and ultimately improve productivity, morale, and overall project success.

SUMMARY

The construction project monitoring and control chapter offers insights into the crucial processes of tracking, evaluating, and regulating project progress to ensure adherence to predefined objectives and timelines. It delves into implementing monitoring systems, such as progress reports, performance metrics, and key performance indicators (KPIs), to gauge project performance against established benchmarks. Emphasising the importance of real-time data collection and analysis, the chapter highlights the significance of identifying deviations from the project plan and promptly implementing corrective measures to mitigate risks and prevent schedule and budget overruns. Moreover, it explores the role of effective communication and stakeholder engagement in facilitating transparency and accountability throughout the construction project lifecycle. By employing robust monitoring and control mechanisms, construction managers can proactively address issues, optimise resource allocation, and foster project success while maintaining quality standards and client satisfaction.

EXERCISE

Safety, health, and environmental considerations are integral to project management. To ensure a safe and healthy work environment, select any construction site:

a) Analyse the causes and effects of accidents on the construction site and propose preventive measures to mitigate the risk of accidents.
b) Discuss the costs associated with construction project accidents, including direct and indirect costs, and explain how these costs impact project budgets and schedules.
c) Outline the organisational measures needed to promote safety, health, and environmental awareness at the construction site and discuss the role of workers, supervisors, and management in implementing and enforcing safety regulations.

MULTIPLE CHOICE QUESTIONS

1. What is the primary purpose of supervision in construction project management?

   A) To ensure compliance with safety regulations
   B) To monitor project progress and quality of work
   C) To manage project finances
   D) To coordinate communication between stakeholders

2. Which of the following is NOT a type of record typically kept in construction project management?

   A) Daily progress reports
   B) Meeting minutes
   C) Employee performance evaluations
   D) Equipment maintenance logs

3. What is the purpose of periodic progress reports in construction project management?

   A) To evaluate project team performance
   B) To inform stakeholders about the project status
   C) To schedule upcoming meetings
   D) To track project expenses

4. What is Lean Construction?

   A) A method of reducing waste and maximising value in construction projects
   B) A type of building material

C) A safety protocol for construction sites
D) A construction equipment brand

5. What is the primary purpose of inspection in quality control?

A) To monitor project progress
B) To identify and correct defects
C) To schedule meetings
D) To allocate resources

6. What is the aim of statistical quality control in construction?

A) To improve communication among project teams
B) To reduce the occurrence of accidents
C) To monitor project finances
D) To identify and analyse variations in construction processes

7. What are the costs associated with accidents on construction sites?

A) Direct costs only
B) Indirect costs only
C) Both direct and indirect costs
D) No costs

ANSWERS TO MULTIPLE CHOICE QUESTIONS

1	2	3	4	5	6	7
B	C	B	A	B	D	C

SHORT ANSWER TYPE QUESTIONS

1. What are the key elements of a construction project monitoring plan?
2. How do you identify and prioritise project risks in construction projects?
3. What standard tools and techniques are used to monitor progress on construction projects?

4. What metrics or key performance indicators (KPIs) are typically used to measure project performance during monitoring and control phases?
5. Can you describe the process of reporting progress and issues in construction projects?
6. What role does personal protective equipment (PPE) play in construction project safety, and how do you ensure its proper usage?
7. How do you implement and enforce safety regulations and standards on a construction site?
8. What are some best practices for managing subcontractors' safety performance on a construction project?
9. What role does technology, such as drones or wearable sensors, play in enhancing construction project safety?
10. How do you measure and evaluate the effectiveness of safety initiatives and programs on a construction site?

LONG ANSWER TYPE QUESTIONS

1. How do you ensure compliance with regulatory requirements and safety standards during project construction?
2. Can you explain the role of technology, such as Building Information Modeling (BIM) or project management software, in construction project monitoring and control?
3. How do you conduct a comprehensive safety assessment before starting a construction project?
4. A construction company is monitoring the thickness of asphalt pavement using control charts. Over the past ten days, they have collected the following data on pavement thickness (in inches):

Day	1	2	3	4	5	6	7	8	9	10
Thickness	4.1	4.2	4.6	4.3	4.1	4.1	4.9	4.8	4.3	4.2

Construct an X-bar chart and R-chart for this data. Calculate the control limits assuming 3-sigma limits.

5. A construction company is measuring the compressive strength of concrete samples. They took ten samples and found the following strengths (in MPa): 26.5, 28.2, 27.8, 30.4, 28.9, 29.5, 29.9, 28.3, 30.7, 26.7. Calculate the mean and standard deviation of the compressive strength.
6. The tensile strength of a construction material is normally distributed with a mean of 62 MPa and a standard deviation of 4 MPa. What is the probability that a randomly selected sample of this material will have a tensile strength greater than 64 MPa?
7. In a construction project, the number of defects found in 20 building blocks was recorded as follows: 2, 2, 5, 8, 2, 1, 4, 2, 3, 2, 0, 1, 2, 3, 1, 0, 3, 2, 3, 2. Calculate the mean, median, mode, and range of defects per building block.
8. Can you discuss the legal and financial implications of failing to prioritise safety on a construction project?
9. Explain the difference between Quality Control and Quality Assurance. Give examples to justify your answer.
10. What do you mean by cost of quality? How budget related to quality is computed on a construction site?

TUTORIAL

Write a 500-word note on the advantages of the Lean Construction method over the conventional project management system. In addition, write a 500-word note on the Safety and Health precautions you would take for a typical 3-storeyed building with a 400 sq. m plinth area.

KNOW MORE

(1) For more information related to this topic scan the QR code.

OR

Type this link in your browser

https://nptel.ac.in/courses/105102206

(2) For more information related to this topic scan the QR code.

OR

Type this link in your browser

https://nptel.ac.in/courses/105104161

(3) For more information related to this topic scan the QR code.

OR

Type this link in your browser

https://nptel.ac.in/courses/105106213

BIBLIOGRAPHY

- Baker, W., Korista, S., and Novak, L. C. (2015). The design and construction of the world's tallest building: The Burj Dubai. *Structural Engineering International*. 25(4), 389-394.

- Ballard, G., and Howell, G. (2003). An update on last planner. In Proc., *11th Annual Conf., International Group for Lean Construction*, Blacksburg.
- Burati Jr, J. L., Matthews, M. F., and Kalidindi, S. N. (1991). Quality management in construction industry. *Journal of construction Engineering and Management*, 117(2), 341-359.
- Chitkara, K. K. (2019). *Construction Project Management.* Tata McGraw-Hill Education: New Delhi.
- Crosby, P. B. (1979). Quality is free: The art of making quality sure. McGraw-Hill: New York.
- Hill, R. C., and Bowen, P. A. (1997). Sustainable construction: Principles and a framework for attainment. *Construction Management and Economics*, 15(3), 223-239.
- Hoonakker, P., Carayon, P., and Loushine, T. (2010). Barriers and benefits of quality management in construction: Empirical study. *Journal of Construction Engineering and Management*, 136(8), 932-941.
- ISO. (2015). ISO 9001:2015 Quality management systems: Requirements. *International Organization for Standardization*: Geneva.
- ISO. (2017). ISO 9000 Quality management. *International Organization for Standardization*, Geneva.
- Jaafar, M. H., Arifin, K., Aiyub, K., Razman, M. R., Ishak, M. I. S., and Samsurijan, M. S. (2018). Occupational safety and health management in the construction industry: a review. *International Journal of Occupational Safety and Ergonomics*, 24(4), 493-506.
- Latiffi, A. A., Mohd, S., Kasim, N., and Fathi, M. S. (2013). Building information modeling (BIM) application in Malaysian construction industry. *International Journal of Construction Engineering and Management*, 2(4A), 1-6.
- Love, P.E.D., Smith, J., Simpson, I., Regan, M., and Olatunji, O.A. (2015). Understanding the landscape of overruns in transport infrastructure projects. *Environment and Planning B: Planning and Design*, 42(3), 490-509.
- Lu, Y., Wu, Z., Chang, R., and Li, Y. (2017). Building Information Modeling (BIM) for green buildings: A critical review and future directions. *Automation in Construction*, 83(1), 134-148.
- Nycyk, M. (2008). Records management practices in construction industries: Australian perspectives. *Records Management Journal*, 18(2), 140-149.
- Sarhan, J. G., Xia, B., Fawzia, S., and Karim, A. (2017). Lean construction implementation in the Saudi Arabian construction industry. *Construction Economics and Building*, 17(1), 46-69.

- Smith, B. S. (2005). Structural design of Taipei 101, the world's tallest building. *CTBUH Journal*, 2005(3), 12-25.
- Sreedharan, E. (2014). Project management lessons learned from the Delhi Metro Project. *Indian Infrastructure*, 6(4), 44-48.

7 CONTRACTS MANAGEMENT BASICS

UNIT SPECIFICS

In the complex world of business relationships, contracts serve as the cornerstone of agreements, outlining the terms and conditions that govern transactions between parties. Effective contract management ensures these agreements are understood, executed, and monitored throughout their project lifecycle. In this unit, you will learn about contract management basics, the importance of contracts, the type of construction contracts, and standard contract clauses.

RATIONALE

Claims and disputes are common in construction projects which needs to be settled quickly for timely completion of the projects.

PRE-REQUISITE

Nil

UNIT OUTCOMES

List of outcomes of this unit is as follows:

U7-O1: Use of contract in construction

U7-O2: Understands common contract clauses

U7-O3: Dispute resolution method

Unit Outcomes	Expected Mapping with Course Outcomes *(1- Weak Correlation; 2- Medium correlation; 3- Strong Correlation)*					
	CO-1	CO-2	CO-3	CO-4	CO-5	CO-6
U7-O1	3	2	1	2	1	3
U7-O2	2	1	1	3	1	3
U7-O3	2	1	1	3	1	3

7.1 CONTRACT MANAGEMENT

A contract is a legally binding agreement between two or more parties (or stakeholders) that creates certain obligations. All parties must intend to be legally bound by the contract terms. Once a contract is formed, all parties are legally bound by its terms and conditions. This means all parties must perform their obligations/ duties under the contract or face legal consequences if they cannot complete the written obligations/ duties. Therefore, it becomes essential for contract managers to draft an unambiguous contract that can lay down the obligations/ duties so that all the bound parties must know their responsibilities and the consequences if not perform according to the requirements. Such contracts are drafted by contract managers who are specialised in the field of contract management.

It is the process of systematically and efficiently managing contract creation, execution, and analysis to maximise operational and financial performance and minimise risk. It involves various stages, from initial contract drafting to ongoing monitoring and, eventually, contract closure.

7.2 IMPORTANT ELEMENTS OF A CONTRACT

A contract must have some essential components covered in the following parts to be legally enforceable. Any one of the components missing can make a contract null and void.

7.2.1 Agreement

Mutual understanding and consent regarding the parameters of the agreement are necessary for the existence of a contract. The contract's language should clarify what is meant to be understood from the outset. Generally, a document bearing the signatures of both parties (or stakeholders) signifies an agreement. However, in other cases, if there is enough proof to demonstrate that there was no actual agreement, the contract may be void.

7.2.2 Unlawful Subject Matter

A contractual agreement can be rendered illegal or unenforceable if the content within it violates (i) legal principles, (ii) state statutes, or (iii) established norms of public policy. Contracts featuring (i) criminal activities, (ii) fraudulent representations, (iii) collusive arrangements, (iv) speculative elements, or (v) gambling-related terms serve as illustrations of unlawful subject matter.

Subject matter contrary to public policy is elusive and challenging to delineate, except in instances where it contradicts the well-being and interests of society or obstructs justice. Contracts that impede competition or involve collusion in bidding to establish a monopoly are considered contracts contrary to public policy. In the event of unknowingly entering into an illegal contract, it does not constitute a basis for seeking redress in the event of loss or damage. Contracting parties are presumed to possess awareness of all legal ramifications before entering into the contractual agreement.

7.2.3 Valid Consideration

In contracts and legal agreements, "valid consideration" refers to the value exchanged between parties. Valid consideration (referred to as 'consideration' in upcoming text) is crucial for a contract to be legally binding.

In legal terms, consideration refers to one party's action in exchange for the other party's action or promise. Contract legal requirements are met when the consideration is genuine, valid, and valuable. The law's role is to ensure the contract's foundation is based on proper consideration without assessing its fairness or sufficiency. Courts don't aim to renegotiate the terms for either party; instead, they seek to understand the actual agreement based on the evidence presented. The only exception to this rule is in matters of established debts or liquidated damages. An existing debt cannot be settled for a lesser amount, even if an agreement was made to that effect, unless there is additional consideration, like an earlier payment date. Promises that are impossible, unilateral, gratuitous, or affected by acts of God are not enforceable under contract law due to the absence of genuine consideration. Consideration can be explicitly stated in a contract, such as an explicit promise to pay a specific amount or perform a particular action, or it may be implied, making it challenging to prove its value.

7.2.4 Competent Parties

State law about the competency of parties to a contract varies. Generally, a person acting in good faith can enter into a legally binding contract if s/he is not a minor, insane, or intoxicated while signing the agreement. A minor may affirm and make a previously made contract binding after attaining the age of 21 years. If a minor gains possession of goods through an illegal contract, s/he is not entitled to keep them. In certain states, a contract with an insane person or one made while inebriated is permissible if the parties were acting with knowledge and intent.

The issue of contractual competency holds significance for engineers involved in establishing corporations. A corporation, being a legal entity, possesses only the powers explicitly granted by the law, and its ability to enter into contracts is circumscribed. For instance, a corporation might engage in a construction contract for a tourist-oriented pleasure resort. Statutes or bylaws strictly define the procedures governing a corporation's contracting activities, and non-compliance with these regulations may render a contract null and void.

If a contract between a company and an incompetent party falls apart, the party may seek payment for their partial services, provided the company has utilised them. However, pursuing this course of action can be both expensive and time-consuming. Nonetheless, it's important to note that there is the slightest possibility of recovering any damages in the case of a void contract with a company.

Competency in contracting is essential to engineers in connection with government agencies. Contracts with Municipal, State and Central Government agencies must be made within the authority of the contracting officers of those agencies.

7.2.5 Provision of the Law

Certain agreements necessitate written documentation and must be "signed by the party to be charged" for legal enforcement. The contracts must be drafted with the following necessary understanding:

i. A contractual agreement about the sale of land, any interest in land, or a lease extending beyond one year.
ii. Commit to using their funds to settle a lawsuit.
iii. A commitment to respond to another person's debt, default or lapse.
iv. Any agreement which is not to be implemented within one year of making it (for example, outlet structure at the end of a commercial building), and
v. A contract for the sale of surplus material or equipment valued at more than a specific amount in rupees, unless the buyer agrees to accept, pay, or offer partial payment.

In adhering to sound business practices, contracts should be documented in written form and duly executed by the involved parties to establish a record, particularly in anticipation of potential disputes. This practice holds particular relevance in construction contracts, given the inherent complexity of the services involved and the multitude of commitments and conditions inherent in such agreements. The written document should explicitly outline the services' scope, with the parties' signatures affirming their acknowledgement and acceptance. Other significant conditions may be incorporated directly within the agreement or delineated in separate accompanying documents.

The signatures to the contract should be the exact names or legal titles of the parties and should be used with the addresses of their places of business. In the case of a partnership, the name of the firm and each partner should be mentioned in the agreement. The signatures of the firm name by one of the partners will be binding on each of the partners, but additional emphasis is given if each of the partners signs the contract.

If a corporation is a party to a contract, the corporate name must be succeeded by the signature of the individual duly authorised to bind the corporation in contractual obligations. This signature necessitates attestation by the designated officer, typically the corporate secretary, affirming that the contracting party possesses the requisite authority to execute the contract. When engaging in contractual arrangements with a corporation, verifying the corporation's legal capacity to enter into the contract and adhering to proper legal procedures in undertaking such contractual actions is imperative.

The signature ought to be accompanied by the inclusion of stamps and seals from the signatory parties. These stamps and seals can take the form of rubber-stamped impressions, embossed on the impressions, or adhesive seals affixed to the document.

7.3 IMPORTANCE OF CONTRACTS

Contracts are essential because they formalise agreements between parties and set out obligations. They play a crucial role in revenue generation by outlining payment conditions, and they improve operational efficiency by clearly stating roles and timelines. Moreover, contracts ensure compliance with relevant regulations and facilitate good relationships through clear communication and collaboration. Some features of contracts are as follows:

i. The contract serves as legal written documents and commitments for both parties
ii. Contract prevents conflicts and mitigates risk
iii. Contract helps to maintain compliance with work
iv. Contract also serves as a communication and collaboration tool between the parties
v. contracts help to increase or generate revenues
vi. It increases operational efficiency
vii. It solidifies the organisation's image

7.4 TYPES OF CONSTRUCTION CONTRACTS

Contracts are legal agreements that define the terms and conditions under which parties agree to perform certain actions or provide specific goods and services. Various types of contracts are tailored to meet the diverse needs of different projects. Typically, the contract can be classified as a competitive or negotiated bid, as explained in the upcoming subsections.

7.4.1 Competitive Bid Contract

A competitive bid contract is a procurement method an organisation uses to obtain goods, services, or construction projects from external suppliers or contractors. A competitive bid contract is awarded to the bidder who has quoted the least amount to perform the desired job. In construction projects where the state authorities are involved as clients, the lowest bidder, the L1 (1st lowest) bidder, gets the job to perform. However, in construction projects where the client is a private company, the contract may be awarded to a party other than the L1 bidder, considering the contractor's experience, reputation, and other factors. The competitive bidding process aims to secure the best value for the organisation by encouraging competition among potential vendors. Competitive bid contracts are commonly used in public procurement, construction projects, and various industries where organisations seek to balance cost-effectiveness with the need for high-quality goods or services. This process encourages competition, transparency, and fairness in selecting vendors or contractors. Typically, competitive bid contracts can be of three types: lump sum contracts, unit price or item rate contracts, and combined lump sum and unit price contracts. A description of each of the contracts will be given in the upcoming subsections.

Lump Sum Contract

A lump sum contract requires the contractor to provide necessary goods and services in exchange for a lump sum payment. This ensures that the completed product meets the required specifications. Once the contract is in force, the lump sum price is fixed regardless of costs incurred by the contractor during the execution of the project. Therefore, the contractor must include contingencies for estimating design flaws and unknown expenditures, the quantity of which is undetermined.

A lump sum contract is preferred when the type of construction work is more or less uniform, and it is impractical to divide the work into various parts due to the amount of operations required to finish the task. A lump sum contract requires extensive plans and specifications that cover complete details and task needs. The owner has a tremendous advantage in such a contract because the tender shows them exactly how much the job will cost. Aside from that, s/he does not need to hire people to track precisely what work has been completed and what materials are given each month.

The lump sum contract approach may be employed in situations where:

i. The quantities of various items can be determined during the tendering phase. In simpler terms, the design and specifications should be fully developed and finalised.
ii. Contractors are willing to bid competitively for projects that entail a proprietary process (such as in a petrochemical plant or bridge) or specialised equipment (such as equipment used in marine construction projects).

The lump sum contract offers several advantages in the realm of construction projects. Firstly, it empowers the client to clearly define the scope of work and create detailed drawings and specifications well before initiating the bidding process. This foresight enables the client to formulate an internal fair price estimate for bid comparison, providing a prior understanding of the budgetary commitment. Furthermore, the lump sum contract fosters an environment of intense competition among bidders, encouraging competitive pricing. For the contractor, this contract type serves as a motivation to adhere to both the specified schedule and budgetary constraints. Notably, the contractor assumes full responsibility for the entire project, leading to a streamlined assessment of bids. Overall, the lump sum contract proves advantageous in promoting clarity, competition, and accountability within the construction process.

The lump sum contract, while having its advantages, also comes with notable disadvantages. Firstly, a significant duration may transpire between the decision to initiate requests for quotations from bidders and the final awarding of the contract, potentially causing delays. Contractors securing projects through low bids may be inclined to recover initial losses by submitting excessive variation proposal orders and claims, impacting the overall project cost. The lump sum contract also often necessitates comprehensive design engineering, making the process more intricate. A lack of adaptability within the contract structure can result in expensive modifications to accommodate unforeseen changes. This rigidity makes the contract vulnerable to attempts at making claims, affecting both time and cost. Including provisions for risk and escalation contingencies, while necessary, can also add complexity to the contract. Lastly, the emphasis on achieving a low bid price may inadvertently lead to suboptimal work outcomes, as contractors may compromise on quality to secure the project.

Unit Price or Item Rate Contracts

In a unit rate contract, the contractor gets paid for the work based on the finished quantities of predetermined work items and supplies provided and used by the contractor; the contractor's bid price for each amount is multiplied. In a unit price or item rate contract, the projected quantities are multiplied by the corresponding unit prices specified in the bidder's proposal.

The bid with the overall lowest cost determines the successful bidder. Payments to the contractor are then made based on the quantities of explicitly specified work items mentioned.

An advantageous aspect of opting for a unit rate–type contract is the potential for an expedited commencement of work, attributed to a shorter bidding cycle, and the flexibility of not requiring finalised engineering details at the contract initiation. However, the drawback lies in the involvement of both the client and contractor in the process, necessitating substantial time for updating, pricing, and frequently reassessing and agreeing upon the quantities of work involved.

A drawback for the contractor arises from the uncertainty associated with determining the total cost of the work until the project reaches completion. Conversely, this approach mitigates potential delays that would otherwise be incurred in generating an extensive set of contract drawings detailing every aspect, a necessity for a lump sum contract.

Combined Lump Sum and Unit Price Contract

When the contractor bids with the lump sum amount for some items and estimates quantities corresponding with unit prices for others, the combination of lump sum and unit price contract is considered. Combining the essential elements of lump sum and unit price bidding in a single contract can often be prudent. This is particularly applicable when the project involves items that can be defined and broken down into units, but the quantities are uncertain. In such cases, a unit price contract is well-suited. Conversely, a lump sum payment approach simplifies matters for all parties involved if the project encompasses special items or structures with a known set of construction types, allowing the contractor to formulate precise estimates and bids. The contractor's bid may include lump sum amounts for specific items while estimating quantities and corresponding unit prices for others. This approach is especially fitting for building construction projects. While unit price terms can accommodate the unpredictable nature of foundation conditions of any building, lump sum bidding is more suitable for the well-planned superstructure of a building. In the case of lump sum plus unit rates, the benefits and drawbacks mirror those of a lump sum contract. However, it is in the client's best interest to include as many unit rate offers as possible in the request for quotation (RFQ). It outlines requirements, specifications, terms, and conditions, inviting suppliers to present pricing and proposals.

7.4.2 Negotiated Contract

Negotiated contracts represent a procurement methodology wherein the delineation of terms, conditions, and pricing within an agreement is achieved through direct deliberations and negotiations between the contracting entities, typically the client and the contractor. Diverging from the competitive bidding paradigm, negotiated contracts forego the public solicitation of bids or proposals, opting for a collaborative approach to achieve a mutually agreeable arrangement. Negotiated contracts find frequent application in sectors where project success relies heavily on collaboration, adaptability, and continuous communication. Although they present benefits regarding flexibility and cultivating relationships, the absence of a competitive bidding process may elicit apprehensions regarding transparency. Consequently, negotiated contracts are meticulously examined to guarantee impartiality and adherence to pertinent regulatory standards. Negotiated bid contracts are typically used in big projects involving new technology and innovations.

Rather than opting for competitive bidding, private owners frequently confer construction contracts upon one or more specifically chosen contractors. The primary rationale for favouring negotiated contracts lies in the adaptability intrinsic to this pricing arrangement, particularly suited for those substantially mirroring previous facilities sponsored by the owner. An owner may prioritise a contractor's expertise and reputable track record, especially if the contractor has demonstrated success in prior collaborations. When adhering to a project completion deadline is imperative, construction may commence before the finalisation of detailed plans and specifications, relying on a trusted contractor. However, this approach necessitates the owner's staff to possess substantial knowledge and competence in assessing contractor proposals and overseeing subsequent performance. The negotiated contracts are further subcategorised into five, explained in the upcoming sections.

Cost plus Percentage of Cost Contract

This is the earliest sort of negotiated contract, with the contractor's profit set at a predefined percentage of the actual cost of the work. Like other negotiated contracts, this type permits the initiation of construction before comprehensive plan development, thereby expediting the completion of urgent projects. Additionally, the owner retains the flexibility to implement desired alterations in plans and specifications as the work progresses. The drawback for the owner lies in the fact that the contractor's remuneration escalates proportionally with the rise in construction costs. Hence, there is a lack of motivation for the contractor to exercise frugality during the construction process. A shrewd contractor might intentionally exaggerate construction costs to secure an amplification in their fee. This can be accomplished through padding payrolls or earning commissions on material purchases. However, it is not advisable for widespread adoption, even though additional work and change orders are managed acceptably.

Cost plus Fixed Fee Contracts with a Profit Sharing Clause

A Cost plus Fixed Fee (CPFF) contract with a profit-sharing clause is a contractual arrangement commonly used in private and government contracting. Let us dissect the fundamental elements:

Cost Plus: Within a cost-plus contract, the contractor receives reimbursement for the allowable costs accrued throughout the contract's execution. These costs encompass direct expenditures, such as labour and materials, and indirect costs, such as overheads and administrative expenses.

Fixed Fee: Apart from reimbursing expenditures, the contractor is remunerated with a predetermined fixed fee established before the project's commencement. This fee covers the contractor's overhead expenses and facilitates a profit margin.

Profit Sharing Clause: A provision for profit-sharing facilitates the distribution of cost savings or underruns between the contractor and the client. In cases where the actual costs incurred by the contractor are lower than the estimated costs utilised for determining the fixed fee, both parties may mutually decide to partake in the realised savings. This contractual arrangement is frequently employed when articulating the precise scope of work at the project's initiation is challenging. In such instances, clients aim to guarantee fair reimbursement for all valid costs incurred by the contractor while concurrently creating an incentive for the contractor to implement effective cost management practices. It is crucial to emphasise that such contracts' precise terms and conditions may exhibit variability, necessitating thorough negotiation and meticulous documentation to secure clarity and equity for both parties. Legal and financial experts are frequently engaged in formulating and reviewing these contracts to safeguard the interests of all involved parties.

Cost Plus Fixed Fee Contract with a Bonus Clause

When the owner prioritises the expeditious completion of the project, a bonus clause within the contract functions as a motivational tool for the contractor to minimise construction duration. This bonus is specified as a predetermined sum, supplementary to the contractor's fees, to be paid for each day the owner gains full access to the completed work before the initially estimated completion date. Conversely, the contract may stipulate a fixed sum as liquidated damages, compensating the owner for each day of delay beyond the initially estimated completion date.

Cost Plus Sliding Scale of Fees Contract

A Cost Plus Sliding Scale of Fees Contract is comparable to a Cost Plus Fixed price (CPFF) contract but has a different price structure. Let's lay down the essential components of a cost plus a sliding scale of fees:

Cost Plus: As in a standard cost-plus contract, the contractor is reimbursed for approved project expenses. This covers direct costs (such as labour and materials) and indirect costs (such as overhead and administrative charges).

Sliding Fee: In place of a predetermined fee, this contract variant incorporates a fee structure that fluctuates by specific performance metrics or project milestones. The fee undergoes alterations during the project's evolution and attainment of distinct stages.

This contractual framework is frequently employed when there arises a necessity to provide incentives for the contractor to achieve or surpass project objectives, adhere to timelines, or meet performance benchmarks. It ensures that the contractor's remuneration is commensurate with the productive and timely fulfilment of the project.

Cost Plus a Guaranteed Ceiling Price Contracts

An argument against using cost-plus contracts lies in the owner's inherent challenge in predicting the anticipated expenditure for the undertaken work. However, this contention is addressed by imposing an upper threshold on the work cost. In this context, the contractor is reimbursed for the expenses incurred during the project, augmented by a fixed fee, provided the cumulative sum falls below the stipulated maximum limit defined in the contractual agreement. Conversely, if the aggregate amount surpasses this predefined maximum limit, the contractor is not entitled to receive compensation exceeding the guaranteed ceiling price. While this contractual approach mitigates certain uncertainties inherent in standard cost-plus arrangements, the plans and specifications governing the project must be meticulously developed to establish a reasonable ceiling price.

7.4.3 Other Types of Contracts

Management Contract

Alternatively recognised as a Construction Management (CM) Contract, a Management Contract constitutes a distinctive contractual paradigm employed within the construction domain. Within the confines of this contractual framework, an owner engages the services of a construction manager tasked with supervising and administering diverse facets of the construction project. Diverging from conventional contracts wherein the general contractor assumes dual responsibilities for both managerial and construction functions, a construction management contract delineates the segregation of these roles.

Management contracts allow owners more direct engagement in construction and better control over subcontractor selection. Legal professionals and construction experts are usually involved in developing and reviewing these contracts to ensure that they suit the specific demands and criteria of the construction project. For example, typically, the construction project requires a third-party quality audit. In such a case, the management contract is signed between the client and the third party to perform the quality audit of the work done by the contractor.

Architect Engineer Management Contract

Originating in the United States during World War II, this contractual approach involves entrusting all planning, design, and management phases to a singular firm comprising architects and engineers. A contractual framework known as an architect-engineer management contract, commonly denoted as an Architect-Engineer (A/E) or Architect-Engineer-Manager (A/E/M) contract, finds application in the construction sector. Within this contractual arrangement, an architect or engineer is engaged to furnish design and management expertise for a given construction project.

Using architect-engineer management contracts proves pivotal in establishing a lucid understanding between the project owner and the designated design professionals. These contracts ensure that the project undergoes development, management, and completion in adherence to the predefined terms and standards. The formulation and scrutiny of such agreements often involve legal professionals specialising in construction and engineering law, aiming to safeguard the interests of all parties involved.

Combined Engineering and Construction Contract

In this type of contract, the owner of the construction project has clear scope of work, and the owner desires to deal with only one party for engineering, design, and construction service. In this, there are two types of contracts: design-built and turnkey contracts.

Design-built contract: This is a contract in which the contractor is responsible for design and construction based on the client's fundamental designs. In other words, design and construction are managed within a single organisational structure, preventing a recurring conflict between the designer and contractor. This makes it easier to apply universal standards. In most circumstances, a cost-plus-fee or lump-sum contract covering design and construction costs may be used. Contracts of this nature are frequently used when a client lacks in-house design and engineering teams, and subcontracting (or outsourcing) the design to a separate firm is deemed improper. In such instances, the contracting agency should be knowledgeable in design and construction. However, different organisations specialising in design and construction can always form a joint venture and bid on such a project with acceptable financial and legal arrangements. Aside from fostering a holistic and complete approach that tends to lower costs, the method also stimulates the development of technical prowess in contractors and minimises the frequency of disagreements and litigation.

Turnkey contract: This contract assigns responsibility for all activities to the contracting agency, allowing the owner to 'turn the key' and take over the facility upon completion. Thus, in such contracts, all operations connected to surveying, specification drawing, design, project planning, building, and test operation are delegated to a single major contracting firm, which may divide the activities and hire additional organisations to do specific tasks. The contract may also involve the facility's operation for a set amount of time. Such agreements have been proven to be especially helpful in projects that require a combination of civil, electrical, mechanical, chemical, and mining engineering and are commonly used in the design and building of industrial complexes such as petrochemical plants and nuclear power stations. Large contracting firms have both technical and managerial skills to undertake such projects. Several large public-sector contracting organisations frequently manage turnkey projects in India and internationally. The advantages and disadvantages of the Turnkey delivery method are shown in Fig. 7.1.

Joint Venture Contract

Imagine a super big construction project, like building a giant skyscraper. One company alone might not have enough money, people, or know-how to handle it. That's where joint ventures come in. Several companies combine their resources and skills, like workers, equipment, and money. They work together on the project like a temporary super-company, sharing the workload, risks, and profits (or losses). Unlike a real company that lasts forever, these joint ventures usually stick around for one big project before everyone goes their separate ways. It's kind of like a dream team for building stuff.

Several companies can join a joint venture for a big construction project. They can use any construction contract the owner agrees to. However, to avoid confusion, these companies need to have a written agreement with each other. This agreement should explain how they'll pay for and manage the project and share the risks, profits, and losses.

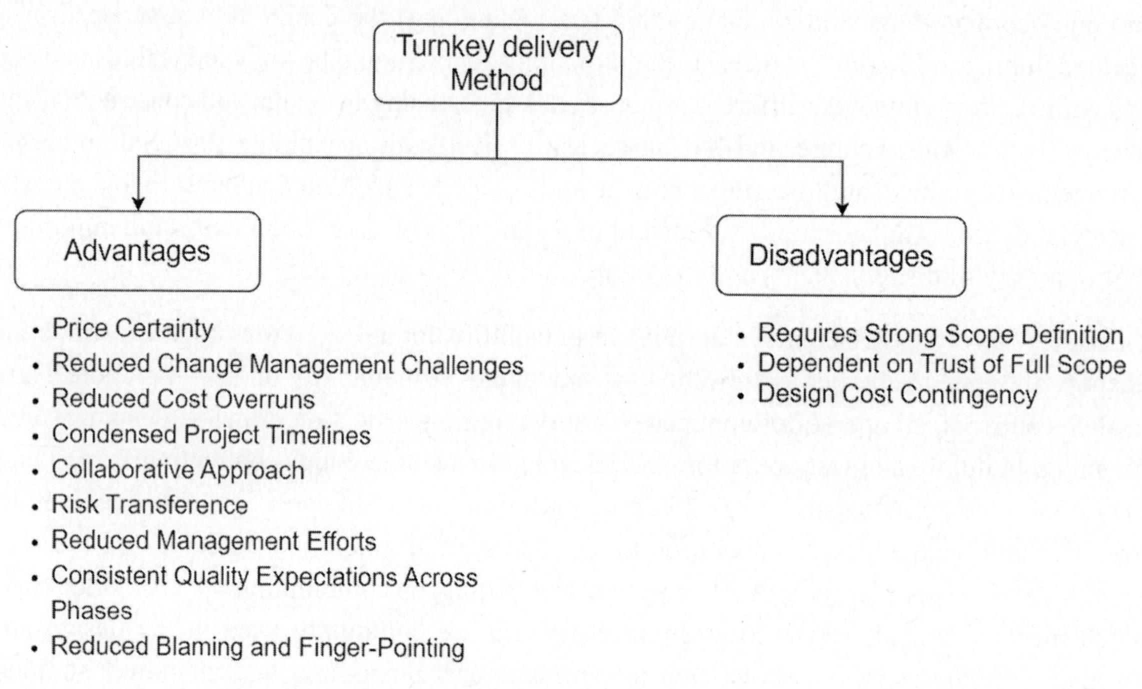

Fig. 7.1: advantages and disadvantages of the Turnkey delivery method

Incentive-Type Contracts for Work Outside the Country

This contractual agreement adopts a cost-plus structure. Common challenges associated with international projects include the volatility of foreign currencies, the presence of remote and frequently rudimentary living conditions, the unavailability of skilled and experienced local labour, and obstacles related to transportation and communication. A contractual arrangement has been devised to enhance the contractor's motivation to execute the project optimally and minimise costs while concurrently imposing penalties for suboptimal performance. This involves a cost-plus-base fee contract with an incorporated incentive provision. In this paradigm, prospective bidders tender their qualifications to the client, wherein those deemed unsuitable for the undertaking are subsequently excluded from the bidding process. Such contractual arrangements' inherent complexity makes them less advisable for domestic projects.

Equipment Rental Contract

Contracts for the lease of construction equipment are frequently essential during construction projects. Such contractual arrangements become imperative when the contracting party lacks the requisite equipment for project execution. Within the framework of cost-plus contracts, the stipulations of equipment lease agreements assume a direct significance for the project owner. Conversely, in the absence of cost-plus arrangements, the resolution of matters concerning equipment rental is confined to the contracting party and the equipment lessee, with the project owner playing no intervening role.

Construction equipment may be subject to leasing arrangements characterised by a lump-sum payment for the entire project duration, a fixed daily or hourly rate, or an arrangement based on the actual ownership cost plus a predetermined profit margin for the equipment owner. The terms of the agreement may or may not encompass all operational costs and the necessary personnel for equipment utilisation. Notably, a recapture clause is often incorporated, allowing the lessee to assume ownership of the equipment upon reaching a specified cumulative rental amount or in the event of a contractual breach.

Guaranteed Maximum Price (GMP) Contract

A Guaranteed Maximum price contract is a construction contract where the contractor agrees to deliver the project for a maximum price established before the construction begins. The guaranteed maximum cost is the highest price the owner will pay for the contracted work. The owner benefits from the cost savings if the actual costs exceed the guaranteed maximum. If expenses exceed the guaranteed maximum, the contractor is typically responsible for covering the overruns up to a certain point.

Guaranteed Maximum cost contracts benefit owners who want cost certainty while allowing some flexibility for changes during construction. It incentivises the contractor to control costs and manage the project efficiently. Legal and construction professionals are typically involved in drafting and reviewing GMP (Guaranteed Maximum Price) contracts to ensure the terms are transparent and fair to both parties.

7.5 COMMON CONTRACT CLAUSES IN CONSTRUCTION

A contract clause is a distinct provision within a legal contract that pertains to a specific aspect of the agreement between the parties involved. Contracts usually comprise multiple clauses, each serving a unique purpose and specifying particular terms and conditions. Including various clauses ensures clarity, mitigates risks, and establishes the rights and obligations of the parties. Different organisations such as NHAI (National Highway Authority of India), IOCL (Indian Oil Corporation Limited), NBCC (National Building Construction Corporation), NPCC (National Project Construction Corporation), CPWD (Central Public Works Department) and state PWD (Public Works Department) have their own set of contract clauses. CPWD contract conditions are frequently employed (as shown in Table 7.1), and we will use them as a reference point in our discussion. Further, some critical CPWD clauses are explained in the following subsections.

Table 7.1: List of CPWD clauses

S. No.	Clause number	Description of the clauses in the contract
1	Clause-1	Performance Guarantee
2	Clause-1A	Recovery of security deposit
3	Clause-2	Compensation for delay
4	Clause-3, 3A	When contract can be determined
5	Clause-4	A contractor is liable to pay compensation even if action is not taken under Clause-3
6	Clause-5	Time and extension for delay
7	Clause-6	Computerised/Electronic measurement book through CPWD ERP portal
8	Clause-7, 7A	Payment on intermediate certificate to be regarded as advances, payment to composite contract
9	Clause-7B	Payment to the third party
10	Clause-8	Completion certificate and completion plans
11	Clause-8A	Contractor to keep the site clean
12	Clause-9	Payment of final bill
13	Clause-9A	Payments of contractors' bills to banks
14	Clause-10A	Materials provided by the contractors

15	Clause-10B	Secured advance on materials and mobilisation advance
16	Clause-10C	Payment on account of an increase in prices/wages due to statutory orders
17	Clause-10D	Dismantled material government property
18	Clause-11	Work is to be executed per specifications, drawings, orders, etc.
19	Clause-12	Deviation/Variation extent and quantity and also pricing
20	Clause-13	Foreclosure of contract due to abandonment or reduction in scope of work.
21	Clause-14	Carrying out part of the work at risk and cost to the contractor
22	Clause-15	Suspension of work
23	Clause-16	Action in case work is not done as per specification
24	Clause-17	The contractor is liable for damages and defects during the defect liability period.
25	Clause-18	Contractor to supply tool & plant, etc.
26	Clause-18A	Recovery of Compensation paid to workers if the contractor fails
27	Clause-18B	Ensuring payment and amenities to workers if the contractor fails
28	Clause-19	Labour laws to be compiled by the contractor
29	Clause-20	Minimum wages act to be compiled with
30	Clause-21	Work not to be sublet, action in case of insolvency
31	Clause-22	Compensation pay
32	Clause-23	Changes in firm constitution to be intimated
33	Clause-24	Lifecycle cost
34	Clause-25	Settlement of disputes by conciliation and arbitration
35	Clause-26	Contractor to indemnify government against patent right
36	Clause-27	Lump sum provision in tender
37	Clause-28	Action where no specifications are specified
38	Clause-29	Withholding and lien in respect of sum due from contractor
39	Clause-29A	Lien in respect of claims in other contracts
40	Clause-30	Water for works
41	Clause-30A	Alternate water arrangement
42	Clause-31	Hire of plant and machinery
43	Clause-32	Employment of technical staff and employees
44	Clause-33	Levy/taxes payable by the contractor
45	Clause-34	Condition for reimbursement of levy/taxes if levied after receipt of tender
46	Clause-35	Termination of contract on the death of the contractor

47	Clause-36	If a relative works in CPWD, the contractor cannot tender.
48	Clause-37	No gazetted engineer to work as a contractor within one year of retirement
49	Clause-38	Theoretical consumption of material
50	Clause-39	Compensation during a war-like situation
51	Clause-40	Apprentice Act provision to be compiled with the project
52	Clause-41	Release of security deposit after labour clearance

7.5.1 Clause-1 Performance Guarantee

The contractor must submit a Performance Guarantee per the General Conditions of Contract (GCC), initially valid until the completion date plus a minimum of 6 months. If the completion time extends, the guarantee must be developed. After obtaining the completion certificate, the Performance Guarantee is returned without interest. For post-construction work contracts, 50% of the guarantee is retained as a Security Deposit, returned each year proportionately.

The Engineer-in-Charge is restricted from claiming the performance guarantee, except for amounts owed to the President of India as specified in the contract. This provision holds even in the presence of other contractual clauses. The Engineer-in-Charge is entitled to claim the total amount of the Performance Guarantee in two scenarios: first, if the contractor fails to extend the guarantee's validity as outlined earlier, and second, if the contractor neglects to pay the President of India any amount due, as agreed or determined under the contract clauses, within 30 days of receiving notice from the Engineer-in-Charge.

When a significant part of the work is done and ready to use, the Engineer-in-Charge gives a temporary completion certificate. This certificate lists any remaining tasks that must be finished as per the contract. If necessary, the Engineer-in-Charge will document a provisional completion certificate with approval from the superintending engineer/ project manager/ chief engineer/ chief project manager. Once the competent authority records the provisional completion certificate for the work, 80% of the performance guarantee is returned to the contractor without accruing any interest. However, suppose a contract involves taking care of buildings, services, or extra work after building or providing those services; in that case, the contractor will return 40% of the performance guarantee without any interest. This happens after the provisional completion certificate is documented.

7.5.2 Clause-1A Recovery of Security Deposit

The contractor whose tender is accepted must allow the government to deduct 2.5% of the gross amount from each payment until the deducted sum reaches a security deposit equivalent to 2.5% of the tendered amount. This deduction is a security deposit unless the contractor deposits the specified amount in Government Securities or fixed deposit receipts. If a bank cannot honour a fixed deposit receipt furnished as part of the security deposit, the contractor is responsible for any loss incurred. The contractor must promptly provide additional security to cover the deficit upon demand.

Any compensations or sums owed by the contractor under this contract can be deducted from the security deposit, the interest earned on it, or any amounts owed to the contractor by the government. Suppose the security deposit is reduced due to such deductions or sales. In that case, the contractor must replenish the amount within ten days in cash or through fixed deposit receipts from the State Bank of India, Scheduled Banks, or Government Securities (if deposited for over 12 months) endorsed in favour of the Engineer-in-Charge. The security deposit will be collected from the contractor's running bills and the final bill at the specified rates.

7.5.3 Clause-2 Liquidated Damages or Compensation for Delays

Liquidated damages are predetermined and quantifiable damages rather than penalties. When contractual parties mutually agree on a specific amount to be paid as liquidated damages in the case of a default, it signifies that the agreed-upon sum has been evaluated by the parties involved. Whether the designated sum constitutes liquidated damages or a penalty is subject to judicial determination. The court examines the parties' intentions based on the knowledge and circumstances surrounding the case. Liquidated damages represent a genuine pre-estimate of the likely damages resulting from a contract breach. Conversely, a penalty is a monetary payment aimed at intimidating the defaulting party to ensure performance unrelated to the damages incurred. Typically, if there is a delay in fulfilling the contract, liquidated damages (LD) at a maximum rate of 1% per month for delays, calculated daily according to the extent of damages incurred due to the specified delays caused by the Contractor, with a cap set at 10% of the total contract price. Compensation for delays, with a maximum rate of 1% per month, is to be calculated daily, considering the extent of damage caused by the contractor's specified delay. The total compensation for delay, as per this provision, is capped at 10% of the accepted tendered value of the work.

7.5.4 Clause-3 Under what Circumstances a Contract can be Terminated

Except for the provisions outlined elsewhere in this clause, the Engineer-in-Charge has the authority, without waiving any other rights or remedies concerning delays, failure to adhere to safety standards, substandard workmanship, claims for damages, or any other contract provisions, to formally terminate the contract by providing written notice. This termination may occur irrespective of whether the completion date has passed. The general termination clauses are as follows:

i. If the contractor fails to comply within seven days after receiving a written notice from the Engineer-in-Charge to rectify or replace defective work.
ii. If the contractor, without reasonable cause, suspends or fails to progress diligently in the work, even after a seven-day notice from the Engineer-in-Charge.
iii. If the contractor doesn't complete the work or a section by the specified or extended date, and the Engineer-in-Charge, after giving a written notice, believes the contractor won't finish it within a reasonable time.
iv. If the contractor persistently neglects obligations, defaults on contract terms, and fails to remedy the situation within seven days of receiving written notice from the Engineer-in-Charge.
v. If the contractor offers gifts or considerations to influence government officials or others in the contract.
vi. If the contractor enters into a contract with the government involving undisclosed commissions unless such details were previously disclosed in writing to the Engineer-in-Charge.
vii. If the contractor obtained the government contract through wrongful tendering, non-bonafide competitive methods, or breaches an Integrity Agreement.
viii. If the contractor, whether an individual or a partner in a firm, becomes insolvent, faces legal actions, or takes steps for liquidation or composition under insolvency laws.
ix. If the contractor is a company and faces winding-up resolutions, court orders, a receiver or manager appointment, or circumstances allowing such appointments.
x. If the contractor assigns, transfers, sublets, or parts with the works without prior written approval from the Engineer-in-Charge.

7.5.5 Clause-12 Deviation/Variation Extent and Quantity and Pricing

The price and quantity variations established by the Engineer-in-Charge are conclusive and obligatory for the contractor, and they are not subject to arbitration.

Clause-12.1: The clause outlines provisions for extending the time for completion of construction works in the event of deviations that result in additional costs beyond the tendered initial value. If the contractor requests an extension due to such deviations, the time extension will be determined in two parts. First, the extension will be proportional to the cost incurred for altered, additional, or substituted work with the original tendered value. Second, 25% of the time calculated in the first part will be granted. Alternatively, the Engineer-in-Charge may consider further additional time if deemed reasonable. This clause adjusts the project timeline somewhat in response to unforeseen changes or additions, ensuring the contractor is granted an appropriate time extension corresponding to the additional cost incurred.

Clasue-12.2: In the event of additional items not specified in the contract, the contractor is allowed a 15-day period from the order receipt or item identification to submit a claim for market rates. This submission should include a thorough analysis of rates, manufacturer's specifications, invoices, vouchers, etc. Failure to submit such a claim results in the Engineer-in-Charge approving rates later, which become definitive. Conversely, when the contractor properly submits a claim for market rates, the Engineer-in-Charge has 45 days to inspect and establish rates based on market conditions and the provided supporting documents. Payment to the contractor is subsequently made per the rates determined through the evaluation process.

Clause-12.3: If contract items surpass the stipulated limit outlined in Schedule F, the Engineer-in-Charge will, following notification to the contractor within 30 days of bill submission containing such items, assess and potentially reduce the rate for quantities exceeding the specified limit. This evaluation considers any responses from the contractor within 15 days of the notice. The rate adjustment, based on market rates, must be completed within 30 days after the expiration of the aforementioned 15-day period. Subsequently, the contractor will be reimbursed by the determined rates.

7.5.6 Clause-15 Suspension of Work

Upon receiving a written order from the Engineer-in-Charge, the contractor must promptly suspend the progress of the works, or any part thereof, as directed by the Engineer-in-Charge. The decision of the Engineer-in-Charge is final and binding on the contractor. This suspension may be enforced for the following reasons: (a) due to any default on the part of the contractor, (b) for the proper execution of the works or part thereof, unrelated to the contractor's default, or (c) to ensure the safety of the works or part thereof. During the suspension, the contractor is responsible for adequately protecting and securing the works as necessary and must adhere to any instructions provided by the Engineer-in-Charge.

7.5.7 Clause-16 Action in case Work is not Done as per Specification

This clause places a responsibility on both the contractor and departmental staff to guarantee the delivery of high-quality work. Under this clause, the contractor may be required to rectify defects in the work at their own cost or redo the work if it does not meet the specified standards or design.

7.5.8 Clause-25 Settlement of Disputes by Conciliation and Arbitration

Conciliation: This provision outlines the dispute resolution process in the contract. If the contractor or Engineer-in-Charge disputes any aspect of the work, drawing, record, or decision, they can refer the matter, along with the claimed amount, to the Conciliator. The Conciliator then requests written statements from both parties describing the disputes and points at issue. If elements of a settlement appear feasible, the Conciliator formulates possible terms and presents them for the parties' consideration. After receiving their observations, the Conciliator may adjust the terms. If an agreement is reached, the parties can formalise it in a written settlement agreement on non-judicial stamp paper. The Conciliator authenticates the deal, providing a copy to each party. The termination of conciliation proceedings follows Section 76 of The Arbitration and Conciliation Act 1996. This process ensures a structured and collaborative approach to dispute resolution, promoting the possibility of amicable settlements. The conciliation process must conclude within 45 days of the reference receipt. The Conciliator can extend this period by an additional 15 days if necessary. If the conciliation proceedings have not been resolved by 60 days from the receipt of the reference, they will be considered officially terminated.

Arbitration: If the conciliation efforts prove unsuccessful or the Conciliator does not present a settlement proposal within the stipulated period, either party has the right to promptly issue a notice using the prescribed proforma. This notice must be communicated to the other party and directed to the Chief Engineer or the Superintending Engineer overseeing the work (as applicable), referred to as the Arbitrator Appointing Authority. The purpose of the notice is to request the appointment of an Arbitrator to address the unresolved matters.

Force majeure: Any delay or failure by either party to perform shall not be considered a default leading to claims for damages if caused by acts of God, fire, explosion, flood, natural catastrophes, government legislation, orders, regulations, etc. The failure of the client/owner to provide the entire site or release funds to the client is also deemed a force majeure event. The time for performance by both parties is extended for the duration of the force majeure event, and efforts are to be made to minimise resulting delays. If the client/owner's failure persists beyond the stipulated completion date, the client, at the contractor's request, may terminate the contract without liability to either party. In such a case, the contractor is not entitled to any compensation.

Contract duration: The stipulated timeframe for completing the works, as outlined in the contract or as extended under specific conditions, is a critical aspect of the contract. The initiation of work shall commence either from the specified period in the contract or from the date of site handover, as notified by the Engineer-in-Charge, whichever occurs later. If the contractor defaults on initiating work as prescribed, the Engineer-in-Charge can forfeit the performance guarantee. This forfeited amount shall be entirely at the government's disposal without prejudicing any other legal rights or remedies available.

Notice to proceed: A "Notice to Proceed" (NTP) is like an official permission slip given to the contractor by the person in charge of a project. It tells the contractor they can start working on a specific project or job. The NTP usually includes essential details about the project, such as what needs to be done, when the work should start, and the contract rules. It covers the project name, location, and a brief work description. The start date is crucial to the NTP because it marks when the contractor can begin. The document also explains the tasks or services the contractor needs to provide and any specific rules they must follow. It even includes contact information for essential people involved in the project. Getting the NTP is a formal step that gives the green signal to the contractors to start their work, ensuring everyone is on the same page about what needs to be done and when.

SUMMARY

The construction contract management chapter comprehensively overviews the essential processes of effectively managing contracts throughout the project lifecycle. It covers key aspects such as contract negotiation, drafting, administration, and compliance to ensure that all parties uphold their obligations and responsibilities. The chapter emphasises the importance of establishing clear and enforceable contract terms, including scope of work, project timelines, payment schedules, and dispute resolution mechanisms, to mitigate risks and promote project success. By fostering transparency, communication, and collaboration among stakeholders, effective contract management facilitates the smooth execution of construction projects, enhances accountability, and minimises legal and financial liabilities.

EXERCISE

Assuming a 4-month delay in a construction contract of 24 months' duration. Form 3 groups for arguing the case for or against levying a penalty on the contractor. Group A will formulate the contract conditions, Group B will act as the Client, Group C will act as the Contractor, and one person will act as the Arbitrator.

MULTIPLE CHOICE QUESTIONS

1. Which of the following is NOT a type of construction contract?

   A) Fixed price contract
   B) Cost-plus contract
   C) Fixed-fee contract
   D) Volunteer contract

2. Who are the parties typically involved in a construction contract?

   A) Only the contractor
   B) Only the client
   C) Both the contractor and the client
   D) Only the subcontractors

3. What is the purpose of a "Notice to Proceed" clause in a construction contract?

   A) To terminate the contract
   B) To inform the client about project delays
   C) To inform the contractor to start work
   D) To request additional funds

4. What does "Contract Duration" refer to in a construction contract?

   A) The duration of the contract negotiation process
   B) The duration of the construction project
   C) The duration of the contract termination process
   D) The duration of the contract signing ceremony

5. What are liquidated damages in a construction contract?

   A) Damages that occur due to water leakage

B) Pre-estimated damages for specific breaches of contract
C) Damages caused by natural disasters
D) Damages that occur during construction

6. What does "Force Majeure" refer to in a construction contract?

A) Unforeseeable circumstances that prevent contract performance
B) Financial penalties for project delays
C) The termination of the contract by mutual agreement
D) Changes made to the contract without consent

7. How are changes and variations handled in a construction contract?

A) By ignoring them
B) By increasing the contract price
C) By terminating the contract
D) By documenting and negotiating them

8. Which of the following statement is false?

A) When time is the essence of contract, the completion time can be extended.
B) When time is the essence of contract, liquidated damage clause can apply.
C) When time is the essence of contract, penalty can be charged for delayed completion.
D) When time is the essence of contract, full payment by employer is not delayed.

ANSWERS TO MULTIPLE CHOICE QUESTIONS

1	2	3	4	5	6	7	8
D	C	C	B	B	A	D	A

SHORT ANSWER TYPE QUESTIONS

1. Why is contract management critical?
2. What is the difference between contract and contract management?
3. What do you understand by the competent parties?
4. What do you understand by the term cost bid contract?

5. What are the advantages or disadvantages of a lump sum contract?
6. Give an example of efficiently using the unit price contract.
7. Why contract is essential?
8. What is a negotiated bid contract and its type?
9. What is the common name for an architect-engineer management contract?
10. What do you understand about liquidated damage?
11. What do you understand by the term subcontract? When and how is it used?
12. How is a turnkey contract different from a design-built contract?

LONG ANSWER TYPE QUESTIONS

1. Enlist and explain essential terms or elements of a contract.
2. Describe how the contract will get terminated or suspended.
3. Describe the obligation of various parties involved in any contract.
4. What are the benefits of a joint venture?
5. Discuss the key parties in a construction contract and their roles and responsibilities. Explain how effective communication and collaboration among these parties contribute to project success.
6. Explain the significance of common contract clauses such as "Notice to Proceed," "Rights and Duties," and "Contract Duration." Provide examples of situations where each clause would be applicable and what its impact would be on the project.
7. Describe the performance parameters typically outlined in a construction contract. Discuss how these parameters are measured and monitored throughout the project lifecycle.
8. Discuss the concept of delays, penalties, and liquidated damages in construction contracts. Explain how these provisions help ensure project timelines and address delays.

9. Define Force Majeure in the context of construction contracts. Explain its significance and the circumstances under which it can be invoked. Provide examples of events that qualify as Force Majeure.
10. Discuss the common challenges and pitfalls associated with construction contracts. Provide examples of contract disputes, delays, and cost overruns, and discuss strategies for mitigating these risks.
11. What are the conditions of contract in a contract document? Why is it recommended to use standard forms of contract?
12. What do you mean by bill of quantity? How is it important for construction project?

TUTORIAL

Imagine you are a project manager tasked with overseeing the construction of a new residential building. Identify and justify your choice and explain which type of contract (fixed-price, cost-plus, or time and material) you would recommend for this project. List the key parties involved in the contract and outline their roles and responsibilities.

KNOW MORE

For more information related to this topic scan the QR code.

OR

Type this link in your browser

https://cpwd.gov.in/Documents/cpwd_publication.aspx

BIBLIOGRAPHY

- CPWD (2023). *The general condition of the contract*. Central Public Works Department.
- Mason, J. (2017). Intelligent contracts and the construction industry. *Journal of Legal*

Affairs and Dispute Resolution in Engineering and Construction, 9(3), 04517012.

- McNamara, A. J., and Sepasgozar, S. M. (2021). Intelligent contract adoption in the construction industry: Concept development. *Automation in Construction*, 122, 103452.
- NBCC (2016). *General conditions of contract*. National Building Construction Corporation.
- Whitticks, E. (2005). *Construction contracts: managing contracts and controlling disputes in a volatile industry*. Gulf Publ. Co.: Texas.

CONSTRUCTION COSTS

UNIT SPECIFICS

In the construction industry, understanding and managing construction costs are pivotal to the success of any project. This unit delves into the diverse facets of construction costs, offering an in-depth understanding of their classification, components, time-cost trade-offs, and interactions within the project lifecycle.

RATIONALE

As delay is expected in construction projects, expediting the construction activities becomes necessary.

PRE-REQUISITE

Basic mathematics

UNIT OUTCOMES

List of outcomes of this unit is as follows:

U8-O1: Understand the different types of construction costs

U8-O2: Crashing of the construction schedule

Unit Outcomes	Expected Mapping with Course Outcomes (1- Weak Correlation; 2- Medium correlation; 3- Strong Correlation)					
	CO-1	CO-2	CO-3	CO-4	CO-5	CO-6
U8-O1	3	3	3	1	1	1
U8-O2	2	3	3	2	1	1

8.1 IMPORTANCE OF CONSTRUCTION COST

i. Construction costs help allocate funds for various project components, including materials, labour, equipment, and overheads.
ii. A detailed cost estimate allows project stakeholders to plan and secure the necessary financial resources for the construction process.
iii. Accurate cost estimates aid in evaluating whether the project is economically viable.
iv. Construction costs are essential for tendering; contractors submit bids based on estimated costs. This helps in selecting the most competitive and qualified contractors. Project owners can negotiate contracts more effectively when armed with detailed cost information.
v. Understanding construction costs allows project managers to optimise project schedules by evaluating time-cost trade-offs. This involves deciding whether to expedite the schedule, which may incur additional costs.
vi. Adequate budgeting allows for proper training, supervision, and quality control measures, ensuring workmanship meets required standards.
vii. Understanding costs aids in identifying and mitigating potential risks that could impact the project's financial health.
viii. Regular monitoring of construction costs allows project managers to track expenditures against the budget, enabling better control over financial aspects.

Construction costs are typically borne by the entity or party responsible for undertaking the construction project. The allocation of construction costs depends on the specific contractual arrangements and agreements between the involved parties. Here are common scenarios for who pays construction costs:

i. *Private developers:* Individual property owners or developers usually bear the construction costs in private construction projects. They fund the project either from their resources or through financing.
ii. *Government:* Public infrastructure projects, such as roads, bridges, and buildings, are often funded by government entities at various levels (local, state, or national).
iii. *Contractors:* In specific contractual arrangements, contractors may front the initial construction costs and then be reimbursed by the project owner. This can happen through progress payments or milestone payments as the project advances.
iv. *Joint ventures:* Large-scale projects may involve joint ventures between private and public entities or multiple private firms. In such cases, the partners share the construction costs based on the terms outlined in the joint venture agreement.

Construction costs exert a profound influence on project timelines, often contributing to delays, and they are intricately linked to considerations of project quality and safety. Delays may occur if there are interruptions in the supply chain, an inability to pay subcontractors promptly, or a lack of funds for critical project phases. Changes in project scope often result in additional costs and can lead to project delays. Inadequate financial planning for scope changes may disrupt the project schedule. When cost considerations precede quality, there may be a temptation to cut corners or use lower-quality materials. This can compromise the overall quality of the construction, leading to issues such as structural deficiencies or the need for frequent repairs. Reduced spending on quality control measures, inspections, and testing can lead to subpar workmanship and construction that does not meet standards. Cost constraints may lead to cutbacks in safety measures and protocols. This can result in a higher likelihood of accidents, injuries, and non-compliance with safety regulations.

8.2 CLASSIFICATION OF CONSTRUCTION COSTS

Costs are broadly categorised into two essential types: direct and indirect. Each type holds unique significance and contributes distinctively to the overall financial landscape of a construction project. This classification provides a structured approach to identifying, allocating, and managing expenditures, offering project stakeholders valuable insights into resource utilisation, budgetary considerations, and financial planning. Exploring the dichotomy between direct and indirect costs is crucial for practitioners, decision-makers, and professionals involved in the multifaceted domain of construction management.

8.2.1 Direct Costs

The construction costs that can be directly computed or associated with a specific activity or work item are called direct costs. The cost of materials, labour, equipment, etc., is an essential direct cost component, as discussed in the following subsections.

Labour Costs

The costs incurred on the labour employed at the site are called labour costs. These costs include the basic pay for workers involved in the construction process, additional compensation for hours worked beyond regular working hours, and extra payments based on performance or meeting specific milestones. Labour costs entail additional perks such as health insurance, pension contributions, other benefits, and employer-paid taxes associated with hiring labour, including social security and Medicare taxes. Training sessions, workshops, or certifications for the workforce, safety programs and training to ensure a secure working environment are part of these costs. Companies also provide workers with transportation, meals and accommodations, which are labour costs.

Material Costs

Material costs include all materials used in the construction process, including raw materials, building materials, and any components or products incorporated into the project. These costs encompass various construction materials, including concrete, steel, wood, glass, plumbing fixtures, electrical components, etc.

Equipment Costs

Equipment costs in construction refer to the costs associated with owning, maintaining, and operating machinery and tools used during a construction project. Ownership or acquisition costs are the initial costs of purchasing or leasing construction equipment. The costs incurred in mobilisation and demobilisation, costs of fuel/oil involved, operator and driver costs and statutory expenses are also counted as equipment costs. The ongoing costs of keeping equipment in good working condition are also part of equipment costs. This includes routine maintenance, inspections, and necessary repairs to prevent breakdowns and ensure optimal performance. Expenses related to storing equipment when not in use are also considered within equipment costs, encompassing rental fees for storage facilities, security measures, and protection against environmental factors. Moreover, costs related to incorporating advanced technologies or upgrading equipment to improve efficiency, safety, and compliance with industry standards fall under the purview of equipment costs.

Subcontractor Costs

Subcontractor costs pertain to the payments made to subcontractors hired for specific tasks or portions of the construction project. More specifically, these costs include the agreed-upon payments to subcontractors for the services they provide, which can vary based on the complexity and scope of the subcontracted work. The main contractor invites quotations from several subcontractors for a specific work (such as waterproofing, woodwork, HVAC, etc.), makes a comparative statement of the bids received, and selects the most responsive bid judiciously. It's important to note that subcontractor costs are distinct from direct labour costs, as subcontractors operate as independent entities and are responsible for managing their workforce and resources. The nature and extent of subcontractor costs depend on the contractual agreements between the main contractor and the subcontractor.

8.2.2 Indirect Costs

Indirect costs, commonly known as overhead, constitute essential expenses associated with conducting work that cannot be directly attributed to a specific activity and, in some instances, cannot be tied to a particular project. An indirect component is conceivable even within material, labour, equipment, or subcontractor costs. Establishing completely distinct boundaries between direct and indirect costs proves challenging. In a broad sense, indirect costs encompass different types of project overheads.

Project overhead costs are not directly tied to a specific project activity but are necessary for the overall operation of the construction project. These costs involve the salaries of project personnel, including engineers, supervisors, and administrative staff stationed at the construction site. To address various risks associated with a construction project from a contractor's perspective, suitable insurance schemes are established in collaboration with insurance agencies, and the costs related to these schemes fall under this category.

Overhead costs also cover conveyance expenses, staff travel and transfer costs, and headquarters personnel visits. Temporary site installations, such as site offices, workshops, stores, equipment fencing, warehouses, storage areas, sanitary facilities, furniture and fittings, temporary roads, car parks, and even residential units and dining facilities for staff, must be established as part of the project. As these cost components cannot be directly computed for a specific task, or, in other words, different construction activities (not only one) use these facilities, they come under indirect cost. The costs incurred for ensuring proper water, power, and sewage facilities are also classified under overhead costs.

Try to find out!

What is the total cost of constructing the new parliament building of India?
Calculate the indirect cost associated with it.

8.3 TIME COST TRADE-OFF IN CONSTRUCTION PROJECTS

Construction projects often operate under tight schedules, and there's a natural desire to complete them quickly. However, expediting the schedule usually involves additional expenditures, such as overtime wages, accelerated procurement, or the need for more resources. Project managers carefully analyse the implications of adjusting project timelines and associated costs to find an optimal balance. They may evaluate the cost implications of compressing or decompressing the schedule. Compression involves shortening the duration of certain project activities to meet specific constraints or deadlines. Decompression, conversely, refers to the extension of activity durations up to their maximum normal duration. It involves relaxing time constraints to allow for more flexibility. The goal is to achieve project completion in optimum duration and minimum cost.

Finding the strategic balance between the duration of a project and its associated costs is referred to as a time-cost trade-off. This trade-off involves considering project completion time against the additional costs required to expedite or compress the schedule. The time-cost trade-off is an essential aspect of project management, requiring careful planning, evaluation, and decision-making throughout the project lifecycle.

The time-cost trade-off, commonly known as crashing, involves shortening the duration of a project by allocating additional resources to specific activities. The goal of crashing is to expedite the completion of the project or specific project activities to meet deadlines or to address unexpected delays. The point at which the project has minimum cost is the optimum point.

The time-cost relationships can be visualised graphically as a time-cost curve, as depicted in Fig. 8.1. Although the cost curve is convex, a linear approximation of the time-cost relationship is used to simplify network scheduling.

An activity can be completed either in its normal duration or crash duration. The minimum direct cost required to complete an activity is the normal cost, and the corresponding duration is the normal duration. The normal duration is the expected or planned amount of time needed to complete an activity under normal working conditions and with the available resources. The shortest possible duration for completing an activity by adding extra resources or taking other measures to expedite the work is called crash duration, and the corresponding cost is called crash cost. Let's consider an example of excavation for a construction project where manual labour is initially used, and later, additional resources, such as excavators, are brought in to speed up the process. The normal project duration is 20 days, the typical duration required to manually excavate a certain amount of soil. By introducing excavators or additional resources, the project manager expects to complete the excavation in a shorter time, in 10 days. The project manager incurs extra costs associated with using excavators but gains the advantage of finishing the excavation in a shorter time.

The linear approximation shown as a dotted line in Fig. 8.1 represents a linear incremental cost per unit of time saved under crashing conditions. The incremental cost for an activity is also called the cost-time slope. Graphically, the slope of the line connecting the normal point (lower point) and the crash point (upper point) is called the cost-time slope of the activity. The cost-time slope represents the additional cost (direct cost) incurred for each unit of time saved in a project schedule. The equation for the cost-time slope is as follows:

$$Cost - Time\ Slope = \frac{Crash\ Cost - Normal\ Cost}{Normal\ duration - Crash\ duration} \quad \textbf{(8.1)}$$

where,
Crash Cost is the cost of the project with crashing applied.
Normal Cost is the cost of the project without crashing.
Normal Duration is the original duration of the project.
Crash Duration is the duration after crashing.

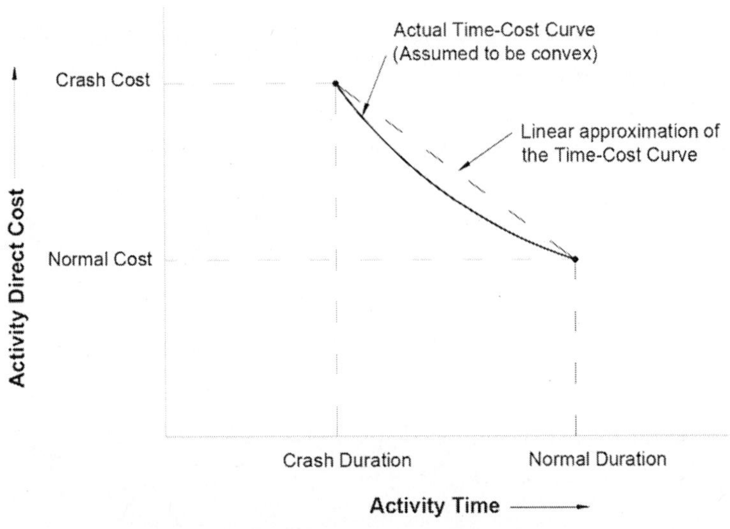

Fig. 8.1: Time-cost curve for an activity

The time-cost trade-off or crashing comprises the following steps broadly:

Step 1: The first step is identifying and crashing the critical activity with the minimum cost-time slope. There are two scenarios for finding the critical activity to crash.

Scenario 1: When there is one critical path

The activity with the least slope along the critical path crashes where no further schedule shortening is possible (either because the activity duration cannot be reduced further or some other activity has become critical along a parallel path).

Scenario 2: When there are multiple critical paths

When there are multiple critical paths, an activity from each path is chosen. It becomes essential to shorten both critical paths simultaneously. Failing to address both paths concurrently can lead to a scenario where the other remains unaffected despite shortening one critical path, thereby keeping the overall project duration unchanged. The one with the least cost-time slope is selected from the various combinations available.

Step 2: The network is revised by adjusting the time and cost of the crashed activity. The critical path is identified again and reverted to Step 1. This process is continued till no more crashing of the project is possible.

Step 3: Determine the optimum duration of the project. It would be the time duration corresponding to the minimum total cost.

The process of crashing is well illustrated in the following examples.

Illustration 1

A small project consists of activities listed below. If the indirect cost of the project is Rs. 120/day, what is the minimum cost, optimum duration, and minimum duration of the project?

Activity	Precedence	Duration (days)		Cost (in Rupees)	
		Normal	Crash	Normal	Crash
A	-	4	2	400	500
B	-	8	5	800	980
C	-	3	2	600	700
D	A	10	6	500	600
E	A, B	8	6	800	950
F	A, B, C	7	4	700	1000

Solution:

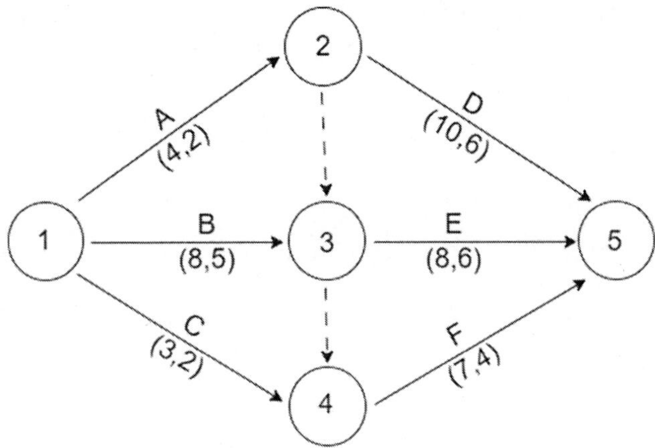

Step 1: Identify the Critical Path

All the different paths for project completion:

Paths	Normal duration	Crash duration
A-D	14	8
A-E	12	8
A-F	11	6
B-E	16	11
B-F	15	9
C-F	10	6

From the Figure and Table of the solution, path B-E has the maximum duration; thus, the critical path identified is B-E. The duration of the project is 16 days. At each step of the process, activities on the critical path are considered for crashing. The cost-time slope of each activity is calculated.

Step 2: Calculate the cost-time slope of each activity

$$Cost - Time\ Slope = \frac{Crash\ Cost - Normal\ Cost}{Normal\ duration - Crash\ duration}$$

Cost-Time slope of A = $\frac{500-400}{4-2}$ = 50

Cost-Time slope of B = $\frac{980-800}{8-5}$ = 60

Cost-Time slope of C = $\frac{700-600}{3-2}$ = 100

Cost-Time slope of D = $\frac{600-500}{10-6}$ = 25

Cost-Time slope of E = $\frac{950-800}{8-6}$ = 75

Cost-Time slope of F = $\frac{1000-700}{7-4}$ = 100

Activity	Duration (days)		ΔTime	Cost (in Rupees)		ΔCost	ΔCost/ΔTime
	Normal	Crash		Normal	Crash		
A	4	2	2	400	500	100	50
B	8	5	3	800	980	180	60
C	3	2	1	600	700	100	100
D	10	6	4	500	600	100	25
E	8	6	2	800	950	150	75
F	7	4	3	700	1000	300	100

The normal duration of the project is 16 days.

The direct cost of the project = 400 + 800 + 600 + 500 + 800 + 700 = Rs. 3800

Indirect cost of the project = 16 × 120 = Rs. 1920

Total cost of the project = 3800 + 1920 = Rs. 5720

Step 3: Crashing the Project

The whole crashing process is as follows:

Activity	ΔCost/ ΔTime	Time shortened					
		0th Cr*	1st Cr*	2nd Cr*	3rd Cr*	4th Cr*	5th Cr*
A	50						
B	60		1	1	1		
C	100						
D	25				1	1	1
E	75					1	1
F	100						1
Critical path		B-E	B-E	B-E	A-D, B-E	A-D, B-E	A-D, B-E, B-F
Activity crashed		-	B	B	B, D	D, E	D, E, F
Days reduced		-	1	1	1	1	1
Project duration		16	15	14	13	12	11
Increased cost/day		-	60	60	85	100	200
Total direct cost		3800	3860	3920	4005	4105	4305
Total indirect cost		1920	1800	1680	1560	1440	1320
Total cost		5720	5660	5600	5565	5545	5625

Cr is denoting Crashing here.*

The First crashing

In this example, the critical path is B-E. The critical activities are B and E, for which the cost of reduction per day is Rs. 60 and Rs. 75, respectively. The activity with the least cost-time slope is crashed. So, activity B is crashed.

Crashing it by a day,

The project length is reduced to 15 days,

The direct cost of the project = 3800 + 60 = Rs. 3860

Indirect cost = 15 × 120 = Rs. 1800

Total cost of the project = 3860 + 1800 = Rs. 5660

Now, the duration of the activity B has changed from 8 to 7 days. At this stage, the critical path also remains B-E.

The Second crashing

The critical path is B-E. Activity B is crashed, as in the first crashing.

Crashing it by a day,

The project length is reduced to 14 days,

The direct cost of the project = 3860 + 60 = Rs. 3920

Indirect cost = 14 × 120 = Rs. 1680

The total cost of the project = 3920 + 1680 = Rs. 5600

Now, the duration of the activity B has changed from 7 to 6 days. At this stage, the critical paths, each with 14 days, are A-D and B-E.

The Third crashing

The critical paths are A-D and B-E. When there are multiple critical paths, an activity from each path is chosen. The one with the least cost-time slope is selected from the various combinations available. The combinations, along with their costs, are as follows:

Critical path	Combinations	Associated cost slope (in Rs/day)
A-D	A, B	50 + 60 = 110
	A, E	50 + 75 = 125
B-E	D, B	25 + 60 = 85
	D, E	25 + 75 = 100

Thus, activities B and D are crashed for Rs. 85.

Crashing it by a day,

The project length is reduced to 13 days,

The direct cost of the project = 3920 + 85 = Rs. 4005

Indirect cost = 13 × 120 = Rs. 1560

Total cost of the project = 4005 + 1560 = Rs. 5565

At this stage, the critical paths remain the same. They are A-D and B-E, each with a length of 13 days.

The Fourth crashing

The critical paths are A-D and B-E. Notice that activity B cannot be crashed anymore. So, the combinations are as follows:

Critical path	Combinations	Associated cost slope (in Rs/day)
A-D	A, E	50 + 75 = 125
B-E	D, E	25 + 75 = 100

Thus, activities D and E are crashed for Rs. 100.

Crashing it by a day,

The project length is reduced to 12 days,

The direct cost of the project = 4005 + 100 = Rs. 4105

Indirect cost = 12 × 120 = Rs. 1440

The total cost of the project = 4105 + 1440 = Rs. 5545

After the fourth crash, the critical paths, each for 12 days, are A-D, B-E and B-F.

The Fifth crashing

The critical paths are A-D, B-E and B-F. Notice that activity B cannot be crashed anymore. So, the combinations are as follows:

Critical path	Combinations	Associated cost slope (in Rs/day)
A-D	A, E, F	50+75+100=225
B-E	D, E, F	25+75+100=200
B-F	-	-

Thus, the activities D, E and F are crashed for Rs. 200.

Crashing it by a day,

The project length is reduced to 11 days,

The direct cost of the project = 4105 + 200 = Rs. 4305

Indirect cost = 11 × 120 = Rs. 1320

The total cost of the project = 4305 + 1320 = Rs. 5625

After the fifth crash, the project duration was reduced by another day, but the cost increased by Rs. 80 over the previous total cost. Thus, a stage is reached where the decrease in duration is accompanied by increased project cost, forcing us to stop further crashing. Combining all the results in a time-cost graph shows the minimum project cost corresponding to a project duration of 12 days.

Results

Normal project duration = 16 days

Normal project cost = Rs. 5720

Minimum cost (after crashing) = Rs. 5545

Optimum duration = 12 days

Minimum duration = 11 days

The associated cost for minimum duration = Rs. 5625

The time-cost curve helps the project manager choose a suitable project schedule.

Illustration 2

The durations and costs for each activity in the network of a small construction contract under both normal and crash conditions are given in the following table. Calculate the least cost for expediting the contract. Determine the optimum duration of the contract, assuming the indirect cost as Rs. 60/day.

Activity	Precedence	Duration (days)		Cost (in Rupees)	
		Normal	Crash	Normal	Crash
A	-	6	3	300	360
B	-	6	4	450	500
C	-	4	2	360	420
D	-	6	3	600	675
E	C	3	2	325	350
F	B, E	2	1	250	285
G	D, F	2	1	310	350

Solution:

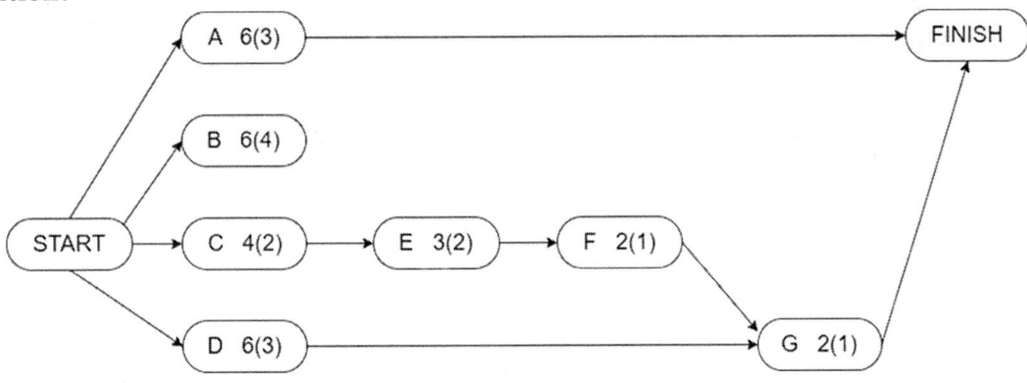

Step 1: Identify the Critical Path

All the different paths for project completion

Paths	Normal duration	Crash duration
A	6	3
B-F-G	10	6
C-E-F-G	11	6
D-G	8	4

From the Figure and Table, path C-E-F-G has the maximum duration; thus, the critical path identified is C-E-F-G. The duration of the project is 11 days. At each step of the process, activities on the critical path are considered for crashing. The cost-time slope of each activity is calculated.

Step 2: Calculate the cost-time slope of each activity

$$Cost - Time\ Slope = \frac{Crash\ Cost - Normal\ Cost}{Normal\ duration - Crash\ duration}$$

Cost-Time slope of A = $\frac{360-300}{6-3}$ = 20

Cost-Time slope of B = $\frac{500-450}{6-4}$ = 25

Cost-Time slope of C = $\frac{420-360}{4-2}$ = 30

Cost-Time slope of D = $\frac{675-600}{6-3}$ = 25

Cost-Time slope of E = $\frac{350-325}{3-2}$ = 25

Cost-Time slope of F = $\frac{285-250}{2-1}$ = 35

Cost-Time slope of G = $\frac{350-310}{2-1}$ = 40

Activity	Duration (days)		ΔTime	Cost (in Rupees)		ΔCost	ΔCost/ΔTime
	Normal	Crash		Normal	Crash		
A	6	3	3	300	360	60	20
B	6	4	2	450	500	50	25
C	4	2	2	360	420	60	30
D	6	3	3	600	675	75	25
E	3	2	1	325	350	25	25
F	2	1	1	250	285	35	35
G	2	1	1	310	350	40	40

The normal duration of the project is 11 days.

The direct cost of the project = 300 + 450 + 360 + 600 + 325 + 250 + 310 = Rs. 2595

Indirect cost of the project = 11×60 = Rs. 660

The total cost of the project = 2595 + 660 = Rs. 3255

Step 3: Crashing the Project

The whole crashing process is as follows:

Activity	ΔCost/ΔTime	Time shortened					
		0th crashing	1st crashing	2nd crashing	3rd crashing	4th crashing	5th crashing
A	20						
B	25					1	1
C	30					1	1
D	25						1
E	25		1				
F	35			1			
G	40				1		
Critical path		C-E-F-G	C-E-F-G	B-F-G, C-E-F-G	B-F-G, C-E-F-G	B-F-G, C-E-F-G	B-F-G, C-E-F-G, D-G
Activity crashed		-	E	F	G	B, C	B, C, D
Days reduced		-	1	1	1	1	1
Project duration		11	10	9	8	7	6
Increased cost/day		-	25	35	40	55	80
Total direct cost		2595	2620	2655	2695	2750	2830
Total indirect cost		660	600	540	480	420	360
Total cost		3255	3220	3195	3175	3170	3190

The First crashing

In this example, the critical path is C-E-F-G. The critical activity is E, for which the cost of reduction per day is Rs. 25. The activity with the least cost-time slope is crashed. So, activity E is crashed.

Crashing it by a day,

The project length is reduced to 10 days,

The direct cost of the project = 2595 + 25 = Rs. 2620

Indirect cost = 10 × 60 = Rs. 600

Total cost of the project = 2620 + 600 = Rs. 3220

Now, the duration of the activity E has changed from 3 to 2 days. At this stage, the critical paths, each lasting ten days, are B-F-G and C-E-F-G.

The Second crashing

The critical paths are B-F-G and C-E-F-G. Notice that activity E cannot be crashed anymore as it has reached the crash duration. The one with the least cost-time slope is selected from the various combinations available. The combinations, along with the associated cost slopes, are as follows:

Critical path	Combinations	Associated cost slope (in Rs/day)
B-F-G	B, C	25 + 30 = 55
C-E-F-G	F	35
	G	40

The combination with the least cost-time slope is Rs. 35/day. Hence, activity F is crashed for Rs. 35.

Crashing it by a day,

The project length is reduced to 9 days,

The direct cost of the project = 2620 + 35 = Rs. 2655

Indirect cost = 9 × 60 = Rs. 540

Total cost of the project = 2655 + 540 = Rs. 3195

The duration of activity F has changed from 2 to 1 day. The critical paths remain the same for this stage for nine days, B-F-G and C-E-F-G.

The Third crashing

The critical paths are B-F-G and C-E-F-G. Notice that activities E and F cannot be crashed anymore as they have reached the crash duration. The one with the least cost-time slope is selected from the various combinations available. The combinations, along with the associated cost slopes, are as follows:

Critical path	Combinations	Associated cost slope (in Rs/day)
B-F-G	B, C	25+30=55
C-E-F-G	G	40

The combination with the least cost-time slope is Rs. 40/day. Hence, activity G is crashed for Rs. 40.

Crashing it by a day,

The project length is reduced to 8 days,

The direct cost of the project = 2655 + 40 = Rs. 2695

Indirect cost = 8 × 60 = Rs. 480

Total cost of the project = 2695 + 480 = Rs. 3175

Now, the duration of the activity G has changed from 2 to 1 day. At this stage, the critical paths remain the same. They are B-F-G and C-E-F-G, each with a length of 8 days.

The Fourth crashing

The critical paths are B-F-G and C-E-F-G. Notice that activities E, F, and G cannot be crashed anymore as they have reached the crash duration. The one with the least cost-time slope is selected from the various combinations available. There is only one combination left, i.e., B and C. The combination, along with the associated cost slope, is shown below:

Critical path	Combinations	Associated cost slope (in Rs/day)
B-F-G	B, C	25+30=55
C-E-F-G		

The associated cost-time slope is Rs. 55/day for the combination B and C. Hence, activities B and C are crashed for Rs. 55.

Crashing it by a day,

The project length is reduced to 7 days,

The direct cost of the project = 2695 + 55 = Rs. 2750

Indirect cost = 7 × 60 = Rs. 420

Total cost of the project = 2750 + 420 = Rs. 3170

After the fourth crash, the critical paths, each lasting seven days, are B-F-G, C-E-F-G and D-G.

The Fifth crashing

The critical paths are B-F-G, C-E-F-G and D-G. Notice that activities E, F, and G cannot be crashed anymore as they have reached the crash duration. The one with the least cost-time slope is selected from the various combinations available. There is only one combination left, i.e., B, C and D. The combination, along with the associated cost slope, is shown below:

Critical path	Combinations	Associated cost slope (in Rs/day)
B-F-G C-E-F-G D-G	B, C, D	25+30+25=80

Thus, activities B, C, and D crashed for Rs. 80.

Crashing it by a day,

The project length is reduced to 6 days,

The direct cost of the project = 2750 + 80 = Rs. 2830

Indirect cost = 6 × 60 = Rs. 360

Total cost of the project = 2830 + 360 = Rs. 3190

After the fifth crash, the project duration was reduced by another day, but the cost increased by Rs. 20 over the previous total cost. Thus, a stage is reached where the decrease in duration is accompanied by increased project cost, forcing us to stop further crushing. If we combine all the results in a time-cost graph, a curve is obtained, as shown in Figure, which shows the minimum project cost corresponding to a project duration of 7 days.

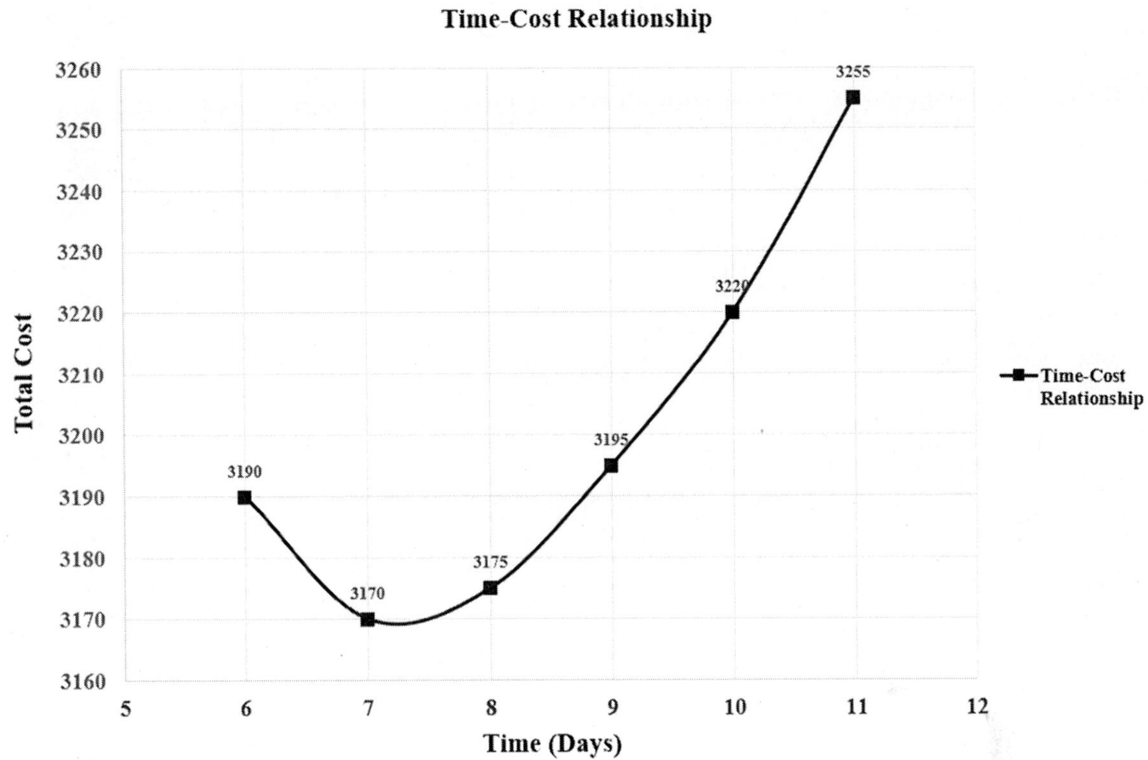

Results

Normal project duration = 11 days

Normal project cost = Rs. 3255

Minimum cost (after crashing) = Rs. 3170

Optimum duration = 7 days

Minimum duration = 6 days

The associated cost for minimum duration = Rs. 3190

The time-cost curve helps the project manager choose a suitable project schedule.

Illustration 3

The primary activities in a construction project and the relationships among them, the normal and crash durations, and the corresponding normal and crash costs are given in the following Table. Find the critical path and time for completion under normal working conditions and plot the direct costs on a graph.

Activity	Precedence	Duration (months)		Cost (in 1000 Rupees)	
		Normal	Crash	Normal	Crash
A	-	8	5	25	40
B	-	9	7	20	30
C	A	6	4	16	24
D	B	7	4	27	45

Solution:

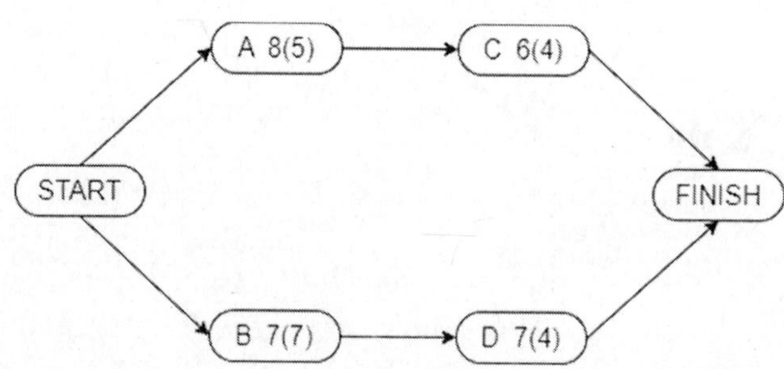

Activity	ΔCost/ΔTime	Time shortened					
A	5						1
B	5		1	1			
C	4				1	1	
D	6				1	1	1
Critical path		B-D	B-D	B-D	A-C, B-D	A-C, B-D	A-C, B-D
Activity crashed		-	B	B	C, D	C, D	A, D
Days cut		-	1	1	1	1	1
Project duration		16	15	14	13	12	11
Increased cost/day		-	5	5	10	10	11
Direct cost		88	93	98	108	118	129

We combine all the results in a time-cost graph, and a curve is obtained, as shown in Figure below.

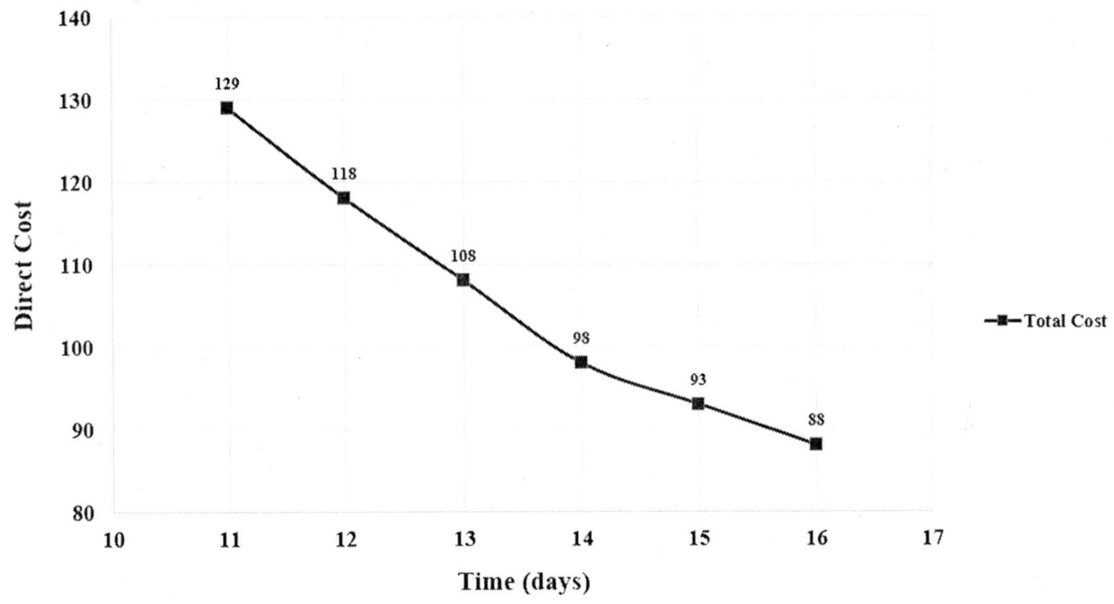

Illustration 4

The precedence requirements, normal and crash activity times, and normal and crash costs for a construction project are given in the following table. The indirect costs are ₹120 per day. Calculate the normal duration of the project and the critical path. Also, calculate and plot the cost-time function for the project on a graph and state the lowest cost and associated time.

Activity	Precedence	Duration (days)		Cost (in Rupees)	
		Normal	Crash	Normal	Crash
A	-	5	4	500	600
B	A	7	5	350	500
C	A	8	5	800	920
D	A	11	7	1200	1400
E	B, C	6	4	600	700
F	C	4	4	500	500
G	D, F	7	5	700	1000
H	E, F	6	5	300	420

Solution:

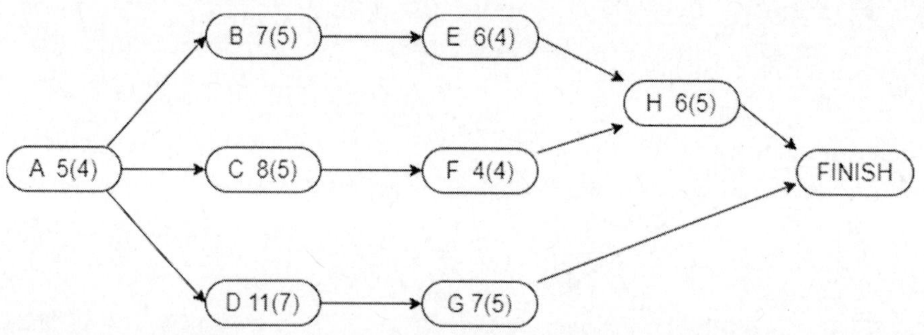

Activity	ΔCost/ΔTime	Time shortened				
A	100				1	
B	75					1
C	40		1			1
D	50					1
E	50			1		
F	-					
G	150					
H	120					
Critical path		ACEH	ACEH	ABEH, ACEH	ABEH ACEH ACFG ADG	ABEH ACEH ACFG ADG
Activity crashed		-	C	E	A	B, C, D
Days cut		-	1	1	1	1
Project duration		25	24	23	22	21
Increased cost/day		-	40	50	100	165
Total direct cost		4950	4990	5040	5140	5305
Total indirect cost		3000	2880	2760	2640	2520
Total cost		7950	7870	7800	7780	7825

We combine all the results in a time-cost graph, and a curve is obtained, as shown in Figure below.

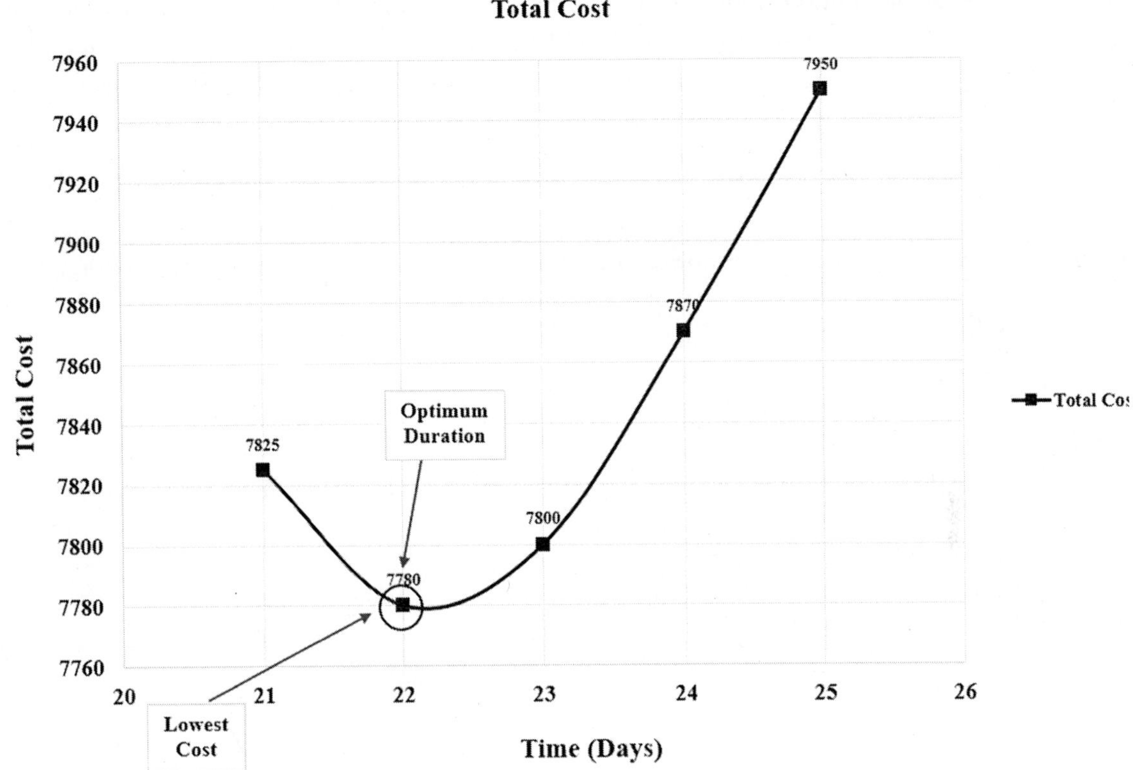

SUMMARY

The construction costs chapter provides an in-depth examination of the various factors influencing the financial aspects of construction projects. It delves into estimating, budgeting, and controlling costs throughout the project lifecycle. Key components such as labour, materials, equipment, overhead, and profit margins are analysed to develop accurate cost projections and ensure profitability. The chapter explores cost management techniques such as time cost trade-offs and crashing schedules to optimise resource allocation and minimise expenses. By understanding and effectively managing construction costs, project stakeholders can make informed decisions, enhance feasibility, and achieve desired outcomes within budgetary constraints.

EXERCISE

Divide students into small groups and assign each group a construction project schedule with critical activities and costs identified. Subsequently, students need to use concepts of compression and decompression to optimise project duration and cost. Students can also consider techniques such as overlapping activities, re-sequencing tasks, and allocating additional resources to critical path activities. Each group should present their proposed compression and decompression strategies, explaining the potential impacts on project cost, duration, and risk.

MULTIPLE CHOICE QUESTIONS

1. Which of the following is an example of a direct cost in a construction project?

   A) Administrative salaries
   B) Office rent
   C) Construction materials
   D) General liability insurance

2. Indirect costs in construction projects typically include expenses related to:

   A) Labour
   B) Materials
   C) Utilities
   D) Equipment rental

3. What is the time-cost trade-off in construction projects?

   A) The exchange of time for cost savings
   B) The exchange of cost for quality
   C) The exchange of quality for time savings
   D) The exchange of time for quality improvements

4. Which technique compresses a construction project schedule to meet a tight deadline?

   A) Fast-tracking
   B) Decompression
   C) Delaying
   D) Re-scheduling

5. What is the primary benefit of compressing a construction project schedule?

   A) Decreased project cost
   B) Increased project duration

C) Enhanced project quality
D) Accelerated project completion

6. Which of the following is a strategy for compressing a construction project schedule?

A) Adding slack to critical activities
B) Decreasing resource allocation
C) Delaying procurement
D) Overlapping activities

7. In a construction project, what does compression refer to?

A) Increasing the overall project duration
B) Decreasing the overall project duration
C) Adding more activities to the project
D) Postponing project activities

8. What is the primary objective of time-cost trade-off analysis in construction projects?

A) To increase project complexity
B) To decrease project duration
C) To confuse stakeholders
D) To delay project completion

ANSWERS TO MULTIPLE CHOICE QUESTIONS

1	2	3	4	5	6	7	8
C	C	A	A	D	D	B	B

SHORT ANSWER TYPE QUESTIONS

1. What are the different types of construction costs?
2. What are the components of construction costs?
3. How do construction costs impact project schedule, quality, and safety?
4. What do you mean by 'crashing' of an activity?
5. Discuss the time-cost trade-off.

6. What do you mean by compression and decompression of an activity?

LONG ANSWER TYPE QUESTIONS

1. Plot and explain the time-cost curve.
2. Discuss the composition of construction costs, including materials, labour, equipment, and overhead expenses. Explain how each component contributes to the overall cost of a construction project.
3. Explain the concept of direct costs in construction. Provide examples of direct costs and discuss how they are allocated to specific project activities.
4. Explain the concept of life-cycle costing in construction. Discuss how life-cycle costs are calculated and used to evaluate the long-term economic viability of construction projects.
5. The following details pertain to a project. The indirect cost of the project is Rs. 3000/week. Determine the optimum duration of the project and the corresponding minimum cost.

Activity		A	B	C	D	E
Immediate Predecessor		-	-	A	A	B, C
Duration (weeks)	Normal	6	8	4	5	5
	Crash	3	5	2	3	3
Cost (Rs.)	Normal	700	400	600	800	500
	Crash	1450	850	1000	1500	1200

TUTORIAL

Refer to a Standard Schedule of Rates of any PWD (available on the Net), and develop the approximate cost of a 3-storey, 400 sq. m plinth area building.

KNOW MORE

For more information related to this topic scan the QR code.

OR

Type this link in your browser

https://nptel.ac.in/courses/105103023

BIBLIOGRAPHY

- Love, P. E., and Irani, Z. (2001). Evaluation of IT costs in construction. *Automation in Construction*, 10(6), 649-658.
- Pheng Low, S., and Yeo, H. K. (1998). A construction quality costs quantifying system for the building industry. *International Journal of Quality and Reliability Management*, 15(3), 329-349.
- Subramani, T., Lishitha, P. T., and Kavitha, M. (2014). Time overrun and cost effectiveness in the construction industry. *Journal of Engineering Research and Applications*, 4(5), 111-116.

APPENDIX

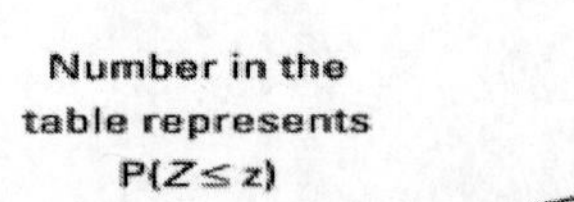

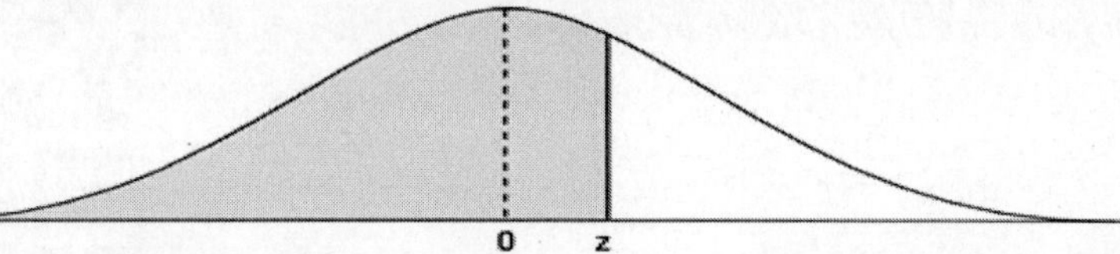

z	0.00	0.01	0.02	0.03	0.04	0.05	0.06	0.07	0.08	0.09
0.0	.5000	.5040	.5080	.5120	.5160	.5199	.5239	.5279	.5319	.5359
0.1	.5398	.5438	.5478	.5517	.5557	.5596	.5636	.5675	.5714	.5753
0.2	.5793	.5832	.5871	.5910	.5948	.5987	.6026	.6064	.6103	.6141
0.3	.6179	.6217	.6255	.6293	.6331	.6368	.6406	.6443	.6480	.6517
0.4	.6554	.6591	.6628	.6664	.6700	.6736	.6772	.6808	.6844	.6879
0.5	.6915	.6950	.6985	.7019	.7054	.7088	.7123	.7157	.7190	.7224
0.6	.7257	.7291	.7324	.7357	.7389	.7422	.7454	.7486	.7517	.7549
0.7	.7580	.7611	.7642	.7673	.7704	.7734	.7764	.7794	.7823	.7852
0.8	.7881	.7910	.7939	.7967	.7995	.8023	.8051	.8078	.8106	.8133
0.9	.8159	.8186	.8212	.8238	.8264	.8289	.8315	.8340	.8365	.8389
1.0	.8413	.8438	.8461	.8485	.8508	.8531	.8554	.8577	.8599	.8621
1.1	.8643	.8665	.8686	.8708	.8729	.8749	.8770	.8790	.8810	.8830
1.2	.8849	.8869	.8888	.8907	.8925	.8944	.8962	.8980	.8997	.9015
1.3	.9032	.9049	.9066	.9082	.9099	.9115	.9131	.9147	.9162	.9177
1.4	.9192	.9207	.9222	.9236	.9251	.9265	.9279	.9292	.9306	.9319
1.5	.9332	.9345	.9357	.9370	.9382	.9394	.9406	.9418	.9429	.9441
1.6	.9452	.9463	.9474	.9484	.9495	.9505	.9515	.9525	.9535	.9545
1.7	.9554	.9564	.9573	.9582	.9591	.9599	.9608	.9616	.9625	.9633
1.8	.9641	.9649	.9656	.9664	.9671	.9678	.9686	.9693	.9699	.9706
1.9	.9713	.9719	.9726	.9732	.9738	.9744	.9750	.9756	.9761	.9767
2.0	.9772	.9778	.9783	.9788	.9793	.9798	.9803	.9808	.9812	.9817
2.1	.9821	.9826	.9830	.9834	.9838	.9842	.9846	.9850	.9854	.9857
2.2	.9861	.9864	.9868	.9871	.9875	.9878	.9881	.9884	.9887	.9890
2.3	.9893	.9896	.9898	.9901	.9904	.9906	.9909	.9911	.9913	.9916
2.4	.9918	.9920	.9922	.9925	.9927	.9929	.9931	.9932	.9934	.9936
2.5	.9938	.9940	.9941	.9943	.9945	.9946	.9948	.9949	.9951	.9952
2.6	.9953	.9955	.9956	.9957	.9959	.9960	.9961	.9962	.9963	.9964
2.7	.9965	.9966	.9967	.9968	.9969	.9970	.9971	.9972	.9973	.9974
2.8	.9974	.9975	.9976	.9977	.9977	.9978	.9979	.9979	.9980	.9981
2.9	.9981	.9982	.9982	.9983	.9984	.9984	.9985	.9985	.9986	.9986
3.0	.9987	.9987	.9987	.9988	.9988	.9989	.9989	.9989	.9990	.9990
3.1	.9990	.9991	.9991	.9991	.9992	.9992	.9992	.9992	.9993	.9993
3.2	.9993	.9993	.9994	.9994	.9994	.9994	.9994	.9995	.9995	.9995
3.3	.9995	.9995	.9995	.9996	.9996	.9996	.9996	.9996	.9996	.9997
3.4	.9997	.9997	.9997	.9997	.9997	.9997	.9997	.9997	.9997	.9998
3.5	.9998	.9998	.9998	.9998	.9998	.9998	.9998	.9998	.9998	.9998
3.6	.9998	.9998	.9999	.9999	.9999	.9999	.9999	.9999	.9999	.9999

B REFERENCES FOR FURTHER LEARNING

- Ba'Its, H. A., Puspita, I. A., and Bay, A. F. (2020). Combination of program evaluation and review technique (PERT) and critical path method (CPM) for project schedule development. *International Journal of Integrated Engineering*, 12(3), 68-75.
- Betts, M., and Lansley, P. (1993). Construction management and economics: A review of the first ten years. *Construction Management and Economics*, 11(4), 221-245.
- Burtonshaw-Gunn, S. A. (2017). *Risk and financial management in construction*. Routledge.
- Cynthia, O. U. (2020). Implementation of project evaluation and review technique (PERT) and Critical path method (CPM): A comparative study. *International Journal of Industrial and Operations Research*, 3(004).
- Fellows, R. F., Langford, D., Newcombe, R., and Urry, S. (2009). *Construction management in practice*. John Wiley & Sons.
- Gurmu, A. T., and Aibinu, A. A. (2017). Construction equipment management practices for improving labor productivity in multistory building construction projects. *Journal of Construction Engineering and Management*, *143*(10), 04017081.
- Harris, F., McCaffer, R., Baldwin, A., and Edum-Fotwe, F. (2021). *Modern construction management*. John Wiley & Sons.
- Hussam, S., Laishram, B., and Johari, S. (2024). Framework to enhance gender inclusion of workers on construction sites. *Journal of Construction Engineering and Management*, 150(4), 04024018.
- Jackson, B. J. (2020). *Construction management jumpstart: the best first step toward a career in construction management*. John Wiley & Sons.

- Johari, S., and Jha, K.N. (2020). "Impact of work-motivation over construction labour productivity." *Journal of Management in Engineering*, 36(5), 04020052.
- Johari, S., and Jha, K.N. (2021). Learning curve models for construction workers. *Journal of Management in Engineering*, 37(5), 0000941.
- Merna, T., Chu, Y., and Al-Thani, F. F. (2010). *Project finance in construction: A structured guide to assessment*. John Wiley & Sons.
- Pretorius, F., Chung-Hsu, B. F., McInnes, A., Lejot, P., and Arner, D. (2008). *Project finance for construction and infrastructure: principles and case studies*. John Wiley & Sons.
- Safa, M., Shahi, A., Haas, C. T., and Hipel, K. W. (2017). Construction contract management using value packaging systems. *International Journal of Construction Management*, 17(1), 50-64.
- Schaufelberger, J. E., and Migliaccio, G. C. (2019). *Construction equipment management*. Routledge.
- Turner, J. R. (2004). Farsighted project contract management: incomplete in its entirety. *Construction Management and Economics*, 22(1), 75-83.

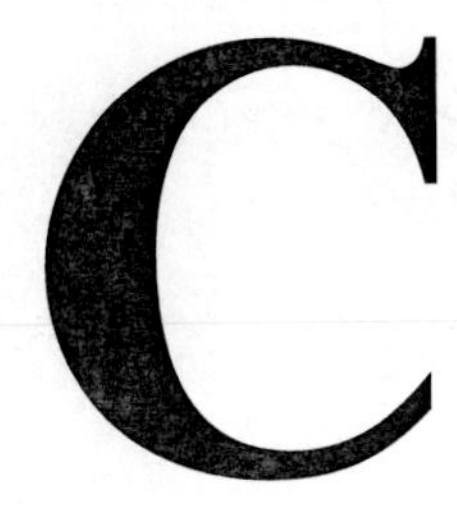

CO AND PO ATTAINABLE TABLE

Course outcomes (COs) for this course can be mapped with the programme outcomes (POs) after the completion of the course and a correlation can be made for the attainment of POs to analyse the gap. After proper analysis of the gap in the attainment of POs necessary measures can be taken to overcome the gaps.

Table for CO and PO attainment

Course Outcomes	Attainment of Programme Outcomes *(1- Weak Correlation; 2- Medium correlation; 3- Strong Correlation)*											
	PO-1	PO-2	PO-3	PO-4	PO-5	PO-6	PO-7	PO-8	PO-9	PO-10	PO-11	PO-12
CO-1												
CO-2												
CO-3												
CO-4												
CO-5												
CO-6												

The data filled in the above table can be used for gap analysis.

D INDEX